How Good We Can Be

Also by Will Hutton

The Revolution That Never Was

The State We're In

The State to Come

The World We're In

The Writing on the Wall

Them and Us

How Good We Can Be

Ending the Mercenary Society
and Building a Great Country

WILL HUTTON

Little, Brown

LITTLE, BROWN

First published in Great Britain in 2015 by Little, Brown

1 3 5 7 9 10 8 6 4 2

Copyright © Will Hutton 2015

The moral right of the author has been asserted.

A CIP catalogue record for this book
is available from the British Library.

Hardback ISBN 978-1-4087-0531-5
Trade paperback ISBN 978-1-4087-0597-1

Typeset in Caslon by M Rules
Printed and bound in Great Britain by
Clays Ltd, St Ives plc

Papers used by Little, Brown are from well-managed forests
and other responsible sources.

MIX
Paper from
responsible sources
FSC® C104740

Little, Brown
An imprint of
Little, Brown Book Group
100 Victoria Embankment
London EC4Y 0DY

An Hachette UK Company
www.hachette.co.uk

www.littlebrown.co.uk

To Jane

Contents

Contents

Preface

The State We're In was that rare thing – a success that came out of nowhere. Nobody expected it, including its author. For six months after its publication in January 1995 – twenty years ago – a book of political economy topped the non-fiction best-seller charts, much to general amazement. An economic journalist in early middle age was plucked from the relative obscurity of the business pages of the *Guardian* and hailed as offering the prospectus for a New Labour government, with the Labour leader Tony Blair referring to its ideas in major speeches in the run-up to the 1997 general election. The party seemed content to allow healing the fissures of British society with a reformed, high-investment stakeholder capitalism driven forward by a newly democratised British state to be characterised as its big idea. It may have abolished Clause 4 of its constitution, which proposed to secure the full fruits of workers' industry 'by hand or by brain' through securing the common ownership of the means of production. But that did not mean it accepted the merits of the market economy as fashioned by Mrs Thatcher. It would create a very different economy and society to hers.

The consensus was that the book captured the zeitgeist. There was a weariness with Thatcherism: the commonly held view was that whatever the doctrine's success the time had come to move on – to invest more, to build, to heal the wounds she had created in British society. The country believed in the renewal of the Labour party engineered by Tony Blair. A non-socialist but reformist agenda of the kind proposed by *The State We're In* was what many were looking for, and surely in broad terms would be what his New Labour party would want to do. Blair came to office on a surge of hope.

Twenty years on, and before another general election, is an opportune moment to review how well what I argued then holds up today and what as a country we might do now – and in passing why New Labour baulked at almost all the reforms I proposed. It was my generation's chance and although there were some gains, in the round it was flunked. As I will argue in the pages ahead, if anything *The State We're In* underestimated the catastrophic economic and social impact of Thatcherism and thus the need for a radical change of course. I certainly understood it was creating growing and potentially dangerous social divisions, and that her laissez-faire deregulation of the City of London was making the British ownership and financial system even more dysfunctional, with a disastrous impact on the attitude of British companies to investment and innovation. I warned of the ongoing relative decline of productive entrepreneurship and the value-generating part of the economy, a growing trade deficit, a cycle of amplifying credit and property booms, widening inequality and mounting social disillusion at the prospect of living within the brutalities of a market society while the social settlement frayed. I thought economic reform would also require reform of the British state and its democracy.

What I didn't anticipate was how financial and labour market deregulation would interact to become one of the drivers of the financial crisis. I certainly thought the gentlemanly capitalists of British finance short-termist and far too powerful – but believed they had an instinct for self-preservation; I had not reckoned that the whole system could be driven to the point of collapse as it was in 2008. I did not foresee how an extraordinary demand for credit would emerge, driven not only by self-fulfilling expectations of rising house prices so that borrowing seemed a safe bet but by ordinary people's determination to protect their living standards as collective bargaining in the private sector collapsed, and how ready deregulated banks and building societies would be to lend indiscriminately to them in the cause of apparent risk-free profit and extravagant personal remuneration for those at the top. I was a critic of demutualisation, but again I did not foresee the degree to which former building societies like Northern Rock and the Halifax would go rogue. Looking back, if I had been told in 1994 that twenty years later five million council houses would have been sold and not replaced, that in the last ten years British companies worth £440 billion would be sold overseas, that privatisation would lead to such extensive profiteering and that one of the fastest-growing sectors would be the contracted-out public sector or public services industry, I would not have been surprised at the trends which were already discernible – but I would have been shocked by the sheer scale and indifference to fairness with which it has all been done. There has been an across the board gigantic sale of public and private assets – a 'cashing out' – in the name of liberalisation, deregulation, openness for business and wealth generation. There has been an astonishing lack of interest in social justice and equity. Yet scant gain has it brought. Nor would that have surprised me.

Many of *The State We're In*'s warnings have been outdone by reality. The mis-selling scandals and excesses of executive pay that I found so shocking seem small in scale by today's standards. Then I was worried about the growth of temporary and agency work: I did not dream of zero-hour contracts. I was aware that the improvement in pension incomes would come under threat and that the next generation of pensioners would become steadily poorer: again I did not foresee the collapse of defined benefit pension schemes. Then I was worried that, in order to assuage shareholders, companies paid out too high a share of their profits in dividends: now the concern is the fixation with billions of pounds' worth of share buy-backs. Re-reading the book, my errors were of under- rather than overstatement. Of course I did not anticipate the digital revolution – but I was aware that necessarily there would be technological change. An economy and society had to have institutions fit for purpose to exploit and benefit from whatever scientific or technological opportunity presented itself – which Britain plainly did not.

But, as Adam Smith famously remarked, there is a great deal of ruin in a nation: a country has a considerable capacity to withstand even calamitous bungling. Britain does have a more entrepreneurial culture than it did twenty years ago. There are clusters of young, fast-growing firms, especially in the South-East – in London, Cambridge and around Heathrow – and around our great universities. There is an embrace of digitalisation. Attitudes towards women, gay people and ethnic minorities have been transformed. Having being winnowed out in the 1980s and 1990s, older people are rejoining the labour force in millions. Educational standards have risen, as has longevity. The economy is more carbon efficient. To characterise the last twenty years as a total failure would be unfair. As I say in this book, Britain still has some assets on which it can build.

But it could have been so much better. Critics of *The State We're In* dismissed my advocacy of stakeholder capitalism, my criticism of the City and my willingness to try intelligently to design better institutions to support long-term, high-investment companies rather than short-term finance. It represented, they charged, a throwback to corporatism, state meddling and an obstacle to the beneficial operation of markets. There was neither need nor demand to reform British democracy – the preoccupation of north London intellectuals – nor any need to try to build a more inclusive, modern social settlement beyond a minimum safety net. That would only be expensive and encourage 'dependency'. Yet the dismissal of such ideas, while carrying on broadly where Mrs Thatcher left off, has led to greater disasters. The banking system did nearly collapse. We did contemplate the break-up of the UK, with the real threat of Scottish secession. Large parts of the country are defined by neglect. It is hard to imagine that anyone can believe that the course of the last twenty years was unimprovable.

Indeed, one of the striking political realities of the summer of 2014 in the build-up to the Scottish referendum was the inability of advocates of the UK to make an emotional case to the Scots to keep the union. The building of an Empire together, dominating the world together, fighting world wars together and the creation of the 1945 settlement all lay in the past. The major achievement of the last thirty years has been the great cashing out, with the attendant rise of massive inequality and decline of opportunity. It was small wonder that the demand for self-government to strike out in a direction in which the Scottish national community might build great things together was so attractive – though in the event it was outweighed by the huge economic risks of secession, the ongoing economic advantages of union and the still strong emotional ties. We are better together and it was good the union held: divided islands worldwide do not fare well. But it served as a warning that the old order has to change.

I am sure some critics on the right will once again dismiss the analysis in this book as anti-free market, unsound and, despite its effort to show how a reformed state must necessarily interact with the private sector for their twin benefit, in practice merely an attempt to reintroduce meddling by the state. They will dislike the call for audacious national goals and the recasting of ownership and finance, and will try to argue that mass flourishing, which all reasonable men and women must support, should rather be founded on laissez-faire individualism than the series of institutional reforms I propose, notably in education, trade unions and local government, alongside how our companies are owned, financed and encouraged to innovate. They are powerful and have held the country in thrall for most of my adult life. It may very well be that the analysis and proposals I present here gain no more leverage in the next twenty years than they did in the last. The UK will make no effort to pull together, to reframe its approach to the economy and to create more social justice. It will continue along the path set by libertarian conservatives. In that case I have no doubt the UK will break up, that it risks another banking crisis that it will be unable to afford, that real living standards will continue to be squeezed and that at some stage there will be a revolt from below as one by one the great institutions we hold in common – the NHS, the BBC, the armed services, the universities and even a fair-minded justice system – fall before the onward march of the individualist libertarian know-nothings and their cheerleaders in our highly partisan media. The blaming of immigrants and Europe for our largely home-made ills is already creating an unpleasantly illiberal, and I would say unBritish and unfair, society. Unless something radical happens – for which I ardently hope – there is all the potential for the mood to become very much worse.

But it could be different – a moment for a change of course. *How Good We Can Be* was written in eleven weeks over the summer of 2014. In the first four chapters I describe, for want of a better phrase, the state we're in now – and the last two chapters and conclusion focus on proposals about how to put it right. First I must thank the fellows of Hertford College for offering me a sabbatical in May 2014 and indulging me in the August and most of September as I scrambled to finish. I was also given varying respites from my column-writing duties in the *Observer* – thanks to comment editor Rob Yates and editor John Mulholland. I asked a number of friends and colleagues whose opinion I respect to read drafts of chapters. So thank you to Birgitte Andersen, Philip Augar, Eric Beinhocker, Alan Bogg, Andrew Haldane, Colin Higson, Gavin Kelly, Eamonn Matthews, Colin Meyer, Philippe Schneider, Muhtu de Silva and Keir Starmer. Paul Gregg and Jonathan Wadsworth read the chapter on inequality and reworked the numbers on the 30/30/40 society that they had prepared for *The State We're In*. Hope you are both around in twenty years' time if I try a third assessment in my dotage! Lindsay Mckie and Avner Offer read the final manuscript and offered valuable last corrections. My agent Ed Victor had long encouraged me to write a book as much as possible just following my instincts and relying on the ideas and knowledge accumulated over the last forty years; for better or worse this is the result. Richard Beswick, my editor at Little, Brown, read the entire book in draft and did what an editor should – but so often doesn't or can't – with multiple suggestions for improvement; so huge thanks to him for his helpful editing suggestions and always upbeat encouragement. Iain Hunt is the senior project editor who managed the book through to publication calmly against very tight deadlines, while Steve Gove copy-edited brilliantly in very short time: my thanks to both. Felicity Bryan came up with the idea for the title. It goes without saying that all mistakes and errors are mine and mine alone.

Last but not least of course there is my family. My three children, all adult now, are a joy to their father; they have watched me write a few books now and know the routine. Jane, my partner of forty years, fought leukaemia over the whole period I was writing, and was often extremely unwell – but was as supportive of what I was doing as she has been of all my projects throughout our marriage. It was her suggestion twenty years ago that I spell out what stakeholder capitalism meant in *The State We're In*; this time round she came up with the telling line about throwaway people. Nothing I have achieved in my career could have been done without the platform and love she has provided. So I unhesitatingly dedicate this book to her.

Will Hutton
10th October 2014

1
The State We Shouldn't Be In

Britain is beset by a crisis of purpose. We don't know who we are any longer, where we are going or even if there is a 'we'. The country is so passionately attached to past glories because there are so few to celebrate in the present. The crisis is compounded since we have been told for thirty years that the route to universal well-being is to abandon the expense of justice and equity and so allow the judgements of the market to go unobstructed. Private decisions in markets supposedly are morally and economically better than any public or collective action. As a result the sense of the 'we' that binds a society together and gives us reason to belong is being lost. We take refuge in looking after number one, because there is no sense in nor reason for doing anything else.

The inevitable consequence is a decline in public integrity and a new carelessness about others. This amoral deficit of integrity takes many guises. It is sky-high executive pay out of proportion to effort or contribution. It is the phone-hacking scandal. It is the too frequent lack of duty of care to workforces and customers alike, betrayed by cases of mis-selling or exploitative work contracts. It is the careless, indiscriminate sale of so many our public and private assets – the great 'cashing out'. It is the unwillingness to find ways of investing in ourselves, while we look so regularly to foreigners to revive our industries or build our infrastructure. It is the crisis of trust in our politicians. It is the uncontested acceptance that our children confront a worse world than we faced ourselves – from the size of mortgage they will need to buy a house to lower pensions. It is the new hostility to openness, and the zeal to blame so many of our home-made problems on foreigners, immigrant workers and the European Union. Perhaps the most dispiriting element in the campaign to persuade Scotland not to secede from the UK was that there was so little inspiring to associate with the union around which people could emotionally rally. A national community must offer reasons to belong or it is lost.

This is all the more tragic because if it were able to regain purpose and integrity, driving forward a cluster of feasible reforms, Britain could be one of the best countries in the world. There is a lot going for this country – from great universities engaging in important research to a deeply held belief in the rule of law, from a stirring entrepreneurialism to the fair-mindedness of our society. When there is some discovery of purpose and the unity it brings – as in the 2012 Olympics – we surprise ourselves with how good we are. There are great international networks, and much affection towards us: poor migrants and the super-rich alike want to live here. In a world where the so-called 'intangibles' associated with knowledge and knowhow are becoming ever more important, Britain is rich in both. Technological and scientific advance, along with the digital revolution, promises to transform the economic and social landscape. We – if that 'we' could be rediscovered – could seize and shape the future.

Yet Britain faces these exciting possibilities with a dysfunctional capitalism and democracy. Not only are we failing to shape this future, our capacity to do so is shrinking before our eyes. A crisis of integrity straddles the country in three principal guises, throttling our vitality and inflaming the worst sentiments and prejudices.

The first site of the crisis is in the organisation of our business and financial system, along with the dominant values of many of those who run it. Britain's business culture, built on companies without engaged shareholders to assume the stewardship dimension of ownership and so myopically chasing short-term performance, is overwhelmingly about extracting value rather than creating it, with the focus on the next deal or risk-free government contract rather than innovation. These are 'ownerless corporations'.[1] Executive remuneration is blind to how profits are made: it simply ensures extravagant personal fortunes if any kind of profit is delivered that will boost the short-term share price. The reward system is meant to drive better performance. Instead it has grown into a Frankenstein's monster that gives business leaders the incentive to put themselves and their own pay first. And, given the numbers, they would need to be saints to do otherwise. Chief executives' pay has risen from 35 times average pay in the late 1980s to 180 times today, with remuneration in 2014 averaging £4.7 million for the CEOs of companies listed on the FTSE 100.[2] Adjusted for the size of companies they run, executive pay in Britain is higher even than in the US.

The lack of proportionality and the way pay goes up on average in both good times and bad has properly created enormous cynicism. The incentive for such executives is to wheel and deal their way to a dynastic fortune with little or no sense of obligation to the society of which they are part or the companies they lead. To build an enduring and innovative company, to accept a broad duty of care to those who work for you or even to pay the taxes that the state intends the company to pay are now in tension with a business leader's prime incentive – to create wealth, defined as the share price and thus his or her own remuneration package. The financial crisis, which impacted more profoundly on the British banking system than on any other leading industrialised country's, was the most complete expression of British capitalism's dysfunctionality.

The second site of crisis flows from the first. British society is ever more fragmented and unequal; the mass of the population are more at risk and insecure than ever before – and this in a country that remains one of the richest in the world. It is true that the interaction of globalisation and new technologies is quickening the pace of change, requiring from workers, whatever their skills, ever faster adaptation and a constant readiness to change. But instead of reshaping the social contract and the institutions of society to allow individuals better to confront the risks of modern life – offering them the chance to build a career or even to have one at all, to buy a house, to face ageing and ill-health with confidence, to bring up their kids well, to enjoy a common infrastructure designed to support them – we seem resigned about the unprecedented fall in real wages for the typical worker, and grimly embrace the dismantling of the social settlement in the name of 'rolling back the state' and promoting self-reliance. Britain could, as I argue later, try refashioning its social deal both to provide business with flexibility and workers with more security. Instead the only discourse is about cuts, 'tough decisions' and the withdrawal of benefits. Extraordinarily the Coalition government has budgeted to reduce public spending on goods and services – in effect the state – in 2018 to the same proportion in relation to GDP as in 1948, despite today's complexities and extra demands.[3] No additional tax is to be demanded of the propertied, the well-off, business or the elite to mitigate the impact. Justice is eclipsed. The vocal right and centre-right blame EU regulations and immigrants as the cause of our ills, crowding out any arguments that genuinely address the origins of our malaise.

Which segues into the third dimension of the crisis: political philosophy, governance and democratic deliberation. Too many on the left still do not celebrate or believe in the idea of great companies or in the capacity of a reformed economic system with better checks and balances to deliver wealth and individual enfranchisement, although the best on the left are beginning to change. The right meanwhile so worship at the shrine of unalloyed capitalism, and are so dazzled by the fortunes of the new financial and corporate elite, they do not believe in the necessity of ensuring that capitalism operates fairly, building countervailing forces or social institutions to support the lives of ordinary people. There is no creative, democratic conversation about how to build a better capitalism populated by purposeful companies within an enfranchised, just society, or how to seek allies at home and abroad to do it. This is all the more extraordinary in the wake of a financial crisis that so nearly triggered a banking collapse and associated depression. The void is filled by a cacophony of opinionated voices and interest groups, so that before the simplistic, populist message from the UK Independence Party (UKIP) – it is Europe and not ourselves that is the problem – the political class cannot find the language to respond. Matters are exacerbated by a parliament that follows not leads, institutions of government that have lost their fitness for purpose and a media that preys on and distorts the national conversation.

If it could but resolve this triple-headed crisis, the country could take off. With reformed institutions it could build on its assets to become the richest and most dynamic country in Europe. After all, Britain has more world-class universities per head of population than any other country, and a strong scientific base. There are surprisingly vigorous and fast-growing clusters of high-tech start-ups and small firms. The triangle bounded by the M3 in the south and M40 to the north and with Heathrow at its centre boasts the highest concentration of high-tech start-ups outside California and Massachusetts.[4] The Internet economy is booming: e-commerce is expected to be worth £140 billion in 2016, proportionally among the highest of leading industrial countries. There is a growing awareness of the importance of innovation and entrepreneurialism. More multi-nationals than the rest of Europe put together choose to locate their headquarters in Britain, which along with the City of London, capital of world finance, provides not only jobs but also a rich market for business services.[5] The manufacturing we still have is resilient and profitable. We speak the world's language, English. The values that would underpin a more inclusive capitalism – justice, fair play, respect for others' opinions, profound belief in democracy whatever the shortcomings in its delivery – are widely held and never far from the surface. These are some of the elements that could constitute a springboard for a national renaissance.

Apologists for the great neoliberal experiment of the last thirty years would argue that these successes are proof positive that it has worked; the task is to stick with it. Of course, in a rich and diverse country there are examples of success. The question is whether such examples are evidence of a wider system that works, and whether we can build on their success throughout the country as a whole. The verdict has to be No, with the minuses outweighing any pluses. Stable companies who can exploit the new technologies, achieve real scale and help the economy grow are conspicuous by their absence, making even more elusive the prospect of an era of stable economic growth following the so-called 'recovery' – which in 2014, after six years, had merely returned the country to 2008 levels of output, the longest recession for more than a century.

In the 1930s, after the Great Depression, Britain could point to major emerging global companies in chemistry (ICI), consumer electronics (Thorn Electrical Industries), cars (Austin and Morris Motors), aerospace (Hawker Siddeley) and so on that could drive growth forward and represent the new. The same cannot be said in 2015. It is telling that Britain can boast only one genuine new high-tech company of global importance: ARM, which provides chips used by 95 per cent of the world's smartphones and has a stock market value exceeding £10 billion. There are fewer than a handful of new high-tech companies worth £1 billion, despite London being the home for 3000 high-tech start-ups.[6]

Britain may have angel investors aplenty, but it does not have a financial and ownership system that enables enough of these start-ups to grow to maturity, especially when it is intellectual capital, frontier knowledge and unproven products and services that require backing. Short-termism, disengagement, lack of technical knowledge and demands for impossibly high returns over a very short period define our system. The chances of these hopeful, innovative start-ups being given the chance to innovate and invest to become the giants of tomorrow are close to nil. It is a scale-up crisis, beginning to attract more and more concern.[7] Companies in the round are as ephemeral, focused on the short term and disposable as another reality TV programme. There is little chance of them stewarding and investing in their disposable workforces. Indeed their workforces are disposable precisely because the firms who employ them are. Britain is too often a world of throwaway companies and throwaway people.

Even in the gilded South East there are shadows of the ills that beset the rest of the country, and which explain the lack of any national belief that Britain is going to become a winner. Inequality is no longer a distant concept, the concern of left-wing intellectuals or Labour people nostalgic for the glory years of the Attlee government. It is a lived reality for millions, disabling their lives, breaking down trust and deepening the fissures in our society. London has always housed both rich and poor cheek by jowl, but the disparity between the crowded flats where young people 'hutch up' to share rooms and the extravagant super-mansions with their underground floors of private cinemas and swimming pools is now approaching the grotesque. A class of workers with neither employment rights nor any means to ensure that their skills are not abused by cheap, untrained imitators has become the fastest-growing element in the labour market. In London their employers need them, at least offering some countervailing negotiating power to what would otherwise be a helpless economic position: in the rest of the country they are at the economic margins.

The economic and social consequences of these failings were masked in the twenty years before the financial crisis in 2008 by borrowing and debt, not so much by the state but by companies and households. Households in particular borrowed to sustain their living standards (in part because of the squeeze on real wages caused by the collapse of trade unions, as I analyse in more detail in Chapter 5) and to share in the apparent never-ending rise in property values, and so simultaneously supported what would otherwise have been a very weak economy. But that safety valve is closing. The stock of debt, tribute to decades of excessive lending, has grown to hitherto unthinkable levels. Household debt was a tiny 15 per cent of national output in 1964: today that has increased nearly nine times to stand at 140 per cent of GDP, a third higher than the range in the Eurozone, the US and Japan. Ominously, two-thirds of British household debt is at variable interest rates, portending enormous financial difficulty when interest rates rise.[8] In the US it is widely observed that middle America, whose real wages have scarcely risen for a generation, has sustained its living standards by borrowing;[9] a similar phenomenon has been at work in Britain.

On top there is now the international struggle to recover from the financial crisis, which in Britain, with the near-collapse of the entire banking system, was especially serious. Worse, the extreme sluggishness of the economic recovery, not just in Britain but in the US, the EU and Japan, suggests that something still more serious is afoot than the aftermath of stricken banks and the overhang of excessive private debt. Professor Larry Summers, former US Treasury Secretary, has recently revived the concept of 'secular stagnation' first coined in 1938 by Professor Alvin Hansen to describe the disappointing US economic performance of the late 1930s, after the initial recovery from the Great Depression.[10] Secular stagnation is much more than just slow growth. It means that firms are insufficiently confident and consumers too cautious to create the investment and demand necessary to generate full employment unless interest rates fall below zero. In other words, unless firms are essentially paid to borrow money to invest, there will be such a shortfall of investment spending that both the potential of the economy to grow, and its actual growth, fall away. The cumulative loss of output of the recession stays lost and the economy gets trapped on a lower growth trajectory.[11]

It was apparent that all was not well even before the financial crisis hit. Rather like a junkie needing ever larger doses of drugs to get high, the western economic system needed ever more credit and rising asset prices to keep demand going – but those very things created the bubble that led to the crash, Now the huge overhang of private debt, in particular between banks as much as between them and the ultimate borrowers, means that the same get-out cannot be used a second time. Meanwhile governments are convinced they should be wedded to austerity; and firms continue to hoard cash. The US recovery has been much less vigorous than previous recoveries, creating fewer jobs than any since the war.

There are multiple explanations for what is happening.[12] Some stress that ageing societies need more saving, and this trend has coincided with a uniquely uncertain moment for firms as the digital revolution transforms business models. It is not obvious in what technology or for what market demand firms should be investing. Some argue that the impact of the excess of private debt is too easily underestimated: the scale of the debt has distorted company and household balance sheets, which both parties are seeking to restore to normality – thus constraining their spending. After all, Japan has suffered such a 'balance sheet recession' for twenty years. Others point the finger at austerity policies which assume an economic resilience that is plainly absent. Still others argue that the technologies of today are cheaper, need less costly investment and in any case generate less employment than in the past. Investment is no longer the economic motor it once was. Adair Turner, former chair of the Financial Services Authority, for example, remarks:

> When General Motors was at its peak, it employed over 800,000 people. Microsoft employs only 100,000, Apple 80,000, and Google 50,000. Facebook has an equity value of $170 billion but employs only 5000 people: and it has recently acquired Whatsapp for $19 billion, a company that employs just 55 people. Information and communication technology is not pure magic, but in its economic effects it is far closer to it than were the technologies of the electro-mechanical age.[13]

What unites the above diagnoses is the role of uncertainty, the growing sense of risk and of the frailties of the post-crash financial system – trends discernible not just in Britain but across the industrialised West. The reasons for secular stagnation are not hard to figure out. The financial crisis was ubiquitous. All companies are under more financial pressure from more disengaged owners. All countries have seen a growth in marginalised workers. Inequality of income and wealth is rising everywhere. All countries have seen an increase in the stock of debt and leverage. All countries are concerned to shrink the size of their public sectors, fashionably resorting to privatisation and contracting out employment. Societies are ageing and saving more. In an era of dramatic technological change, firms cannot be certain what the best technological bet will be. But the adverse consequences of these trends have gone further and deeper in Britain than elsewhere. This is why the country has endured the most protracted period of depressed output since the nineteenth century. The recovery of 2013–15 is more of a short-lived snapback to former levels of output, helped along by an artificial housing boom, than the portent of a sustained growth in output and productivity. On too many key economic and social variables, as I detail in the pages ahead, Britain is the worst in class, the principal exhibit for the prosecution. Partly because of our economic structures and culture, and partly as a matter of choice, these phenomena with few exceptions are more deep-rooted in Britain than elsewhere.

Above all it is a crisis of ideas. After the failure of twentieth-century socialism it is not possible to argue that the correct response to the failings of contemporary capitalism is to introduce a form of collectivism. But equally, after the financial crisis, to argue blindly for more markets, privatisation, flexibility, weakening of the social contract and roll-back of the state is no less implausible. Economists may place different emphasis on what lies behind today's secular stagnation, but all agree that economic policies, priorities and indeed institutions need to be rethought. The truth is that it was the growing dysfunctionality of contemporary capitalism, a process most advanced in Britain, that in the run-up to the crisis was already weakening the propensity to invest and innovate – a fact that is now obvious to all.

Twenty years ago, in *The State We're In*, I set out a prospectus for the reform of British capitalism. It should become stakeholder capitalism – embedding committed ownership, the employee's voice, institutions to support innovation and investment, a recast social contract and the creation of a more deliberative, responsive democracy. All were interlinked. If the case was strong then, it is stronger now. What is locking our economy below its potential is that its fundamental structures force companies and individuals alike to manage risk by themselves – not to share it. If we want to benefit from the opportunities before us, we need a better-designed capitalism that takes fairness and justice as seriously as it does incentives and efficiency. Innovation and a spirit of risk-taking need to imbue our entire society; this is a goal we hold in common and perform in common, and it needs to be supported in common.

Secular stagnation, in short, is what happens to dysfunctional capitalism. It is neither transformative technological complexity nor growing longevity nor more saving that are at the root of our problems: indeed, framed correctly, all are rich with possibilities for offering us better, richer lives and increased well-being. At any stage since the Enlightenment two hundred and fifty years ago launched the modern era and its explosion of wealth and growth it has been possible to be pessimistic as old forms give way to new. Would jobs as, say, ostlers or sail-makers be replaced, asked anxious contemporaries, as the car and steam ship superseded horses and sailing ships? Of course they were. The lesson of history is unambiguous. The capacity of women and men to use science and technology to master nature for human betterment is the driver of wealth and productivity. Human wants and ingenuity are infinite. Moreover the process is only in its beginnings and will only gain momentum over the years to come: scientists proclaim how little rather than how much they know. There are multiple transformations ahead, which will generate growth, investment, employment and opportunity. But it is those economies and societies with the best-designed institutions and most appropriate values that will fare best. The task in Britain is to recognise this truth – and reform our capitalism from top to toe so it becomes the servant of a better society rather than its master. To understand the opportunity better, I next want to examine General Purpose Technologies and their transformative economic and social role.

What really drives growth and well-being

General purpose technologies (GPTs) are the generic technologies that change the world. Digitisation – the capacity to turn disparate dimensions of reality into digits, and for computers to make instant sense of them – is set to become the defining general purpose technology of all time, trumping even the transformative impact of steam and electricity. It will create almost boundless possibilities and opportunities to reshape and improve our economy and society. There are accompanying new dangers about the amount of information that public and private organisations will potentially have about individual citizens and indeed each other – this is also a world of hacking, endangered privacy and vulnerable security. But that should not disguise the larger truth of the march into reality of what used to be confined to the pages of science fiction – and nor will those risks stand in its way. With the right framework, policies, values and institutions Britain could become through such technologies a vastly richer, more enfranchised and fun place to live and work. The challenge is to shape this future rather than be shaped by it.

Innovation theorists have defined a GPT as a single generic technology that is developed through continuous improvement but which comes to have multiple and wide usage with many spillover effects.[14] GPTs up until now have been largely confined to four areas – transport, power, communication and agriculture – but have had enormous ramifications beyond their particular provenance. So, for example, the first great GPTs – the domestication and cross-breeding of animals along with the cross-fertilisation and husbanding of plants, so vastly increasing their yields – may have been confined to agriculture, but by offering secure and plentiful supplies of food they allowed human beings to break away from being hunter-gatherers and settle in cities and towns. The creation of the three-masted sailing ship in the fifteenth century and the railway in the nineteenth not only revolutionised transport, but in so doing opened up continents, transformed trade, created maritime Europe and later invented the metropolis and suburbs. Latin American gold, shipped across the Atlantic in three-masted galleons, caused the great European inflation that was one of the causes of the Protestant Reformation.

Steam and electricity were forms of energy that would transform the economic base, creating first the factory and later universal cheap lighting and dense concentrations of industrial power. The printing press and the computer transformed the ability to communicate; the printing of books allowed information to be disseminated to millions quickly and authoritatively – it was printed books that spread the exciting news of untold

Latin American silver and gold to hundreds of thousands of Spaniards who became colonists, and printed bibles that spread the challenge of Protestantism – and the computer is of course the indispensable technology of our own times. In all these cases the GPT arose in one particular domain, but its applicability and many usages spilled over to others. It is not hyperbole to argue that it is GPTs, rather than the dynastic ambitions of monarchs, emperors and dictators, great wars or even the clashes of ideology and religion, that have driven the world forward.

What is becoming ever more apparent is that digitisation and explosive computing power affect not just a few areas of society from which their impact will radiate, but all of them simultaneously. We are living through an economic inflexion point like no other. What lies ahead will be more transformative than anything humanity has lived through so far because digitisation impacts on all human desires, needs and appetites; it encompasses communication, agriculture, industry, energy, education, health and transport. It is only possible, for example, to create the driverless car, train or plane – and to re-imagine transport completely – because of our new capacity to turn widely disparate dimensions of reality into digits. A driverless car works because images can be turned into digital representations which are then recognised and interpreted by computerised sensors; the car's location on the road, the varying obstacles in its vicinity and the actions of other cars are all understood by the vehicle as a thinking, sensing, interacting robot on wheels.

Equally words, numbers, images, sounds can be digitalised and then sent through fibre-optic cables and the air as wireless signals for our mobile phones, tablets and personal computers to process. Monumental amounts of data are held in digital clouds that can be networked simultaneously on a previously unimaginable scale. Our smart mobile phones have become indispensable instruments of communication; on top of texting, emailing and old-fashioned phone conversations, they allow us without any fixed connection to be proactive members of myriad networks, paying our bills with them, watching TV and radio on them, using them to control the sensors in our houses and cars from afar.

Digitisation remakes the compass of our understanding and invents new frontiers of possibility, and in so doing promises to refashion the economics of almost everything. The understanding of our bodies and the varying molecules that constitute matter, whether human, animal, mineral or plant genetic structures, are being transformed by digitisation and computers. The potential to improve yields from plants, the efficacy of drugs and the capacity to release power are as transformatory as any of the earlier GPTs. What is new is that these advances are not just happening in one domain but across all domains, with jumps in one area feeding back into others. Computers are now so powerful that vast arrays of data from myriads of sources (big data) can be combined and recombined through so-called machine learning to make new connections, new insights and new understanding.

Nor is this where the progressive scientific dynamic stops. Science marches on exponentially; we are forever – to adapt Isaac Newton's famous formulation – standing on the shoulders of what others have achieved in order to see further. We may think we know a lot about nature and the physical world, our bodies and the universe beyond; scientists will acknowledge they are only scratching the surface. In every discipline knowledge is growing exponentially and each discipline is interacting with others; medicine, biochemistry, chemistry, engineering, physics, robotics, photonics, mathematics and computer science are all cross-fertilising, combining and recombining their insights and advances. There will be new materials to build the artefacts around us; new ways of creating energy; the customisation of medicine to individual needs – and so it goes on, with digitisation allowing advance to accelerate.

If there were nine GPTs in the twentieth century, expect the number to double in the century ahead. It is a dramatic moment in world history. Nothing will be left untouched. We will live in smart cities, achieve mobility in smart transport, be powered by smart energy, communicate with smart phones, organise our financial affairs with smart banks and socialise in ever smarter networks. It is powering a new industrial revolution of localised micro-production – the new 'makers'.[15] Twenty-first-century life will be like none ever lived before.

Think through the implications of just one corner of the emerging future – the driverless car. One of the reasons Google is investing so much in developing driverless cars is that whoever owns the communications system that controls them will own the twenty-first century's equivalent of the telephone network or money clearing system: this will be a licence to print money. The benefits are endless. Roads will be able to carry more traffic while at the same time being safer. Personalised door-to-door transport will become hugely pleasurable: your car will deliver you to your home or place of work and then park itself without you. Road accidents will plummet. Energy efficiency will be transformed. Insurance rates will fall, even the need for insurance will decrease. Personalised transport, ordered by your mobile phone, will gradually replace mass transport networks.

Of course this future can only be disruptive – and with disruption comes not only opportunity and the new but dislocation and loss. One futurologist has suggested that taxi, bus and truck driving will become extinct occupations, casualties of driverless vehicles – along with traffic police, all forms of home delivery and waste disposal, jobs at petrol stations, car washes and parking lots.[16] The cars themselves will be made by robots in automated car factories. The only new jobs will be in design and marketing, and in writing the computer software that will allow the cars to navigate their journeys, along with the apps that will enable our mobile phones to use them better.

That is just one sector. The advent of thinking machines threatens routine work across the board. The automated checkout at supermarkets is becoming as familiar as the bank ATM. From staff-free ticket offices to students who can learn online without going to college, it seems there is no corner of economic life where people are not being replaced by machines – a trend that will accelerate. For example one important study, evaluating the impact of computers and robots on 702 American occupations, suggests that over the 'next decade or two' as much as 47 per cent of all US employment could be at risk of being automated and performed by machines; not only in transport and logistics but across a wide range of service sectors.[17]

But this is nothing new; the defining feature of modernity is that new industries and jobs replace outmoded ones. The question is whether modernity is now taking a darker turn. It is not just that Apple, Facebook, Amazon and Google are not mass employers as Tesco, Ford or General Motors once were. They represent a new world in which technology could remove the mass of people from worthwhile economic activity; good jobs and full-time employment could become the preserve of an educated, computer science literate elite. It is millions of low-skill, routinisable 'lousy' jobs that are under threat – the common expectation of those predicting that within thirty years robots and machines will replace half the American, and by inference other industrialised countries', workforces.[18] Such predictions about the growing importance of machines are broadly right. The debate is whether the conclusion is optimistic or pessimistic: does the new technology, optimistically, create new vistas and new jobs or does it, pessimistically, presage a dystopian future of 'lovely' highly skilled jobs for the few and joyless unemployment and underemployment for the many?

The future is bright – if we can seize it

Techno-pessimism comes if one shares the view of those who believe that while automation and robotisation are certainly coming, there are no new worthwhile transformational technologies to be automated. All the obvious human needs – to move, to have power, to communicate – have been solved through cars, planes, mobile phones and computers. These were the 'low-hanging fruit', and they have been plucked. We have come to the end of the great GPTs that changed the world: there are none to carry us forward even while the old activities are being robotised and automated.[19]

It is a view argued with some sophistication by Professor Robert Gordon. For him the most important event in the history of the world was the invention of steam power, followed by that of the internal combustion engine. But by 1970 the 'rainbow benefits' of the great inventions and their spin-offs of the second industrial revolution – steel, oil, petrochemicals and electricity – had occurred and could not happen again. As he writes, 'the spread of air conditioning, commercial air travel, and the interstate highway system represented the final implementation of technologies invented in the 1870s'. There was a surge of productivity growth in the middle fifty years of the twentieth century, he argues, as the great technologies were implemented, but productivity growth in the US has regressed today to where it was in the early decades of the last century. He is not predicting a further slowdown, but rather sees the current low levels as the norm and the productivity surge of middle of the last century as an aberration. Add four great headwinds – inequality, an ageing population, the increasing ineffectiveness of education in delivering productivity and unmanageable public debt – and his case is complete.[20] This is why productivity has slowed down and will continue to stay low. American venture capitalist Peter Thiel is even more downbeat: 'We were promised flying cars – we got 140 characters.'[21]

This techno-pessimism is an important dimension of the secular stagnation thesis – but the stagnationists and pessimists are wrong. Peter Thiel is already confounded. In the spring of 2014 there were the first prototypes of flying cars whose arrival he doubted. True, they are as clumsy as the prototypes of driverless cars assembled in March 2004 to show off their paces in the Mojave Desert in response to the first of the US Defense Advanced Research Project Agency (DARPA)'s grand technological challenges to American society – but today nobody would write off the notion of driverless cars. It will be the same story with flying cars.

The techno-pessimists are far too quick to set boundaries to human wants and imagination, too narrow in their understanding of what drives innovation and too crabbed in their view of human ingenuity and our desire to live better. As has been argued by others, the 'innovation-as-fruit' theory – that technology essentially presents itself as a harvest of intellectual fruit to be picked – does not capture what innovation has always been about. Innovators throughout history have ceaselessly rearranged and recombined what was currently known to throw up new insights, processes and capabilities: James Watt was a recombiner, creating a much more efficient steam engine, as was Steve Jobs with his brilliant recombining of the varying pre-existent technologies to create the iPhone: 'Digital innovation is recombinant innovation in its purest form. Each development becomes a building block for future innovations. Progress doesn't run out: it accumulates.'[22]

Precisely. The authors of *The Second Machine Age* (Eric Brynjolfsson and Andrew McAfee), from which that quote is taken, are right. Progress accumulates not only because of the recombinant nature of innovation – but because of the hunger of the scientist and theorist to quest for the new. The prominent economic historian Professor Joel Mokyr argues just this:

> as science moves into new areas and solves issues that were not even imagined to be solvable, there are inventors, engineers, and entrepreneurs waiting in the wings to use the new knowledge and design new gizmos and processes based on it that mostly will continue to improve our lives. The interplay between science and technology creates a self-reinforcing or 'auto-catalytic' process that seems unbounded.

He singles out materials as just one area where there are giant jumps ahead:

> what is happening to materials now is nothing short of a sea change, with new resins, ceramics, and entirely new solids designed *in silico*, being developed at the nano-technological level. These promise the development of materials nature never dreamed of and that deliver custom-ordered properties in terms of hardness, resilience, elasticity, and so on.[23]

Just so. As I argued earlier, science is both developing explosively and jumping across old disciplinary boundaries to create new from the new – a process better enabled by digitisation.

Nor is this a recent development. Exploring the patent record of US companies in the nineteenth century, it is obvious that firms exploited a knowledge base far removed from their own fields of technological expertise to create new patents and thus new goods and services.[24] Innovation is socially created and grows exponentially.

It may take time for digitisation to work its magic; after all it was a full sixty years before the transformative impact of steam began to be widely felt. But the wave of transformation brought about by petrochemicals and electronics took only forty years. All the signs are that digitisation will work through the system even faster – within thirty years.[25] It is much more likely that what we are currently experiencing is a hiatus while the whole system adjusts both to the speed and possibilities of the disruptive change. It has been argued that one cause of the uncertainty besetting business is that at the moment the trans-formative possibilities are almost too wide-ranging. When disruptive change crosses company boundaries and there is so much uncertainty, there has to be an accompanying trans-formation in the way companies develop strategy and take decisions. There has to be more openness, more exchange, more iterative reciprocation if only to avoid costly mistakes. No single organisation can hope to get more than half the bets right consistently: the way to improve is to pool knowledge collaboratively with others in open exchange. This is 'open innovation'.

Yet the current institutional structure is rooted in a pre-dictable, less volatile universe that is more closed. What is required is a sharing revolution to drive forward the processes of open innovation – a reappraisal, as I shall argue in Chapter 5, of everything from the law relating to intellectual property rights to the exchange of data.[26] But learning how to do this will take time, even as the twenty-first century witnesses more technological and scientific advance than in the last five hundred years.

This should not shake the view that digitisation is the most general purpose of all technologies. Moreover, human beings have an infinite capacity to create new wants to use the advances. In this respect I am as unashamedly optimistic today as Keynes was in 1930 when he wrote the 'Economic Possibilities for our Grandchildren', wildly predicting, as it seemed to contemporaries, that in a hundred years living standards would be four to eight times higher than they were at the time. He has been triumphantly vindicated.[27]

If anything the disruptive drive is accelerating. The stock of intangible assets that in one way or another embody knowledge – from computer programs to intellectual property rights, training programmes to the value of brands – surpassed the stock of tangible assets (bricks, mortar and machines) some fifteen years ago, around the turn of the century. In 2011 (the latest year for which figures are available) the UK market sector invested £126.8 billion in intangible assets, 44 per cent more than the £88 billion invested in tangible assets.[28] The fastest-selling luxury car in the US, for example, is now the battery-powered, tablet-operated Tesla that is transforming consumers' notions of what a car should be. Yes, it is a recombination of existing ideas to produce an innovative first. But it is also even more of a knowledge good than the cars it is replacing: it is more 'intangible' than 'tangible'.

Nor is that where the transformation stops. The Tesla is creating new opportunities for the makers of batteries, new battery power stations, in fact the entire infrastructure needed to support electrical cars. What is happening is creative destruction: the elimination of the old and the creation of the new – and with it there will be many job opportunities. The Tesla story will be reproduced many times over. Jeremiah predictions of joblessness overdo the losses and underestimate the possibilities. Growth and jobs will emerge unexpectedly and unpredictably, as they always have. Here is my own stab at identifying four broad areas of the economy where rapid change is taking place and large numbers of jobs are likely to be generated.

The first is the growth of micro-production, the death of scale and the personalisation of provision. There is going to be a huge growth in micro-producers – micro-brewers, micro-bakers, micro-film makers, micro-energy producers, micro-tailors, micro-software houses and micro-providers generally – who will deploy the internet of things (building artefacts – things – with micro-printers receiving digital information over the internet) and micro-production techniques to produce goods at prices as if they were mass-produced, but customised for individual tastes.

The second is in human well-being. There will be a boom in advising, coaching, caring, mentoring, doctoring, nursing, teaching, and general enhancement of human beings' capabilities. Medical provision will broach new boundaries, as replacement organs, skin and limbs open up new specialisms and industries. Taste, sight and hearing will be vastly enhanced. Deafness and blindness will be conquered. We will live longer, with old age advisers offering advice on how to live well in one's hundreds and memory enhancers alleviating memory loss. Mental well-being will become another growth industry. Geneticists will open up a 'live-well' economy. Instantaneous language translation will break down language barriers.

The third is in addressing the globe's 'wicked issues'. There will be new forms of nutrition and carbon-efficient energy, along with ways of using water more economically, to meet the demands of a world population of nine billion in 2050. Space exploration will become crucial to find new minerals and energy sources. New forms of mining will allow exploration of the earth's crust. The oceans will be farmed and seabeds mined.

And fourth, digital and big data management will foster whole new industries – personalised journalism, social media, cyber-security, information selection, software, computer science and the removal of digital clutter.

Doubtless futurologists will come up with different sectors, jobs and potential technologies: everyone is making what can only be informed guesses. What we do know is that two-thirds of what we consume today was not invented twenty-five years ago. The pace of change, obsolescence and renewal is accelerating, so in the years ahead even that benchmark will be surpassed. Firms and individuals will be on their mettle to open up, innovate and constantly reinvent themselves. The downside is that, unless we develop countervailing forces, there will be more inequality in incomes, life chances and opportunity as the gap opens up between routine and skilled work. There is also an ominous tendency in an information economy for the first movers if they achieve scale to grow to a position of monopoly; competition policy has to be faster, aggressive and more intelligent. Digitisation opens up extraordinary vulnerability over personal privacy, as exposed by whistleblower Edward Snowden's revelations about the scale of surveillance by the US National Security Agency; again this requires a new vigilance and entrenchment of citizens' rights. But the larger message remains. The economy is set to reinvent itself. The future does not need to be dystopian. There will be much work and many jobs to do.

Seizing the moment

The question is how to organise ourselves best to benefit. Traditional classical economics is not much of a guide. Centred on the conception that markets necessarily and always create points of equilibrium, this brand of free market economics has neglected the restless, ceaseless, disruptive nature of innovation and the uncertainty and dislocation it inevitably generates. This has disabled understanding of the innovation process; for example, the impact of general purpose technologies on economic life has been abstracted away, as has the role of the state in ambitiously driving them forward, directly and indirectly.

It may be true, for example, that the empirical evidence is that the public sector has played a key role in every GPT in the twentieth century in which the US is globally competitive, but economics ignores it.[29] One famous example is the technologies, ranging from micro-processors to liquid-crystal displays, from lithium-based batteries to the internet itself, that were incorporated into Apple's iPod, iPhone and iPad, as detailed by Professor Mariana Mazzucato. All were seeded by public sector research spending, not only in the US. The genius of Steve Jobs and his co-founder Steve Wozniak was to see how the results – of DARPA's and NASA's sponsorship of ever smaller silicon-based microchips, of Europe's state-backed CERN programme and federal-backed university research into emerging touch-screen capacities, of the Department of Energy's sponsoring of lithium-ion batteries, and, of course, of the internet itself, the DARPA-initiated decentralised control network that would allow the US air forces communication systems to survive nuclear attack – could be integrated into Apple's handsome, well-designed devices.[30] But the state in economics is portrayed as a problem, getting in the way of the market. The idea that the state might be an essential part of the innovation process, designing institutions, sharing risk and frequently spearheading risk-taking itself by spending money and commissioning new ideas has been foreign to the economic canon. Trying to promote the market as the solution to lifting research and development neglects the reality that the rate of return to society from R&D

is up to twice as high as private returns from research: more reliance on private research in free markets in reality means less frontier innovation than society needs.[31] Necessarily the state has been involved, in one way or another, in all the great GPTs over the centuries – whether it was the Pentagon initiating the internet or Protestant princes in Germany placing large orders for the bible to fund the new printing presses.

Breaking out of the risk of secular stagnation and taking advantage of the opportunities offered by new technology thus demands a wholesale rethink about how capitalism is structured, how it relates to society and state and how all three can be reinvigorated. This is what this book will attempt in the chapters ahead. As matters stand Britain is incapacitated. The country is 159th out of 174 countries in the international league table for investment; business investment has been on a downward trend for the last fifteen years.[32] Germany, Japan, France and the US all outspend Britain on research and development (R&D).[33] Exports languish far below what we need them to be – standing at half the £1 trillion target for 2020 – while the trade deficit, at 4.5 per cent of GDP in 2013, was the highest for twenty-five years.

Britain does not have the structures to support innovative risk-taking on the scale that is needed to provide a vibrant economy for all. The necessary interdependencies between public and private to change the calculus of risk and reward that would unleash more investment and innovation are simply not understood in the national conversation. The call for 'open innovation' induces bewilderment. In any case, even if the wider systems were more supportive, there is such a shortage of trust and integrity that it is hard to build the relationships between firms, and between firms and government, that might allow us to figure out what to do, how to react and in what to invest. Government is portrayed as intrusive, a burden, a source of mistakes and a crowder-out of private initiative. It is true that government makes mistakes, but its mistakes do not trump the need for it to shape and design markets to stimulate more innovation and to ensure that the gains from the new are shared round equitably. Such propositions remain a source of controversy rather than being understood as a necessity. Rather than no government we need smart, agile government.

But there will be no change until our business, financial, official and political elite start to recognise these shortcomings and take the lead in demanding smart collaboration between public and private – along with some sacrifice of their own interests and wealth – to recast corporate and financial relationships to deliver a high-growth, high-innovation, high-wage Britain. To do that demands a sense of a shared destiny and a shared belief in what Britain can become, underpinned, as I will argue next, by a shared belief in justice, in openness, and that the objective must be to create a society in which everyone has the opportunity to secure their well-being.

This would entail a recovery of the open Enlightenment values and spirit that so animated the first Industrial Revolution – a belief in the future, underpinned by reason, that is collectively shared and expressed, a sense of fairness and open access to all. Thus could Britain attain the audacious goals around which the nation can rally. Britain should aim to be, say, Europe's innovation leader so that, in every field from smart cities to smart health, we are the number one. We should be a beacon for how to live well. At present our aim seems little more than to reduce public debt, submit to whatever the financial markets wish and keep out as many foreigners as possible – unless they want to buy our homes or our companies. It is a dispiriting, shrunken and defeatist view of what being British can and should be.

In the absence of inspiring goals, we have what we have: a

first-order banking crisis, whose legacy will extend for years; widespread, sullen disaffection represented by influential political movements in England and Scotland – UKIP and the Scottish National Party (SNP) – that want fundamentally to recast the basic political settlement that shapes our lives. It may be that the Scots voted to retain the union with the rest of the UK, but 45 per cent of the electorate voted for secession; equally, any vote to stay inside the EU will be won, if it is won at all, by a small margin. Economy and society are not working, and the answer – wrong in both Scotland and the rest of the UK – for too many citizens is Scottish independence and leaving the EU. The right answer is much more uncomfortable and harder to accept: it is that by allowing our dysfunctional capitalism to develop as it has, there are too few checks, balances and outright obstacles to a significant part of our business and financial elite choosing to plunder our companies and our country rather than invest in it – and too feeble an attempt to allow the mass of our people to flourish.

The themes of *The State We're In* are no longer the musings of an interested if maverick outsider. If they are not addressed, in twenty years' time I will be writing an even more mournful tract – a requiem to a once great country that refused to confront the truths about itself, allowed its elites to continue with their wanton progress, shrivelled the imagination and aspirations of its citizens and, surrendering to right-wing populism, disintegrated as a coherent economic, social and political whole.

2

The Eclipse of Justice and the Diminution of Britain

Human beings are social animals. The society of others is what gives our lives pleasure and meaning. We love, work, hang out and create belief systems and moral codes by which we live in association with others. Our well-being is not something we can create in isolation. The logic of the emotions we feel and demonstrate is to signal to others, and of course ourselves, the depth and intensity of our reaction to what others are doing and saying. The integrity of this interaction requires trust in a relationship of mutual respect, and this works best in a spirit of tolerant give and take around common values.

The central value is fairness. Every human being possesses an innate sense that he or she should get back proportionally from an interaction what was invested. A smile or greeting returns a reciprocal smile or greeting; a frown and anger invite a reciprocal distancing. Reward and punishment alike should be accorded in proportion to whatever good or bad outcome we have delivered.[1] The origin of the good life is thus human exchange in an atmosphere of mutual tolerance and a mutual respect for fairness around which the principles of justice are based. This is the foundation stone of society, exchange and business. Freedom and autonomy of action must take place within such a social, moral, just framework. Thus can people's capabilities be so enlarged that they can, in philosopher Amartya Sen's famous formulation, 'live the kind of lives they value – and have reason to value'.[2]

The British were pioneers in trying to create a free, just, tolerant society based on mutual respect and the rule of law. The Magna Carta in 1215 was a world first, establishing that even the monarch had to operate within a framework of law, which then led over the centuries to the development of common law and the jury system. It was the struggles of the English Civil War – in part provoked by the desire to defend the common law from incursions by the Crown – that launched the idea of checked, balanced and later representative government within a framework of the rule of law. Later came the Toleration Act, with its respect for religious freedoms, and freedom of expression and the liberty of the individual were entrenched by the Enlightenment.

The concept of academic freedom within autonomous, self-governing universities, along with the post-war creation of the National Health Service and the universal welfare state, were all building blocks in the emergence of a British society that in the context of its times advanced the cause of justice, tolerance, freedom and democratic accountability – along with institutions that tried to offer fairness in the provision of health, education and the alleviation of need. The famous kindness and tolerance which defines the Church of England – so that even an atheist like Richard Dawkins will acknowledge he is a cultural Anglican – was in part created by this history, indeed importantly helped to shape it, and produced the accompanying culture. The BBC, with its duty to report impartially and objectively, is another embodiment of core British values. Self-deprecation, a love of irony, a willingness to queue, neighbourliness, fair play in sport and a suspicion of high theory are all offshoots of this central cultural timber.

In the second decade of the twenty-first century the British are being reinvented to think and behave very differently. The simple pro-market, individualist nostrums of Thatcherism, too little qualified or challenged by New Labour, have begun to metamorphose – egged on by a destructive, vengeful centre-right press – into a mix of crude libertarianism, scepticism of all things initiated by the state and distrust of the public realm. We do not act together: we look out for ourselves as individuals. Justice, equity, tolerance and proportionality are all in retreat and a more brutal, selfish and amoral society is emerging. Yet, as I will argue in later chapters, the values under assault are indispensable both economically and socially; they undergird more purposeful companies that build the trust relations on which fast-moving innovation and high-performance workplaces depend and support any kind of social settlement that tries to deal with poverty, the undeserved bad luck of life and lack of social mobility. Eviscerate these values, and what is left is an impoverished transactional, short-termist capitalism and a mean society. Britain is becoming the laboratory for a libertarian, anti-social justice experiment. It is a game being played for very high stakes.

The manifestations of the new culture are all around. It is compromising basic principles of justice – that it should be accessible to all with indivisible rights to a fair trial – through radically limiting the extent of legal aid. It is wildly extravagant and disproportionate pay for executives. It is allowing understandable concerns about the new scale of inward immigration (partly offset by the rising numbers of outward migration) to transmute into concern about any immigrant and any foreigner that too often verges on racism. Fair criticism about the BBC morphs into ceaseless attacks, because necessarily as an institution that attempts objectivity it cannot report on the world through the same distorted prism as the centre-right press. The inevitable shortcomings in any one NHS hospital, a service employing over a million people, become the excuse for attacking its entire existence because, above any other British institution, it embodies equity and justice – toxic notions to the centre-right and new libertarians. The Human Rights Act, incorporating the Convention of European Human Rights into British law, is criticised for qualifying British parliamentary sovereignty even when the human rights it protects – for example the right even for a suspected terrorist not to be imprisoned without being charged or offered a trial – are fundamental to any canon of rights. The Conservative party now proposes that its recommendations become 'advisory' rather than binding, in essence a withdrawal; the intention is for British justice to be made by the Conservatives controlling the House of Commons following their instincts, rather than internationally agreed principles. The welfare state is not lauded for its strengths but instead is continuously assailed for its seemingly limitless weaknesses, notably that it encourages a culture of dependent entitlement of the kind portrayed by the infamous Channel 4 documentary series *Benefits Street*. Church leaders who inveigh against the injustices of our society are regarded with amused indifference as emissaries from planet God – literally a universe apart, and in such decline that their moral intensity is eccentric, or from the perspective of the right, motivated by political malevolence.

This is not to argue that every part of Britain's matrix of attempted justice has attained perfection: renewal and institutional reform are an ongoing necessity. Neither the NHS nor every corner of the criminal justice system, notably the police, could or should be defended to the last – and the same could be said for all the institutions listed above. But the critics' attacks are not constructive, aimed at reform and reconstruction; rather they are designed radically to undermine what those critics would characterise as a corrupt liberal value system that supports them – and so delegitimise them that they can broken up, privatised, starved of resources or ignored. In the critics' terms, for example, the NHS promotes a socialist ethic. The BBC is inveterately liberal. Institutions that promote citizens' welfare – from the Trussell Trust, which runs 400 food banks and feeds half a million children, to the Howard League for Penal Reform – are respectively dismissed as friends of do-goodery and over-generous welfare or as soft on punishment, undermining the new individualistic culture the libertarians seek to promote.[3]

It was ironic that it fell to Rupert Murdoch's daughter Elizabeth, giving the McTaggart Lecture at the Edinburgh television festival in 2012, to argue that what was happening was to establish profit and the market as the only valid 'sorting mechanism' in society. But 'it's us, human beings, we the people who create the society we want, not profit', she insisted. The consequence, she said, was an 'unsettling dearth of integrity across so many of our institutions'. Integrity had collapsed, she argued, because of the collective acceptance of a libertarian belief in an individualist calculus of profit and loss. Ramming her point home, she continued, 'it's increasingly apparent that the absence of purpose, of a moral language within government, media or business could become one of the most dangerous own goals for capitalism and freedom'. This same absence of moral purpose was wounding companies like News International, she thought, making it more likely that it would lose its way as it had with widespread illegal telephone hacking.

She is right. The words that have mattered for a generation are efficiency, flexibility, shareholder value, business friendly, and wealth generation. The words relegated to the margin have been those associated with justice. It is not just companies like her father's that have been damaged; it is our entire economy and society.

The criminal justice system in peril

This eclipse of justice suffuses the public domain, so that moral purpose becomes expressed not in terms of what is just, but what can be paid for. The Coalition government justifies its drive to reduce public spending because of the alleged immorality of burdening our children with debt. But morality does not extend to allowing justice to inform the character of the spending cuts made in the here and now – so that unsurprisingly the criminal justice system has become one of the principal sufferers. Legal aid will have been cut by 30 per cent between 2012 and 2015, with more to come. Seventy per cent of cases dealt with by the probation service are to be contracted out privately, despite two major public service contractors, Serco and G4S, being investigated for fraud at the time of writing – G4S for overcharging electronic tagging of prisoners on probation and Serco for escorting prisoners to and from jail. The prison service budget was slashed by a quarter between 2010 and 2013; officer numbers have been cut by 30 per cent, estimates the Howard League, so the ratio of officers to men has fallen from one in three in 2000 to one in five today. Prison numbers are so high (around 86,000, just below the all-time high of 88,000) that they exceed available prison space by 13 per cent. The number of prisons reporting that they offer purposeful activity as part of the route to rehabilitation fell from three-quarters in 2009 to a half in 2013. Riots are becoming ever more frequent: the riot squad was called up 203 times in 2013, compared with 129 times in 2012. In the year to May 2013, 91 prisoners took their lives out of desperation, up from 60 in the twelve months to December 2012.[4]

Similarly the Crown Prosecution Service, a key component of our public capacity to ensure justice, is increasingly a broken reed. Reeling from the cumulative 27 per cent cuts in its budget since 2012, it is beset by high staff turnover, inadequate resources and rock-bottom morale. The Bureau of Investigative Journalism calculates that the CPS has lost 23 per cent (202) of its barristers, 22 per cent (518) of its solicitors and 27 per cent (296) of its higher court advocates.[5] Police routinely complain in private that its lawyers turn up to cases without having had the time to read painstakingly assembled evidence. Judges criticise it for fielding barristers inadequate to the task, or for its inability to disclose key papers in a timely way. Too many high-profile cases seem to fail.

Similarly the police since 2010 have been required to cut spending by 20 per cent in real terms – an unprecedented reduction. By 2015, reports Her Majesty's Inspectorate of Constabulary (HMIC), police staffing numbers will have fallen by 34,000 – 16,300 of them police officers to reduce the force to 2005 numbers – as part of finding cumulative savings of £2.53 billion. Despite the best efforts of police forces to restructure and use new technologies so that front-line policing has been as little affected as possible, the HMIC warns that the loss of three posts in twenty must begin to impact on neighbourhood policing.[6] There has been a massive sale of police assets. For example, London's Metropolitan Police is selling its iconic headquarters New Scotland Yard that houses 2500 staff to move to a new office that can only accommodate 1000 on the assumption that 1500 Scotland Yard staff jobs can comfortably be abandoned or performed elsewhere. Necessarily, operational efficiency is impaired. Car pools, for example, have been relocated to distant parts of London so that the response time to crimes is necessarily slower. Response to 999 calls is already 30 per cent slower on average across all forces. Morale is at rock bottom as the possibility of doing a good job recedes, let alone the prospect of promotion and advancement. British policing has not distinguished itself in recent years with a succession of disasters: ongoing evidence of institutional racism, abusing stop and search powers (see below) and not acting swiftly over charges of widespread child sex abuse. The Police Federation has become a byword for its willingness to protect indefensible working practices. Reform is vital. Nonetheless Britain needs policing just as it needs the entire criminal justice system, and for that resources are an imperative. There are more awesome spending cuts ahead that will further undermine the infrastructure of the entire criminal justice system. The easy to do reductions and restructurings have been done: we are now cutting into the bone. Day to day order and the delivery of justice are at risk.

Yet it was Winston Churchill as Home Secretary who declared to the House of Commons in 1910:

> The mood and temper of the public in regard to the treatment of crime and criminals is one of the most unfailing tests of the civilisation of any country. A calm and dispassionate recognition of the rights of the accused against the state and even of convicted criminals against the state, a constant heart-searching by all charged with the duty of punishment, a desire and eagerness to rehabilitate in the world of industry of all those who have paid their dues in the hard coinage of punishment, tireless efforts towards the discovery of curative and regenerating processes and an unfaltering faith that there is a treasure,

if only you can find it in the heart of every person – these are
the symbols which in the treatment of crime and criminals
mark and measure the stored up strength of a nation, and are
the sign and proof of the living virtue in it.[7]

It was a classic statement of a British approach to justice. Today
Churchill would be accused of being part of the human rights
industry, soft on criminals, insufficiently aware of the need
for deterrence and unwilling to accept hard choices over
public spending. A public figure who urged proportionality of
response and humanity in the criminal justice system today
would be derided and mocked; it falls to the ageing former
Tory cabinet minister Ken Clarke to make the case and soak up
the tabloid mockery. Otherwise notions of justice are submerged under a new vengefulness, reinforced by extreme
individualism and distrust of the state.

Law and justice are no longer enshrined as inviolable public
goods that are qualified at our peril; rather, the amount of
money available to spend on them is whatever the Treasury
allocates once tax revenues are forecast and the target for elim-
inating the deficit is set in stone (a process examined in more
detail in the Conclusion). If you want justice, the message is to
expect to pay for it yourself rather than have an embedded
civic right to expect others to help you because they might
one day need the same help.

Moral individuals and a good society in the prevalent worldview are those who do without the state. The public sphere is
derided and positive public action to promote the common or
international good is acceptable only if it involves less, rather
than more, government. Nationhood is not defined as creating
the jurisdiction for self-determination so that government can
build an interdependent great economy and just society.
Rather nationhood is defined by being the locus for hostility to

the other – the immigrant and foreigner – beyond concerns for justice. The open society and justice are in retreat.

The roll-back of justice at work

If such notions are being weakened even in the justice system, expect them to be slaughtered elsewhere. The world of work is another target for the roll-back of justice. What began in the 1980s as a legitimate attempt to rebalance the power relationships between over-powerful trade unions, wedded to an entitlement culture and hostile to the idea of the market economy, and management, has transmuted into the organisation of employment at the bottom as forms of subjugation, and at the top as the opportunity for gothic levels of greed. Forced labour, a contemporary form of slavery, has become so prevalent in the food, construction and agricultural industries that the Joseph Rowntree Foundation has commissioned a report with precisely that title.[8] Immigrants in particular are vulnerable, being essentially held in bondage by the agencies and gangs who bring them into the UK with the promise of work and subsequently terrorise them into working to pay off excessive debts, with the threat that they will be denounced to the authorities as illegal immigrants if they dare to complain. The report suggests the numbers are probably in the tens of thousands, with Home Office analysis later in November 2014 estimating that total UK slave numbers lie in the 10,000 to 13,000 range. That such a phenomenon even exists is a stark signifier of much deeper underlying trends, which has amazingly prompted an anti-slavery bill. A lightly regulated labour market in which the injunction is for individuals to be self-reliant has become a playground for new forms of twenty-first-century exploitation.

Zero-hour contracts, in which workers agree beforehand to

make themselves available only for hours that they are called upon to work by their employer, are another manifestation of the same phenomenon. The number of such contracts has doubled in five years to an estimated 1.4 million.[9] There is no 35- or 40-hour week complete with holiday, sickness and pension benefits. There are no employment rights, redundancy payments or rights for representation at work. There is simply an hourly wage rate for whatever work is available, with the worker as a disposable commodity. It is a technocratic name for a very old and unfair labour market phenomenon: casualisation. The risk of fluctuating patterns in work is moved from the firm, which has the resources to smooth risks from week to week, and instead placed on the shoulders of individuals whose capacity to manage risk and uncertain income is tiny.

Even job seekers must now accept zero-hour contracts as the price of being in receipt of job seeker's allowance. This is not an income that could be used when taking out a mortgage to buy a flat or house – or even an income which allows the worker to budget for rent and food. It simply gets the claimant off the state's books and into the mayhem of payday lenders and food banks. There are some – students or early retirees with a pension – for whom zero-hour contracts can work; but for the most part such agreements are first cousin to forced labour. Importantly, business secretary Vince Cable in June 2014 moved to prevent employers from insisting that a zero-hour contract can be exclusive to one firm: workers will be entitled to hold such contracts with more than one firm. It is a welcome move, but the power imbalance remains stark. Workers are still throwaway commodities, not trusted partners.

The labour market has become brutalised, as I will explore in more detail in Chapter 4. Some of this is the consequence of legislative change in which justice takes a back seat: thus for example workers who wish to make a claim against an employer at an employment tribunal now have to pay a succession of fees which may not be refunded even if they win their case. The decrease in the number of cases has been stunning, with claims running at around a fifth of the level before the fees were introduced.[10] Defenders would say it is an overdue rebalancing of justice and a reduction in frivolous cases; however, in a world in which so many advantages lie with employers it makes the just workplace even harder to attain.

This transformation has occurred partly because companies themselves find they can no longer sustain concepts of career and employee development. This is a consequence of the way companies are owned, managed and governed, where again notions of justice – as I discuss in the next chapter – are in retreat. The decline of career – the idea of progressively gaining wisdom, salary and status the longer one works – has become ubiquitous. Everyone is confronted by the transient, impermanent nature of their work.[11] Part of this is because the pace of technological advance and the capacity to routinise work with computers are growing so rapidly, part because no business model is secure; but part is because so many businesses know their existence is likely to be transient and so do not conceive of themselves as being productive social organisations that will last. Companies know they can be taken over at any moment: key commercial contracts are time limited and will run out, not necessarily to be replaced; yesterday's promising hiree is tomorrow's square peg in a round hole. Nobody can expect upward progression in any firm as a matter of course; skills and experience may suddenly become redundant. A new rootlessness – whether among unskilled, unemployed boys playing video games while heavily using drugs or their elders scratching a living as self-employed 'consultants' – has become the common currency.

This should be the recruiting sergeant, if not for rising

trade union membership, then at least for some bottom-up movements to fight back. But there is a fatalism that it can be no different. Society's belief that there should be justice in the round, let alone in the idea of just work and just rewards, is in retreat; there is thus scant social or cultural support for any challenge to the present situation. The very legitimacy of a trade union movement that could offer some countervailing power is undermined by an insistence that only individual workers acting by themselves should expect just outcomes; workers' collective voice is neither a legitimate part of dialogue in the workplace nor of the wider public conversation.[12]

The liberal society and social contract in peril

The roots of our allegedly liberal society do not prove to be very deep. Tolerance of other people's differences is a core element of a liberal order, but a good society is one where we engage with the complexities of intolerant prejudices rather than believe that because it is understood they are wrong, the liberal job is done and that change automatically follows. In these terms our alleged liberality becomes no more than disinterested indifference rather than the product of genuine conviction and a felt need to act. Thus multiple ways remain in which women's subordinate relationship to men continues to be embedded in culture and practice despite the apparent advances of feminism and legal entrenchment of equality; women disproportionately work in low-paid parts of the economy and even holding the same job are paid less than their male counterparts – despite the Equal Pay Act being law since 1970. Fifty-two per cent of women reported harassment or bullying at work in one of the largest-ever surveys, with a further 12 per cent reporting sexual harassment – despite the law on harassment.[13] CEO of the English Premier League Richard Scudamore was able to apologise for his private sexist texts, revealed by his temporary PA in May 2014, including the 'irrationality' of women – and still retain his job. The Equality and Human Rights Commission reports that black people on average are six times more likely to be stopped and searched than white people.[14] There are only two black football managers of the 92 clubs in the Football League. So it goes on.

The good society is one in which, through argument and deliberation, we create law and justice as a moral system enshrining human dignity and accept mutual responsibilities – and then live by its injunctions across the board. The shortcomings on race, gender or sexual orientation are but the most conspicuous examples of a more general weakness. A passion for justice should inform the way we organise our legal system, work, pay, company organisation and social settlement alike. The aim is to live with dignity, to be able to make the best of one's capabilities and to expect that the consequences of undeserved bad luck – what moral philosopher Ronald Dworkin called brute bad luck – will be compensated by society in a mutual compact.

Unsurprisingly even the notion of a social contract is in peril. What constitutes a good society? What are our responsibilities and obligations to one another? To what extent is our humanity about looking solely after ourselves or being part of something we call society? The last vestiges of an approach to organising society based on a social contract informed by a concept of justice have been shredded. In its place there is an emergent system of discretionary poor relief imposed from on high, in which every claimant is defined not as a citizen exercising an entitlement because they have encountered one of life's many hazards, but as a dependent shirker or scrounger.

The Coalition government believes it is working with the

grain of public opinion. Fairness demands, it protests, that the recipients of Britain's allegedly enormous welfare bill play their part in the urgent programme to eliminate Britain's budget deficit. Austerity must hit everyone. The welfare system, so the argument goes, has become a colossal scam encouraging systematic cheating and, worse, a culture in which idleness is rewarded and work penalised. It does not matter that fraud is trivial in scale, running at 0.7 per cent of total benefit spending.[15] To magnify hugely its salience is part of a systematic onslaught so that support for social solidarity as a principle is disappearing. The terms on which millions have made their plans and life choices are being torn up. The automatic link between inflation and the uprating of benefits has been scrapped for at least three years from 2014. The tax relief available to those building retirement pensions is to be further withdrawn. This comes on top of the capping of benefits, whatever the need, the restrictions on housing benefit and the much resented 'bedroom tax', further limiting of incapacity benefit and the shrinking of access to child benefit. The newly unemployed are only eligible for benefit once they have shown they have looked for work – bureaucratic meanness at a time when a person is at their most vulnerable and despondent.

But life is risky and hazardous for everyone. The bad luck of a broken family, unemployment, poor health, the unexpected expenses of old age, mental illness and physical incapacity can hit anyone, however hard-working and anxious to stand on their own two feet. A good society recognises these risks and insists they should be shared and insured against in an agreed system of collective insurance. The great thinkers of the Enlightenment proposed that if society was to transcend theocracy, anarchy or despotism, then it had to be underwritten by such a social contract embodying notions of social justice. To organise society as an individualistic war in which each person was pitted against another was barbaric, while other models, slavishly following the rules of one religion or one supreme leader, denied freedom.

The heart of fairness is to establish a proportional relationship between contribution and outcome to which everyone consents. It is justice in economic and social practice. People have made calculations about how they are to handle the costs of old age, bringing up their children, physical incapacity or the lack of work in their area on the basis of social contributions that they reckoned on being an inviolable part of the deal. Now millions of British have helplessly found – something for which no one voted – that the deal is being downsized. A social contract is a bargain over time. I pay my taxes and national insurance contributions. I should get benefits back when I need them.

Of course, the design of a social contract matters. It should recognise labour market realities and not undermine incentives; it should restrict itself to insuring against inevitable risks and hazards; and it should be supported by taxation that never becomes onerous, while at the same time the government does its level best to promote economic growth and jobs. Nobody aims to create the culture supposedly depicted in Channel 4's *Benefits Street*. But equally the current punitiveness towards benefit cheats, with the Director of Public Prosecutions suggesting in 2013 that prosecutions be brought forward under the Fraud Act where sentences could exceed those of rapists, is to broach a new disproportionality in our priorities for justice.[16] It is only because so many benefits have not been earned by contributions and are seen as hand-outs that it is felt necessary to patrol potential cheating so vengefully. The system should be based on insurance payments earned through working: a benefit should be the due desert for contributions rather than a discretionary handout policed by the threat of enormous prison sentences.

Roosevelt famously insisted that workers paid for his social security with earmarked hypothecated taxes: 'with these taxes in there,' he said in answer to critics who worried that his proposed benefits would go to everyone rather than just the very needy, 'no damn politician can scrap my social security programme'.[17] Everyone had paid in; everyone should get their just payment if they qualified. So it has proved. Britain has been wide open to the dismantling of its system: there is no broad-based understanding that national insurance contributions deliver pensions and unemployment benefit that no 'damn politician' can unwind. Instead national insurance is widely perceived as just another 'stoppage' – in effect a tax.

A conservative apologist would say that on many measures Britain has never been better off: we are richer, more of us are in work and we live longer. My reply is that, for all the inevitable good that must be found in a country of sixty-two million people, the big picture is sobering and darkening. Too many British institutions – from the police to the City of London – have plainly lost their way. They are not trusted, because their grip on justice – and thus their ability to behave with integrity and deserve trust – has grown ever more shaky. There is widespread disillusionment with the political system. Too many people feel there is no chance they can live lives they have reason to value, or that the future is likely to be better than the past, or that there is any potential redress for such problems. Too many parts of the country feel deserted, neglected and left behind. A conservative would blame the decline of Europe, of which Britain is part, and the rise of Asia: of course living standards are squeezed. My response is as it was twenty years ago. Our difficulties are made at home.

If we do not put justice at the heart of our preoccupations and translate it into the way we organise ourselves, we may expect disaffection, social restlessness and the erosion of trust. We are reaping what we have sown.

3

The Vandals Within

Twenty years ago, Britain's greatest industrial companies were ICI and GEC. A third, Rolls-Royce, secure from hostile takeover by a government golden share that entitled the government to override other shareholders and block an unwanted bid, had a board that was committed to research and development and to investing in its business. ICI and GEC, under colossal pressure from footloose shareholders to deliver high short-term profits, tried to wheel and deal their way to success. Neither now exists. Rolls-Royce, free from concerns about hourly movements in its share price, has gone on to be one of our last remaining great industrial companies.

Britain has far too few Rolls-Royces. Concerned that the explanation lay in the way British companies are owned, Business Secretary Vince Cable invited economist John Kay to conduct a review into 'equity markets and long-term decision making'. His report, published in 2012, more than confirmed the concern. It identified a lengthening list of companies – Marks and Spencer, Royal Bank of Scotland, BP, GlaxoSmithKline, Lloyds and BAE – which along with ICI and GEC have made grave strategic errors, taken ethical short cuts or launched ill-judged takeovers, hoping to benefit their uncommitted tourist shareholders. Their competitors in other countries, with different ownership structures and incentives, have survived and prospered. Intriguingly ICI and GEC both had German immigrant founders in the nineteenth century, and were as central to Britain's Second World War effort as their German rivals BASF and Siemens. Siemens is now Europe's largest engineering company, BASF the world's largest chemical company. Their British rivals have disappeared. Yet the criticism of the ownership and financial system that produced such devastating failure is trivial.

Over the last decade, a fifth of quoted companies have evaporated from the London Stock Exchange, the largest cull in our history. Virtually no new risk capital is sought from the stock market or offered across the spectrum of companies. As the Kay Review remarks, the stock market is more a vehicle for getting money out of companies than putting it in. Britain has no indigenous quoted company in the car, chemical, glass, industrial gases, industrial services, and building materials industries – to name but a few. They are all owned overseas, with their research and development and strategic direction travelling abroad as well.

The stock market is ever more a casino. A share is now held for an average of less than six months, although the average is defined by extremes: long-term shareholding continues, if its prevalence is shrinking, while short-term trading has become hyper-frenetic. Seventy-two per cent of stock market trading is done by hedge funds, high-frequency traders or investment banks trading on their own account.[1] In the US the impact of computerised high-frequency trading has been to reduce the average period shares are held to twenty-two seconds.[2] The story is similar in the UK: in fact many transactions take place in a fraction of a second. This business is served by a vast

industry of intermediaries – agents, trustees, investment managers, registrars and advisers of all sorts – who have grown fat
from opaque fees. The entire apparatus has become a mechanism to drive highly short-term expectations of profit into the
boardroom, and into its assessments of what investment projects it should authorise.

Andrew Haldane, chief economist of the Bank of England,
and Richard Davies have measured the degree to which shareholders are so myopically preoccupied with short-term profits
that they value profits made immediately much more than
those made in, say, five or ten years' time, even allowing for the
rational cost of waiting. They find that share price valuations
are only explicable if the stream of profits in the future is
judged to be worth in today's terms between 5 and 10 per cent
lower than if they were rationally valued. This may not sound
much, but cumulatively the impact is devastating.

For example, a project that would in reality pay back all its
cash outlay within nine years would be judged by the stock
market not to be worth bringing forward because cumulatively
it undervalues each year's profits by 10 per cent. Over thirty-
five years the valuation is one thousandth of an investment's
real value.[3] A later study shows that unquoted companies have
four to five times more capital assets for every pound of
turnover than companies whose shares are quoted on the stock
market, a huge differential that can only be explained by the
disastrous impact of stock market myopia on company investment decisions.[4] Yet, as observed earlier, directors' pay has
been linked ever more closely to share price performance,
offering them the prospect of stunning fortunes (a subject to be
explored in more detail in Chapter 4). As a result, R&D,
investment and innovation are consistently undervalued.
British companies are now hoarding some £800 billion in cash,
cash they would rather use buying back their own shares than

committing to investment. We have allowed a madhouse to develop. An important reason for the crisis in business investment and innovation is the way our companies are owned or, rather, *not* owned.[5]

Every aspect of business strategy is affected. It is now a common place, for example, that Britain's big four supermarket chains are suffering from the challenge of German discount retailers Aldi and Lidl. A typical basket of prices in British supermarkets is up to 20 per cent higher than their German competitors, a pricing policy imposed by the need to generate the financial returns required by footloose shareholders. Aldi and Lidl, privately owned, can price more keenly. Nor is this anything new. In the 1950s and 1960s Japanese motorcycle manufacturers were able to price similarly keenly against British manufacturers for exactly the same reasons, eventually killing indigenous British capability. It is often remarked that openness to foreign ownership has transformed the British car industry. What is less remarked is that the foreign companies that have achieved this transformation – Tata and BMW – are themselves privately owned while the Japanese companies are similarly anchored in long-term ownership structures.

It is a crisis of commitment. Too few shareholders are committed to the companies they allegedly 'own'. They consider their shares casino chips to be traded in the immediate future. Even long-term holders will consider lending their shares in the profitable stock lending business to be used by the share borrower as short-term trading chips. In effect shares are no more than a contract offering the opportunity of dividends in certain industries and countries; this requires no engagement in how those profits and dividends are generated. British company law has historically required directors and investors alike to do no more than look after their fiduciary interests, a duty interpreted as keeping the share price and the value of invested assets as high as possible from year to short-term year. In 1991 at least half of British shares were owned by British pension funds and insurance companies making long-term investments, which mitigated some of the short-term biases to the system. Today that proportion has collapsed to under 15 per cent, with 41 per cent of British shares being held overseas.[6]

There have been some vain efforts to correct the system's momentum. The 2006 Companies Act, for example, broadened the obligations of a company director to 'have regard for' the long-term interests of the company, its supply chain, customers and employees, rather than just the share price. But with ever fewer shares being held by long-term investors and the balance being traded with ever shorter time horizons, 'having regard' for other concerns than the share price has in practice been overwhelmed by the dynamics of the way shares are owned.[7] Directors are compelled to interpret their job as maximising short-term profits, which override any other consideration.[8]

The company is conceived as nothing more than a network of short-term contracts. Any shareholder – from a transient day trader to a long-term investor – has the same standing in law. American directors' ability to defend their company from hostile takeover or the requirement on German directors to live with trade union representatives on their supervisory boards are seen as obstacles to enterprise that Britain must not go near. But companies and wealth generation are about co-creation, sharing risk and long-term trust relationships; Britain's refusal to embrace these core truths is toxic.[9]

Companies were originally invented in the late sixteenth and early seventeenth centuries as legal structures that enabled groups of investors to come together, committing to share risk around a shared goal and so make profit for themselves, while in the process delivering wider economic and social benefits.

Incorporation – to create a company – was then understood to be associated with obligations: a company had to declare its purpose before earning a licence to trade. The East India Company, for example, England's earliest company, was given the monopoly of English trade in Asia but with the reciprocal obligation that it operate English ships and construct manned forts along the trade routes to protect other English trade. There existed a mutual deal between company and society. Other companies were incorporated in the same way.

The shortcomings of the modern British business, financial and regulatory model are visible almost every working day – yet they occasion only spasmodic criticism. Given the lack of popular interest, politicians see little mileage in courting business hostility for little political gain, and insiders do not want to rock the boat. So it goes on. Over the year up to the spring of 2014, as I draft this chapter months later, has come the usual dispiriting litany of predatory foreign takeovers, the underpricing of privatised public assets, the shrinking of Britain's corporate tax base, more dismaying evidence of systemic malpractice in our banks and the substitution of British capabilities by overseas companies. Yet almost nobody seems to turn a hair. The injunction is that Britain must be 'open for business' – code for being systematically stripped of skills, technology, brands and, more importantly, pride. What pride can one have in a country that is prepared to sell anything if the price is right?

A year in the life

The period begins in February 2013 with Centrica, the privatised utility that owns British Gas, pulling out of a proposed partnership with EDF Energy to replace the Hinkley Point and

Sizewell nuclear power stations – a deal which offered the prospect of a 10.5 per cent rate of return, guaranteed for thirty-five years with a gain-sharing arrangement with the government if the returns were ever to exceed 13.5 per cent. Centrica's public line was that rising costs and delays made the project unattractive; in fact Centrica needed a rate of return at least a quarter higher, its then chair Sir Roger Carr has acknowledged, in order to assuage its shareholders. The implication was that the government would have to lift its price guarantee by nearly a half – plainly impossible. Those were returns more commensurate with a fast-growing retail business, say, or a high-tech company, than a solid energy utility producing a vital public good.

Into its place in the autumn of 2013 stepped two state-owned Chinese nuclear power companies, the heart of the Chinese communist state, with the party insisting that it would only allow them to participate if the British government agree it could be the majority shareholder in building subsequent nuclear power plants. It was a naked power play by a rising power that is politically and economically hostile to two key British allies – the US and Japan – but one to which Britain meekly assented: ownership is not meant to matter.

Mr Cameron even took it upon himself to say that no country would be more open than Britain to Chinese investment or prepared to argue China's case in the West,[10] with his Chancellor mouthing the tired formula about the deal securing vital jobs and investment. What it rather showed was the bankruptcy of the system of British business organisation, together with the extravagance of the targets for return that are habitually set, which so inhibit investment and innovation – together with the limitations of privatisation. When EU approval was finally offered in October 2014, the total new build cost of Hinkley in 2012 prices was estimated to be around £16 billion (on current prices extending to £24 billion), figures that

Centrica could use to justify its concerns about high and rising costs – although with fixed assets of nearly £16 billion and little long-term debt its participation would still have been feasible with its pro-rata share of any debt peaking in a worst case at £6 billion. To the degree it was not, its pull-out showed that only governments can assume the financial responsibilities of long-term investment on this scale. Energy privatisation simply meant that the French government, the majority owner of EDF Energy, and the Chinese government were doing what the British government should have done, and still had to do through offering a minimum price guarantee. Centrica meanwhile went on to spend £500 million buying back its own shares, so supporting its share price and the share price-related remuneration of its directors' team, notably through the exercise of rights to buy shares at attractive prices under long-term incentive plans. Its priorities could hardly have been clearer.

In the summer of 2013 came the sale of the industrial systems company Invensys – Britain's last representative in this important industrial sector – to the French company Schneider for £3.4 billion. In a way the sale was inevitable: Invensys was the result of a bodged merger a decade earlier between BTR and Siebe – two once substantial British manufacturing companies – and the combined group was falling behind its competitors. The BTR-Siebe merger was a classic British defensive stratagem. The transient management team at BTR, a company that grew by acquisition and deals, needed a story to tell to their no less transient shareholders about how they planned to develop their company; merger is a quick way of providing an answer and realising 'value', because under British corporate law shareholders assume no responsibility for the firm they own, thus rendering British companies in effect 'ownerless'. Footloose, often anonymous shareholders can be relied upon to sell. The City's investment banking industry is built on a flow of such deals, and is continually putting up ideas and propositions to managements. In fact most mergers fail, as BTR's and Siebe's did – but no matter. Mergers give managements a story to tell, and are good for City fees and bonuses.

This is not a new story. Successive ill-conceived mergers, coupled with a lack of engagement among owners or bankers, led to the eventual demise of the car company British Leyland, with the government stepping in at the last because no one else would or could: union intransigence grew in part because of the lack of any long-term vision to support the company, and in reaction to endless redundancies and retrenchment. It was a story that featured in *The State We're In* along with that of Lord Hanson, a prominent Thatcherite businessman, who in the 1970s and 1980s built a £10 billion business essentially by asset stripping: buying companies and then insisting on target rates of return of 20 per cent and paybacks for new investment of four years. Such figures became a common benchmark; but no industry nor firm can deliver such returns continually and systematically.[11] Lord Hanson was to retire in 1997, having in one of his last acts spooked ICI into breaking itself up into two 'focused' chemical and drugs companies in order to avoid his attentions. ICI has now been taken over in turn by the Dutch firm AkzoNobel, while the drugs business, which became AstraZeneca, was in turn to receive a takeover bid nine months after the sale of Invensys. Nor did Hanson Trust, for all the accolades it garnered in the 1980s and 1990s, fare much better. Lord Hanson's much reduced company was sold to rival German company Heidelberg Cement a decade later, in 2007; the entire British building materials industry, like the car industry, had as a result fallen into foreign ownership. Hanson was a passionate eurosceptic and believer in British-style capitalism: it is fitting that his diminished company should end in German hands.

BTR at the time had been trying to emulate Hanson, but found like him that ultimately a framework requiring the attainment of high targets for return and a quick payback is unsustainable and self-defeating. The merger with Siebe bought time, but it was not used. By the time Sir Nigel Rudd took over as chair, Invensys was the smallest of the global industrial systems businesses. In other countries with different financial and ownership systems, countries where business building is regarded as the prime aim of business, Sir Nigel might have considered options to grow the company. But Sir Nigel is famously a product of the British system, a deal-maker who believes the ultimate arbiter of value is to secure the highest share price in a takeover. He had sold Pilkington to Nippon Glass in 2002 while chair and then in 2008 sold Boots to a private equity firm, who promptly relocated the headquarters to Zug to save corporation tax. The deputy lieutenant of Derbyshire and freeman of the City of London had no doubts about his duty: it was to sell Invensys, complete with tax losses, to the highest bidder, as he had done with Pilkington and Boots. The purchaser, Schneider, openly acknowledged that it would transfer production and R&D to France, and set any of its UK profits against Invensys's accumulated tax losses – so that the British taxpayer would partly pay for French acquisitiveness.

Britain's industrial systems sector was now wholly foreign-owned too. BTR, like Hanson, had swallowed up British companies, running them down until there were no more left to buy that could meet its leech-like targets; then it was extinguished as well. A defender might argue this was creative destruction, the term coined by the economist Joseph Schumpeter to describe the tension in capitalism between unceasing destruction of the old and thus the creation of space for the new. A more objective onlooker would say it was just destruction – except for those individuals, including Sir Nigel, who became very rich and respectable along the way.

Rich and respectable Deloitte and Touche, one of the Big Four accountancy firms, then hit the headlines in October 2013 when it received from the Financial Reporting Council the largest fine (£14 million) ever imposed on such a firm, for its role in helping the MG Four plunder the remnants of MG Rover before it went into receivership in 2005 with debts of £1.3 billion and 6,500 job losses. Essentially four of the company's directors organised payments to themselves of over £40 million during their four-year tenure, with Deloitte fined for creating two tax evasion schemes that served only to create fees for Deloitte and benefits for the directors.[12] They simply plundered the company, and although they were banned from being directors again, kept all their booty. It was the end of the great British Leyland saga: yet one more piece of evidence, if any more were needed, about the poverty of the way Britain organises the ownership and management of its great companies – and the value system of too many who direct them.

And as if on cue, before 2013 came to an end the same value system was exposed in the financial services industry. Lloyds was fined a record £28 million by the Financial Conduct Authority for the period between 1 January 2010 and 31 March 2012 – during which the government held a 39 per cent stake in the bank – for having lax controls and giving its staff incentives to treat its customers as milch cows. Extravagant 'champagne' bonuses were offered to staff who could loot their customers with policies cynically designed to offer nothing of value. It was no less than organised theft. Lloyds a few months later would set aside another £1.8 billion for mis-selling insurance products.

Then in January 2014 came the privatisation sale of 60 per cent of the government's stake in Royal Mail at 330 pence per share. This raised a mere £2 billion, when the jump in the share price to over £6 in the days after the sale suggested that the proceeds could have been at least £1 billion more – and still left investors something to go for in terms of a post-privatisation price rise.

The purpose of the privatisation, averred Michael Fallon, Thatcherite industry minister at the time, was to allow Royal Mail to enjoy all the benefits of being a PLC – access to private capital markets, along with the 'disciplines' of having to meet private sector standards of efficiency which the British public would enjoy in an improved service. He would never sell off the Royal Mail 'cheaply'. The benefits of being a PLC were taken as axiomatic, as if all the examples above – and so many more – had never happened.

But Thatcherites don't look at evidence and have suspended thought: they just worship at the shrine. There was no imaginative attempt to create the Royal Mail as a trust or a public interest company along the careful and thoughtful lines on which the German Bundespost was privatised, allowing it to combine a capacity to build the business strategically with anchored ownership but with access to private finance. Nor was there any attempt to retain a golden share in public hands to ensure that whatever the future pattern of ownership, the Royal Mail would remain true to its core purpose. Instead assurance was sought from sixteen 'long-term' investors that in return for being favoured with more shares at the advantageous price, they would stick with Royal Mail.

But as Royal Mail's disgracefully low flotation price soared, the privileged long-term shareholders – under no legal, regulatory or cultural obligation to remain committed or to keep a promise that in any case could not be made binding in a British context – simply could not resist selling. Only four, at the time of writing, retain their original allocation. The National Audit

Office (NAO) chided the government for its extreme 'caution', for selling as much as 60 per cent of its holding when a mere 50 per cent would have achieved its objective and protected the taxpayer from potential mispricing by holding back 10 per cent for sale later.[13]

What the NAO could not say was that the mispricing – attacked ferociously a few months later by the business select committee – was part of the ideological motivation behind the sale. Earlier Royal Mail had been gold-plated for privatisation, relieved of its vast pension fund deficit, and the pricing of stamps had been freed from regulation – the quid quo pro for having to provide a universal service – to give investors the prospect of ever-rising profits. But what was ever wrong with having a profitable public service, in its last year declaring over £500 million of pre-tax profits, in public hands? The taxpayer has received a one-off payment of £2 billion, with perhaps another £1.5 billion to come when the last 30 per cent is sold, but has forgone an annual profit stream in excess of £500 million, set to rise in perpetuity. None of the investment banks advising the government – led by Lazards and Goldman Sachs and pocketing a cool £12.7 million for their calamitous advice – would have accepted such a deal for their own business or their own families. They were preying on precious British public assets.

But worst of all is what lies ahead. Thames Water was sold way back in 1989 for a similarly paltry £922 million; it recorded pre-tax profits of £550 million in 2013. It has paid out £1.4 billion in dividends alone since 2006. Rarely in British history have taxpayers and society been so systematically traduced while so willingly colluding in their own impoverishment. Thames Water foretells what will happen to Royal Mail. The story in 1989 was the same twenty-five years later. We were promised a utopia of private sector efficiency in which the water industry's new owners would create a first-class water system at much lower prices than the government ever could. The industry could escape Treasury constraints and borrow freely. Regulation would be light touch. The 'dead hand' of government should be got out of this industry as out of every other.

Thames is certainly a different company today, proudly boasting that 99.98 per cent of its sampled water meets quality standards and of a rolling investment programme to meet its regulatory obligations. And has it borrowed! It is crippled with debt, which has jumped from £1.8 billion to £8 billion over the past decade under its foreign owners – first the German utility RWE and, since 2006, a group of private equity funds domiciled in Luxembourg, marshalled by the Australian bank Macquarie.

Macquarie is the bank whose every effort is organised to outflank regulators and tax authorities, and so to make extra for itself – thus its nickname as the millionaire factory. But the game cannot start unless it owns a monopoly business, such as Thames Water, that reliably generates profits and cash. Where tough questions about corporate behaviour are rarely asked, it is an invitation to be looted, and so we have been.

Responsible owners would steward their company with more care. Thames Water has done what the regulator has asked but no more. It has not been concerned to make the water system more resilient, with, say, back-up reservoirs to guard against climate change; restrictions on water use because of drought are becoming habitual. Nor has it managed its affairs so that it has spare capacity for the unexpected or to fund a big project like the proposed £4 billion twenty-mile Thames Tideway Tunnel, seventy metres under the river, to conduct overflow sewage out to sea – and for which it is seeking Treasury guarantees. Instead it is a vehicle whose overriding priority is shareholder and management enrichment.

By maxing out on debt, it can offset the consequent high interest payments against tax, so that in 2012 it paid no tax whatsoever – indeed it received a £5 million tax credit – even while paying £279.5 million of dividends, subject, of course, to minimal Luxembourg taxation. If over the last ten years Thames had made no dividend payments and instead used the cash to build up its reserves, one calculation shows it would have accumulated £4 billion to build the tunnel with no extra borrowing, and thus no additional water charges. In these circumstances the private equity groups behind Thames would have merely seen their investment grow by about two-thirds since 2006 rather than enjoyed a tenfold increase – a much fairer deal all round.[14]

As it is, the Treasury has endorsed the way Thames has been managed by offering it the get-out-of-jail-free card of an infrastructure guarantee. Such guarantees to deliver infrastructure investment that would not otherwise take place are plainly important, but they throw into sharp relief the co-dependence that exists between the public realm and the private sector – and one that is too little acknowledged in regulation, in corporate structure or culturally. After all, Thames Water is a utility providing fourteen million Londoners with water. In law, however, it is no more than a private equity plaything whose obligations to London are secondary to whatever wheeze will enrich its shareholders, who now include both Abu Dhabi's and China's sovereign wealth funds.

Many of England's and Wales's water companies are run the same way: eight out of twenty-three local and regional water companies in England and Wales are owned by private equity groups and a further ten are foreign-owned. *Money Down the Drain*, a report by the think tank CentreForum, hammers home the concern. 'Since 2005 prices for water have been too high, more than required to run a decent service for customers whilst providing a reasonable return for investors. This has led to very high profits for water companies,' it writes. 'These profits, which are funded out of consumer bills, have not been spent on improving customer service or for investing in infrastructure but have been transferred straight to shareholders who have seen extraordinary returns on their investment.'[15] This powerful report, complete with a supporting foreword by Sir Ian Byatt, the former director of Ofwat, the water regulator, has of course been completely ignored. Suggestions for a different corporate structure follow in Chapter 5.

We can thus anticipate the Royal Mail in twenty-five years' time, probably very much earlier. It will be taken over and owned by a group of private equity investors in some tax haven, thus avoiding UK tax on what will be huge dividends. It will be loaded with debt. Universal provision will only be sustained at the price of sky-high stamp prices. Already it has warned that its universal service obligation may be impossible to sustain given the cherry-picking of profitable postal services in cities by its rival TNT. It will not be an international logistics company challenging the Bundespost. It will be a once-great British institution whose fate will echo so many others – vandalised, looted and hollowed out to enrich directors and footloose shareholders. It could even be taken over by another European public postal service, rather as German and French public utility companies have taken over our electricity and rail industry.

AstraZeneca is likely to be another. In May 2014 the litany was completed when the US drugs company Pfizer launched a £63 billion bid – the largest ever in British history – for AstraZeneca. There was no industrial advantage to this bid, nor any promise to enlarge the combined group's R&D. Pfizer was clear that its objective was to take advantage of tax arbitrage – so-called 'tax inversion' – rebasing its European operations in the UK to take advantage of UK corporation tax at 21 per cent compared with the US's 35 per cent. This would allow it legitimately to distribute the many billions it held offshore to avoid US corporation tax as dividends to US shareholders. It would promise to keep 20 per cent of the merged companies' combined $9.4 billion R&D in the UK for five years only, but CEO Ian Read openly acknowledged that AstraZeneca's R&D spend – running at $3.4 billion (£2.1 billion) – would be cut in the UK. It would dismember the company just as it had done three earlier acquisitions, buying growth rather than creating it for itself. Indeed any shareholder who had sold to Pfizer would have done better to stay as an independent pharmaceutical company. Mergers, recall, nearly always destroy value.

It was obvious that the bid would be bad for Britain, bad for the pharmaceutical industry and bad for vital investment in the lower-margin drugs – integral to the medical ecosystem – that Pfizer tends to avoid because its mission is the maximisation of shareholder value, and thus directors' bonuses. Its target is to produce high-margin drug blockbusters like Lipitor, to lower cholesterol, or Viagra. Yet while the British public, most opinion formers and the leaders of the scientific establishment – both the Royal Society and the Wellcome Foundation voiced their disquiet – quickly understood what was at stake and the fecklessness that would lie behind the shareholders' judgement, the British business establishment decided that the UK should be 'open for business'. Shareholders should make the ultimate decision free from political interference, such as the public interest test mooted by the Labour party, and which it rightly judged could only find against the merger. But during the attempted bid not one business leader deviated from the line that shareholders, whoever they were and whatever their priorities, should decide the fate of companies. No reform should be entertained to stop the predatory behaviour or change the dynamic; and no move from government was deemed legitimate beyond creating a climate in which enterprise should flourish – shorthand for low tax, low regulation and letting anything happen. In essence business leaders were not going to concede any ground on which the 'anti-business' Labour party might capitalise.

In the event Pfizer was overconfident that the British system would deliver it the company it craved without too much difficulty; it neither offered enough to provide a knockout blow to force the AstraZeneca board to recommend the bid to shareholders within the time limits allowed for the bid, nor enough to assure the government that the public interest would be protected. UK public opinion had come out massively in favour of the British company – even if it had extensive interests in the US and Sweden – and was deeply and correctly suspicious of Pfizer and its motives. French CEO Pascal Soriot was a scientist committed to his company; his Swedish chair Leif Johansson was no less willing to take the long view. Just enough long-term shareholders – including an important Swedish bloc – backed them for the company to retain its independence. But as it became clear that the bid was not going to go ahead, shareholders representing many more votes declared their unhappiness. After all, AstraZeneca's defence rested strongly on projections of good profits ten years hence – which myopic financial institutions do not value.

It was a fine balance, in which public opinion – correctly much more sceptical about big bids than many in British business and the City – created a climate in which the government simply had to be tough in its scrutiny of the bid. For example it indicated it might insist on much more expensive assurances – a ten-year rather than a five-year guarantee over the location of UK-based R&D – if it was to give its blessing. Even so, if, say, Sir Nigel Rudd had been chair and Sam Laidlaw (the outgoing CEO of Centrica) the CEO, the best guess is that, true to British business culture, they would have done the deal. It took a Frenchman and a Swede to resist.

AstraZeneca remains independent for now, but the promises that it has made to develop the business and keep the share price high will now have to be kept. Pfizer is reported to be considering its options. Nobody, given all we know about the British system, can be sure the story will end well.

The peculiar character of British finance

The deformities of British finance are systemic. The boom–bust cycle of British credit; the lack of finance for small business; the proclivity for takeovers and deal making; the incentives for mal-practice and mis-selling; all are inter-connected. Above all, the financial system shapes how firms are owned, and thus their character, the cost of their capital, their strategic direction and commercial options. In this sense the financial system is the driving, mobilising part of the economy.

I made those points in exactly the same terms twenty years ago. Nothing since has materially changed. So, for example:

> The system is deeply inhibiting to anything but short-term risk. Its effects can be seen from the lowest level of capital-ist endeavour to the highest and most complex. It could be the proprietors of a small firm having to surrender their house as collateral to the bank in order to secure working capital, and then having to pay fees in advance as well as a large mark-up in the rate of interest on the loan. It could be an individual innovator securing the support of a venture capitalist, and then being forced to prepare the company too

early for flotation on the stock market in order to repay the venture capitalist's original investment ... The system forces large companies to pay high and steadily growing dividends to a shifting cast of large shareholders, mindful of securing their loyalty against the approach of a predator ... British companies, compelled to set their prices to earn enough to pay back their expensive capital, have to surrender market share to competitors whose financial structure allows a lower cost of capital and who can set their prices accordingly.[16]

Capital is relatively expensive in Britain for two main reasons. The first is that the entire system is organised around a web of transactional market relationships in which investors and lenders can quickly disengage from a relationship by selling; hence the importance of the stock market, and hence the trillions of pounds of bank deposits traded between banks in the interbank market. This – as in all financial systems – enables the system to take more risks than it otherwise would, because the assurance of liquidity means the provider of finance has the comfort of knowing that exit would be relatively easy. However, the problem is twofold. First there is unknowable risk and myopia: human beings value rewards in the near term more than the distant, not least because they know there is existential, unknowable risk that is not reducible to probabilities. The certainty of a financial return now is more valuable than the possibility of a higher return later. And secondly, the right of early exit, along with its easy execution in highly liquid markets, creates an asymmetrical power relationship: a borrower or investee has to pay more to secure commitment from the lender or investor.

This has an identifiable impact on the cost of capital, the target rates of return, the periods over which investment projects are expected to pay back the cash invested and the amount of profit to be distributed in dividends. Other countries' financial systems are less transactional, more commitment-oriented, and one way or another give managements more incentives and scope to grow their companies. This translates into a measurably lower cost of capital, lower target rates of return, longer payback periods and lower dividend payouts than the British. Twenty years ago I quoted Professor David Miles, then an adviser to the Bank of England and now a member of its Monetary Policy Committee, who calculated in 1993 that the stock market consistently valued future returns lower than it should: profits expected in five years' time, he computed, were undervalued by 40 per cent so that longer-term cash flows were valued at about half the rate of near-term cash flows.[17] Today Andrew Haldane and Richard Davies find the same result.

Occasionally clues surface that, if anything, matters are worse. For example, a survey of 250 FTSE 100 executives in 2011 conducted by PriceWaterhouseCoopers (PWC) asked respondents to rank two options: whether they preferred a return of £250,000 over one year or £450,000 over three years. A majority reported they would opt for £250,000, implying an annual discount rate of over 20 per cent.[18] At least, twenty years earlier, only 40 per cent of the manufacturing companies in the CBI survey I quoted opted for returns of 20 per cent or higher. Haldane and Davies also find evidence to suggest that, comparing the period from 1995 to 2005 with the ten previous years, myopia rose. Back in 1994 I was worried about high dividend payout ratios; those continue, but in addition companies feel they have to launch programmes buying back their shares to keep share prices higher than they would otherwise be. In 2012 (the most recent year for which there are statistics), following a well-established trend, UK listed companies spent £12.4 billion on buying back and cancelling their own shares compared with the £5.9 billion they raised from the stock market through Initial Public Offerings and rights issues.[19] Companies as powerful as Shell or

Tesco feel they have to do the same as Centrica; the share price has become the alpha and omega of British finance.

All this made British finance expensive enough twenty years ago, raising the cost of capital, while paradoxically giving the system less capacity to bear risk associated with innovation and investment, while displacing risk and insecurity on to company workforces. The flipside was that it made it more likely to finance property – which has predictable and generally rising value – or short-term loans to support takeovers, mergers and buyouts. Thus the proclivities of the financial system to create rising property prices and merger booms while avoiding lending to risky small businesses – and I warned about this in the early 1990s! On top, because British finance was closely integrated with the rest of the world, the providers of finance ranked propositions for investment projects and potential returns in Britain with those available overseas. A bias to expensive capital was made more expensive again. Today, after the property boom of the 2000s and – perhaps more extraordinarily – the new housing boom in 2013/14, along with new depths plumbed by business investment, those proclivities are even more pronounced. The cost of capital against whatever prevailing interest rate is ever more expensive.

But there was more. 'Financial systems,' I wrote, 'are themselves part of a still wider system of political and social relationships.' Finance in Britain had a very particular social standing because it embodied gentlemanly capitalism, and with it an indissoluble link to conservatism and the Conservative party.

The gentlemanly ideal is difficult to define – it is part of its mystique – but there is no doubting its motivating power for generations of Englishmen. A gentleman does not try too hard; celebrates sport, games and pleasure; he is fair minded;

he has good manners ... is steady under fire ... The gentle-man is a human island, simultaneously aware of the nuances of rank while recognising the importance of integrity and rep-utation in his relationship with his peers. The civilisation fostered by such values is extraordinarily favourable to finance, commerce and administration – but not to industry.[20]

The City of London was – and even after the financial crisis remains – the apex of gentlemanly social power. Gentlemen defend its privileged autonomy, the wisdom and unchallenge-ability of what goes on there and its alleged crucial economic importance to the country. It may be that the way British PLCs are owned, financed and managed – along with the attendant implications for technology, skills, pay and the weakness of Britain's knowledge economy that grow out of the City's prior-ities – is destructive; but no other order can be imagined. This is Britain's precious economic asset, and the modulated accents which with an air of intelligence explain why no other order can be imagined take for granted centuries of assurance and deference from the rest of the country. They also guarantee that political conservatism, first cousin to gentlemanly capital-ism, is seen as economically sound: this world understands these complicated matters.

Gentlemen are at the top of the social pyramid; gentlemen are conservatives; they run the financial system: ergo the Conservative party is the natural custodian of the country and the body politic. The Tory party; social standing; the City of London; financial freedoms; euroscepticism; what is consid-ered economically and financially 'sound'; all are connected by the same cultural golden thread. Boris Johnson, for example, as Tory mayor of London, exemplifies the connections. But while gentlemanly capitalism remains powerful, the bonds are fraying. Many in the City want to stay in the EU, have been horrified by the excesses of the financial crisis, do not define themselves as Tory gentlemen but rather as global professionals – and want to build businesses and create genuine wealth. The prospects of finding allies for reform twenty years ago seemed faint. There are better prospects in 2015.

The inevitable boom and bust

Seen through this prism, the financial crisis of 2008 was inevitable. The City was a more joyful, careless and enthusiastic participant in the wild fifteen years up to 2008 than any other leading country's financial system. Indeed it exploited the edifice constructed since the 1960s – eurodollar markets, the ending of exchange and capital controls, Big Bang (so that investment and commercial banking could be undertaken by the same bank in London, unlike New York) – to become the heart of the so-called global shadow banking system where so much traditional banking activity was done by unregulated non-banks. The market in trillions of dollars of dodgy securitised assets and bogus means of insuring risk – credit default swaps – could not have grown so large without London. It was where the London Interbank Offer Rate and the daily benchmark fix of foreign exchange rates were set, and as we now know, manipulated. This was all too easy in London's barely regulated markets – foreign exchange manipulation was even apparently connived at by the august Bank of England. This was where the world's banks came together to create the international financial crisis; indeed without London and its attitude to finance it is doubtful that the scale and intensity of the crisis could have been so great.

Yes, there were global imbalances – Asia created huge surpluses that Europe and the USA needed to borrow, and it fell to banks to recycle the money. Yes, banks deluded themselves into believing they could use the shadow banking system and its alleged means of hedging risks to grow their balance sheets to gargantuan size with less capital than they would otherwise have needed, thus making fabulously high returns on shareholders' funds and legendarily high bonuses. And yes, free market economics that predicted that a market like that of contemporary finance – with multiple actors and abundant information – could never make mistakes, as long as it was lightly regulated, sealed the deal. But all this needed a geographical location, infrastructure and a regulatory system ready to accommodate the new falsehoods – and of course the seal of economic, financial and political respectability. That was provided by the gentlemanly financiers in London.

Other leading countries greatly expanded the volume of credit and debt in relation to GDP over those years of madness, and other countries' banks assumed what we now know were impossible risks. But none managed it on the scale of the British. In 1994 the Royal Bank of Scotland was a conservatively run regional bank with national aspirations. In 2008, its balance sheet assets (and of course its liabilities) alone exceeded Britain's GDP. British bank assets in total climbed from around twice GDP in the early 1990s to more than five times in 2008 – while the free shareholders' capital holding up this mountain of debt shrank in proportion.[21] Britain ranked alongside Iceland with an oversized weak banking system: Iceland's was to collapse completely. London was Reykjavik on Thames, as the then LSE Professor Willem Buiter famously joked.

The British financial system had a propensity to create ever larger credit and property booms: by the mid 1990s the impact of globalised finance, along with that of securitisation, was already discernible. It all seemed obviously unsustainable, because of its impact on the real, non-financial economy. But would Britain's financiers be so greedy and crazed that they would bankrupt their own institutions? It seemed unlikely. The crisis would surely flow in the other direction – the hollowing out of the real economy becoming so apparent that eventually finance would have to be reformed. In the event it proved impossible to underestimate British finance's capacity for fecklessness.

The lords of the universe became supremely over-confident, indulged by a credulous Labour government that was bewitched by the City's apparent success and desperate not to appear 'anti-business' by challenging this alleged jewel in Britain's economic crown. Chancellor Gordon Brown even thought to earn credit by suggesting in his June 2007 Mansion House speech that the rest of the economy should borrow from the City's dynamism and innovativeness. Even when queues of depositors tried to withdraw cash from stricken former building society Northern Rock in September 2007, the political and financial establishment did not want to confront the truth behind Britain's first bank run for more than a century. Britain's financial system was so overstretched, so undercapitalised and so fundamentally unsound that one bank run could trigger a domino effect that would cause the entire British financial system to implode.

What followed is well known. By the spring of 2009 Britain had assembled more than £1 trillion in special liquidity measures, guarantees of inter-bank lending, asset protection and extra capital to save its banking system.[22] The Bank of England's balance sheet exploded, becoming proportionally larger than even in wartime. It had been a reluctant intervention; the Governor of the Bank of England, Sir Mervyn King, had initially wanted to let the bankers pay the price for their own folly, before he was persuaded that would bring the entire system down, and that he should at least authorise the release of special liquidity for distressed banks, starting with Northern Rock. The Chancellor, Gordon Brown, had tried to do anything he could rather than inject public money into the capital base of the banks, or worse take a bank like Northern Rock into public ownership – a course of action he only authorised after all other avenues of rescue had been exhausted. Still fearful of using state power in September 2008, before the awesomeness of the crisis became exposed, he brokered the anti-competitive takeover of HBOS by Lloyds rather than 'nationalise' HBOS. It was only when the entire system stood on the point of collapse in 5 October 2008, with the now disgraced chief executive of RBS – Sir Fred Goodwin – saying that his bank could continue trading for only a few more hours given the scale at which huge wholesale deposits were being withdrawn from the bank, that Mr Brown finally acted.

Had RBS defaulted on its hundreds of billions of deposits, the cascade effect on an enfeebled, undercapitalised banking system would have been a calamity. The entire edifice would have collapsed, ensuring a monumental depression. Brown launched what was to be the trillion-pound bailout. Even as it is, GDP has returned to 2008 levels only six years later. Estimates of the cumulative lost output range up to £5 trillion and the economy is likely to remain below its trend rate of growth at least until the end of the decade.

Yet although they were initially shocked, the gentlemanly capitalists quickly recovered their poise. One of the more extraordinary episodes during the crisis was the commissioning by the Labour government of Sir Win Bischoff, then London chair of Citigroup Europe, in July 2008 to lead a group of City notables to recommend to government what could best be done to help the City promote its future competitiveness – hardly, for most sane people, the most obvious preoccupation on the eve of the most serious financial crisis for a century.

The group deliberated throughout the crisis, witnessing at first hand the trillion-pound support package, but still had the nerve to argue – knowing how near the entire system had come to collapse – that the British financial services industry was an incomparable asset and that apart from requiring banks to hold more capital, in essence nothing should be done to change or reform the system. Certainly there should be no tougher regulatory regime, and government and the financial services industry should work closely together to promote the latter's business and reputation; banking and its innovative products, it declaimed, were not socially useless, as Lord Adair Turner, then chair of the Financial Services Authority had averred, but of extreme economic and social importance. Britain should move in lockstep with international regulators, with whom it should lobby to be as unambitious as possible in any regulatory reform.

In commissioning the report, Alistair Darling, Brown's successor as Chancellor, who at heart was an Edinburgh gentlemanly capitalist, was covering his party's back. Northern Rock had just been taken into public ownership, but he still wanted everyone to know that Labour remained as friendly towards the City as ever. Sir Win, who was to go on to chair Lloyds and now heads the Financial Reporting Council, was happy to oblige even as the events of autumn 2008 unfolded. The overwhelming majority of the group's members were City folk: they had 662 years of work experience between them, three-quarters of which had been in financial services. Mr Darling co-signed the report. Gentlemanly capitalism, despite the disaster that had engulfed it, was alive and kicking.

But an unexpected reckoning of a sort was to happen with the formation of the Coalition government. The Liberal Democrats insisted that the price of coalition was a volte-face on the banks, and a commitment to serious banking reform – the first section in the Coalition agreement. There was to be an investigation into how to reduce risk in the banking system, the possible separation of investment and commercial banking and the promotion of credit flows to small and medium-sized enterprises. Robust action was to be taken on unacceptable bonuses. Diversity and competition in banking was to be promoted. The regulatory system was to be overhauled. It was all that Sir Win and Mr Darling had so strenuously opposed. The head of All Souls College Oxford, Sir John Vickers, former chief economist of the Bank of England, was invited to head a five-person commission with a majority of non-bankers – again in stark contrast to Bischoff – and it duly made the case both for the banks to carry considerably more capital and for a ring fence to be established between commercial banking and highly leveraged investment banking by 2019. It would take an inordinately long time, but it was reform.

And yet. The open question is whether the dynamic of the system needs even more fundamental attention. The banks too are ownerless corporations with their own footloose shareholders; part of the reason they expanded their balance sheets so aggressively and recklessly was that over the fifteen years before 2008 they had succeeded in trebling the rate of return on equity – for which directors were handsomely rewarded with bonus packages dependent upon the consequent rising share prices. The financial carnage that resulted was stunning. RBS and Lloyds, the latter having taken over HBOS, were in October 2008 both effectively insolvent without government capital and guarantees. Barclays only survived without state support courtesy of a £6.5 billion injection of capital from Qatar, accompanied by £450 million of fees and commissions; at the time of writing the Serious Fraud Office is investigating the involvement of then CEO Bob Diamond and a number of other executives in the deal. Indeed banking has become synonymous with misconduct ranging from the mere indulging of malpractice to the criminal. The total bill in fines, litigation and provisions for mis-selling to customers for Britain's five largest banks since 2011, calculate professional services firm KPMG, is £28.5 billion.[23] Lloyds alone has provided £10 billion against the mis-selling of personal protection policies along with its fine from the FCA, while the other banks have reserved another £12 billion. Twenty years ago I was inveighing against systemic mis-selling of pension products by insurance companies, the need for high-margin revenue streams to support profits and the way the focus on the share price overwhelmed a duty of care to customers. Now history is reproducing itself as farce.

The Vickers reforms are a beginning not an end; they may reduce the risk of another systemic banking collapse but they do not eliminate it. Only the separation of investment and commercial banking will do that, along with a great deal more equity capital. Nor do the reforms impact on the most important defects of British finance – its capacity to inflate both booms and busts (pro-cyclicality in the jargon), its hard-wired bias to support all forms of property lending to excess, its cavalier attitude to ownership, its embedding of short-term horizons in corporate thinking, the high cost of capital and the under-nourishing of small and medium-sized businesses (SMEs). Thus, despite the Coalition's ambitions, the PLC remains the dominant organisational form in which banks do business; there has been no flourishing of mutuals – indeed the demise of the Co-operative Bank hammers a further nail into their coffin. The few 'challenger' banks encouraged since the crisis have grown almost entirely through lending to buy-to-let property companies. Credit to SMEs has fallen by a third since 2008.

Nor should this be any surprise. The banks are as much creatures of the way the financial system organises company ownership as are PLCs more widely. They too have to deliver breathtakingly high returns to their footloose shareholders, and the reward system is constructed to incentivise just that. An incoming chief executive like Antony Jenkins of Barclays – 'Saint Antony', as he is mocked by his detractors – may want to instil a duty of care into his bank, ethical behaviour in all branches of its business, less extravagant pay more closely related to genuine performance and a sense of wider responsibility to the community in which Barclays trades. Barclays under his leadership published its 2015 Citizen Plan, complete with eight key metrics ranging from improvements in its lending and access to finance to promoting skills and the environment. He monitors progress carefully – but few of his shareholders care. One, Scottish Widows, will only vote in favour of proposals that maximise shareholder value.

Jenkins confronts the deep structures of British ownership and finance; it is an uphill battle, but at least one business leader is trying. For him and others to succeed, the financial system, along with Britain's system of corporate ownership, need much more root and branch reform. But that will mean accepting a remoralisation in British business. Both law and culture should require the acceptance by business leaders that duty of care, stewardship, and commitment to business purpose and wider economic and social good are part of their leadership responsibilities. Britain's gentlemanly capitalists may have lost some their swagger and are on the defensive, but they will resist to the last.

Why are the prospects of change so slim?

The cast of characters we have already encountered supply the answer. Sir Nigel Rudd genuinely and passionately believes that he was doing his duty in selling Pilkington, Alliance Boots and Invensys abroad to the highest bidder: he has never voiced more than the mildest criticism of the way the system operates. You can be sure Sir Win Bischoff genuinely believes that the City of London, despite the insolvent banking system of 2008 going on to generate £28.5 billion of fines, litigation costs and customer redress, should suffer no substantive regulatory or structural reform. Notwithstanding the debacle over the sale of Royal Mail shares and the lesson of Thames Water, former industry minister Michael Fallon will continue to believe that its privatisation as an unalloyed PLC was the only way to move the organisation into the private sector.

It is a small army, occupying boardrooms, editorial chairs, advisory roles to government and of course the Conservative party. They are 'the New Few', as Ferdinand Mount, former head of the Downing Street Policy Unit under Lady Thatcher, puts it. In the name of choice, freedom and individual autonomy they preach that private is always best and the state should be smaller because public initiative is assumed always to be self-defeating. Transactions in markets driven by self-interest reliably produce a better outcome than any public or regulatory agency. Shareholder autonomy is taken to be axiomatically a good thing. They accept the state should be smaller, regulations less strict and taxes as low as possible. The good businessman has an obligation to minimise his company's tax payments because the state only squanders money. Indeed, privately many would share the view of Sir Richard Branson, one of our most charismatic businessmen, who extols the virtues of operating from a tax haven; it allowed Virgin to 'move from business to business without massive tax liabilities ... if we had not done it the way that we did, Virgin would be half the size it is today'.[24]

This financial and business elite is both aggressively self-confident and curiously self-pitying. It is completely certain, whatever the evidence to the contrary, that it is right in every respect on the economy and business. After all Britain has created a job-generating, business-friendly economy that is the envy of Europe – hence London is a magnet for European immigration. The country is not embroiled in the travails of the Eurozone. Yet self-pity, usually privately expressed but bubbling to the surface at the annual conference of the self-appointed guardians of British-style free enterprise, the Institute of Directors, is rarely far away. Why do people not celebrate enterprise more? Why is there so much sniping at business and profit? Chancellor George Osborne caught the mood at the 2014 conference at the Royal Albert Hall, claiming extravagantly that the principles of free enterprise and business were 'up for grabs' for 'the first time in his adult life'. He urged business to put its head above the parapet, and make the argument for 'an enterprising, pro-business, low-tax economy that delivers prosperity for the people and generations to come'. The IOD's director general, Simon Walker, took up the theme: business was in a 'generational struggle' to defend free market principles.[25]

Walker and Osborne, for all their fighting talk, know very well why business is on the defensive. It has a lengthening record of disasters behind it, with extravagant pay encouraging wild risks and short-cuts without any accountability – and the hard work of creating genuine value largely neglected. Ferdinand Mount, hardly a leftist anti-business fifth columnist, adds his own examples to the list sketched by John Kay in his review or those earlier in this chapter, beginning his book with HSBC's extraordinary purchase in 2003 of Household – in effect a bankrupt bank – for £9 billion, which had to be entirely written off six years later. Yet not one of the executives involved, all paid bonuses worth many millions of pounds, suffered any reproach or paid any financial penalty.

The list of parallel disasters is legion. BP may be the victim of an out-of-control US legal system, making it liable for up to $43 billion for its negligence in the Gulf of Mexico oil spill – but its problem was that it was negligent, in part to serve the share price. Tesco disclosed in September 2014 that serious accounting irregularities had caused it to overstate profits by £250 million, triggering a criminal investigation by the Serious Fraud Office and the departure of senior executives. Moreover although business proclaims its devotion to enterprise, it is curiously risk-averse: British business in the main has become very good at extracting value from pre-existing assets, mis-selling products and services to a gullible public and skimming margins from transactions large and small. It prefers nothing better than a contract from government with guaranteed margins. Thirty per cent of British government expenditure is devoted to procuring goods and services from the private sector, one of the highest proportions in the industrialised world.[26] The total value of all the grants, subsidies, tax credits and reliefs to Britain's companies, including the profits made by the procurement companies in the public services industry – corporate welfare – is estimated at around £85 billion annually.[27] The cost of monitoring all this sub-contracted and contracted-out work is huge; cost overruns in ICT projects are endemic, running at 30 per cent on average, while more generally in the medium term the additional costs of outsourcing contracts run at between 10 and 40 per cent.[28]

It should thus be no surprise that more of Britain's top fifty firms and more firms absolutely – some 154 – have connections to politics and government paying advisers or consultants than even in Russia or Japan.[29] British firms chase government contracts, not only in defence and construction but in the lush new business of contracted-out services. Notwithstanding their dreadful record of cutting corners, false invoicing and poor delivery, G4S and Serco are among the fastest-growing companies on the UK stock market. The doctrine is that they could not be worse than the state, despite the growing evidence, some of which is cited earlier, that they are both more expensive and less effective in the round than the public sector they replace. Yet British firms are careful to hire former ministers, current and former MPs as board members or consultants to keep in with their favoured source of business – the government. For example, over the last ten years no less than seven former health ministers and six former defence ministers took up such roles with health companies and defence contractors respectively.[30]

Little of the scale of corporate welfare receives the degree of critical press or media coverage that is deserved: the great centre-right newspapers and their growing host of commentators are essentially uncritical cheerleaders for the anti-state mantra of choice, individualism and freedom. The most animated, forceful element in the Conservative party echo the same refrain. The 2010–15 Conservative party in government experienced more backbench revolts than any other since 1945; it was a badge of pride for MPs such as Dominic Raab, Mark Pritchard, Jacob Rees-Mogg, Mark Reckless and Douglas Carswell (before both Reckless and Carswell resigned their seats in September 2014 to seek re-election for UKIP) and their ilk that they had stood up for real conservatism – freedom, as they would put it – rather than the faux version offered by David Cameron. Their object is exit from the European Union and for Britain to pursue its vocation as the Hong Kong of Europe – a giant entrepot with minimal regulation and welfare, celebrating 'freedom' as it has throughout its history. 'Enterprise' will be set free.

This is the new elite – cousins to gentlemanly capitalists, but without the saving grace of a sense of obligation to those below them that informs Ferdinand Mount's writing. Their vision of the good society is one in which the top 0.1 per cent is free to do 'enterprise' with little or no accountability, while huge personal rewards are accrued. Notions of stewardship, duty of care and wider responsibility to the society of which they are part are not in their lexicon. Wealth must be created, they intone repeatedly, before it can be distributed, never questioning why the British system is so incapable of growing small companies to large or why so many large companies create so little wealth except for those who run them. They bestride the country: the vandals within.

They are succoured by the vigour and simplicity of conservative ideas, and its happy coincidence with their own self-interest. But their ascendancy has been boosted by the disintegration of other centres of countervailing power – partly as a direct result of the new elite's assault on their power base and partly because of their own weaknesses. There is no cohesive working-class elite and voice: the network of strong trade union, civic and social leaders who articulated a coherent contrary argument, representing ordinary people, have largely evaporated. Local government has been stripped of power, money and prestige while trade unionism outside the public sector barely exists – again organisation is made harder by anti-trade union laws and the change in the underlying economic structure. Large industrial sites employing tens or thousands have disappeared: it is much harder to recruit members in small dispersed companies in the service sector.

But trade unions bear some responsibility for their own plight. What is striking is that unions no longer seem to offer a ladder upwards for men and women who not only represent their members but offer a view of economy and society that, if not based on a socialist ideal that we now know to be unworkable, is based on the same values of equity and fairness and offers a feasible alternative. Anger and grievance are rarely marshalled to deliver effective campaigns or change opinion;

there are too few examples of successful unionism in practice (although in Chapter 6 I shall discuss some potential ways forward). The collapse of socialism has robbed the working class of a realisable, easy to understand project. In its place many people have opted for sullen acceptance, directing their rage at foreigners, overpaid business executives and Westminster politicians – the constituency from which UKIP has drawn its support.

Organised religion meanwhile is marginalised by an increasingly secular society. Equally the class of knowledgeable professionals – whether in government, universities or even in the private sector – who represent professional standards and knowhow and have an independent platform from which to speak – have been relegated to the fringes. The professional civil servant, engineer, lawyer, consultant, professor, planner, scientist or even arcane meteorologist are no longer seen as custodians of a professional ethic of integrity or objective knowledge. The civil servant who dares to challenge a minister's ideological convictions as unworkable; the doctor who insists that patient care requires trained rather than agency nurses; the scientist who warns that weather patterns are changing; the planner who professes a belief in urban and transport planning rather than markets – all are to be derided and challenged as no more than lobbyists for a vested interest. There are not patients, students, or passengers served by skilled and devoted professionals: there are only customers, and the market/privatisation framework can be applied universally – from universities to children in care, from hospitals to human resources. We have been taught that professionals cannot be trusted and relied upon to offer objective opinions within a duty of care and professional ethic: they require to be measured by targets which they are incentivised to meet. Only thus will resources be deployed efficiently. Professionals do not understand the business case or the need to husband scarce resources; they and their opinions can be marginalised or ignored.

Equally the clerisy of well-read individuals, creative artists and academics prepared to engage in public argument, participate in public life and challenge the new orthodoxies – and who might stiffen the ranks of the professionals, working-class and faith leaders – is thinner and less influential than it should be. Too many academics hunker down for the dictates of the next research excellence framework rather than enter the public domain. There are dissenting plays, protest films and challenging novels – but far too few, given the size of the target there is to hit. Too many have been co-opted, readier to engage in a tax-evasion scheme than to stir the young with anthems of hope, love and prospects for a better tomorrow. There is not enough energy to contest what is happening.

This is not fertile ground for a progressive culture, new alliances and a politics that challenges today's business and financial structures. The Labour party is criticised for its compromises and timidity in challenging all this, but a strong party of the liberal and centre-left can only emerge if it is succoured by equally strong elements in civil society. Messrs Blair and Brown could have been braver in office, as I will discuss; but it was not as though there were powerful constituencies who both had better ideas and were pressing to offer economic and political support for their implementation. Labour's weakness is society's weakness to generate opposition and a coherent alternative.

Change is stirring

Yet there are counter-trends. Opinion is less one-sided and more in flux: there are the first stirrings of potential change. A majority of business leaders will shake their head at the thesis of this chapter; a growing minority will accept there is force in the criticism, that business must reform and be prepared to dissociate themselves from a 'generational struggle' fought on terms that are indefensible. I have already quoted Elizabeth Murdoch, daughter of Rupert, damning the purpose-free, amoral culture of News International in her 2012 MacTaggart Lecture. Paul Polman, CEO of Unilever, has unilaterally stopped quarterly reporting. Unilever, together with BT, supports the calls of Blueprint for Better Business to build companies as purpose- rather than profit-driven. Rick Haythornthwaite, the incoming chair of Centrica, is keenly aware that his company needs to earn a licence to trade by putting the customer and citizens' interests higher up its agenda. Richard Branson, despite his tax avoidance, declares that there has to be a change of course, particularly on the environment. Richard Lambert, former director general of the CBI, has said publicly that chief executive pay is so stratospheric that CEOs risk becoming aliens in their own land. Antony Jenkins, CEO of Barclays, as I wrote earlier, is trying to recast his bank's values and broaden its priorities. Vincent de Rivaz, as I write in Chapter 6, has struck a social covenant with the unions on the Hinkley nuclear power site. Sir Ian Cheshire, chief executive of Kingfisher, along with a group of business leaders including Steve Marshall, executive chair of Balfour Beatty, publicly co-signed an open letter calling for a higher minimum wage. Lady Lynne Forester de Rothschild is founder of the Coalition for Inclusive Capitalism, aiming to create a more broadly based prosperity and to enlist the great global asset management groups to the cause. There is renewed enthusiasm for Catholic Social Policy in the Catholic community, emphasising that business must have a social purpose and respect the dignity of work. The Governor of the Bank of England (a Catholic), as I write in the next chapter, has warned that justice and a social contract are needed to underwrite successful capitalism. Andrew Haldane, whose speeches are cast very much within the argument of this book, is the Bank of England's chief economist. Even in the US there is dissent from the orthodoxies of the last thirty years. Jack Welch, former CEO of General Electric and the author of the idea that the sole purpose of the company should be maximising shareholder value, has recanted and now says it is the 'dumbest idea in the world'.[31] Alan Greenspan, former President of the US Federal Reserve and prominent conservative, thinks that the biggest danger facing the US is inequality.

What is crystallising opposition to the New Few, the gentlemanly capitalists and their political outriders on the libertarian right of the Conservative party, not to mention the threat of UKIP, is the stance Britain should take over the European Union. Nobody is an enthusiast for a federal Europe; many have doubts about the ambition, set out in EU treaties, for 'an ever closer union' and some of the EU's regulatory initiatives appear intrusive. There is little admiration for the euro. But the bulk of British business does not want to leave the European Union, as UKIP and a significant part of the Conservative party now openly advocate. The City is emphatic in that it is best to be inside the Brussels system influencing legislation that will necessarily have a big impact, and is aware that so many multinationals run their European operations from London because it gives them access to the European single market while enjoying British opt-outs. The single market is a considerable achievement, and there is also a recognition across the British business community that it requires regulation to make it single: Britain should not be a Norway or Switzerland essentially shadowing what the EU decides but without any influence. Nor does business see a tension between trading with the rest of the world and trading with the European Union: the two are not in opposition. Becoming the Hong Kong of

Europe is portrayed as fanciful, even absurd. There was a very adverse reaction to the threat of eurosceptic Tory MP John Redwood, made at the 2014 Conservative party conference, that those business leaders who spoke up for British membership of the EU would pay 'a very dear economic and financial price'.[32] This is not the relationship business expects with the pro-business party of the centre-right.

Broadly, British business thinks the status quo perfectly acceptable and does not want to risk exit. It is alarmed at both the prospect of an EU referendum, the need for which has been fanned up unnecessarily, and, worse, that it could easily be lost. Put the EU question together with the growing recognition that business itself has to change, and there is the first substantive crack in the elite business and financial establishment for a generation. Some of the rage at Britain's elites is understandable, but the target is too broad.[33] The more intriguing analysis is how the elite is fragmenting. It no longer speaks with one voice.

There is also movement from below. The growing criticism against companies who do not pay their fair share of tax, represented by the success of UK Uncut, is perhaps part of the reason why Pfizer encountered such hostility in its bid for AstraZeneca. Food retailers fear the collapse in their reputation if they sell doctored or improperly labelled food. There is a drumbeat of support for a higher minimum wage. The society the new elite want to build is not the society the mass of citizens want to live in or a growing part of the business community believe is fair and sustainable, even if the project still dominates the economic and political landscape. There are allies for change at the top of the business and financial establishment, even if they are in a minority. What moves societies is both ideas and lived experience. Ideas are changing – driven by lived experience, especially of inequality, which is where our inquiry goes next.

4
Inequality at a Tipping Point

Inequality is like a slow-growing but untreated cancer; it can grow with little apparent effect for a long time while the sufferer lives in happy ignorance. Occasionally there may be unexplained physical weaknesses and complaints that suggest something is awry, but other, less alarming explanations than cancer seem both more likely and comforting. Then suddenly the cancer begins to metastasise with catastrophic effects, but it is too late to stop its now obvious spread, and the implications are often fatal.

Societies, unlike individuals, do not die. But the cancer of inequality produces results that are equally catastrophic, if in different terms. Trust evaporates. There is no sense of common purpose. Creative social, economic and political interaction and deliberation becomes impossible. Capitalism distorts itself and ceases to innovate. Electorates become vulnerable to extreme populism from left or right.

So far Britain has tried to explain the riots of August 2011, say, or the growth of food banks, in less alarming terms than potentially catastrophic poverty, but in truth they were warnings of trouble ahead. In 2015 it is becoming clearer that we are arriving at a tipping point – a moment when unchecked inequality of both income and wealth is about to metastasise into a serious economic and social cancer. It is inequality that is behind the unsustainable growth of poverty, ill-health and the welfare bill. It is inequality that has propelled the escalating demand for credit, warning that underneath the economic surface all was not well had there been concern to look. It is inequality that has helped create our fragile banking system and its still feral proclivities. It is inequality that is disfiguring the housing market, with house prices out of reach for first-time buyers as waiting lists for social housing extend to 1.7 million,[1] and a new class of multi-millionaire buy-to-let landlords have become an unwelcome part of the social tapestry. It is inequality that has turned too many aspirant entrepreneurs and top managers in our society into seekers of easy profit, with calamitous consequences for investment, innovation and productivity – a situation evident before the financial crisis and even more so now. It is inequality that is contributing to the collapse in trust in politicians and the democratic process; they are, runs the popular cry, all the same.

Ever since Mrs Thatcher's election in 1979 Britain's elites have relegated concerns about inequality below the existential question of how to restore our capitalist economy to economic health, a matter deemed to transcend all other considerations. The language of the socioeconomic landscape, as I observed earlier, has been commanded by words like efficiency, productivity, wealth generation, aspiration, entrepreneur, pro-business and incentives. To the extent they are significant at all, preoccupations with inequality have been seen as of second-order importance. Some Conservative politicians, notably Boris Johnson in a high-profile speech, even defend inequality on the grounds that it is the natural consequence of some having higher IQ and energy than others, which translates into entrepreneurial success.[2] Inequality is thus the price that society pays for the economic vitality brought by its high-energy, high-IQ individuals, along with the rewards they expect and deserve.

Boris Johnson and his fellow Conservative apologists may argue that the rich deserve their income and wealth – the rich certainly think that – but the sheer disproportion between what is now earned by the top 0.1 per cent and what they contribute economically undermines the conceptions of proportionality and due desert that define fairness. Inequality has now reached levels that have become a challenge to us as moral beings. Fairness is not a soft concept like apple pie and motherhood, one to which we are well disposed but which has no analytic traction. Rather fairness, as I argued in Chapter 2, is a deeply ingrained human instinct: a normative view, with which every human being is endowed, that there should be a proportional relationship between what you do – good or bad – and the consequences. In the justice system of every civilisation there is a tariff of punishment that escalates in proportion to the seriousness of the offence; similarly every civilisation has a tariff of reward that reflects society's view of the proportional contribution that has been made. There are, in short, just or due deserts.

Of course adjustments are made to reflect luck and accident, especially luck that you have made yourself by your own diligence or lack of it. Readers will recall the reference in Chapter 1 to Professor Ronald Dworkin's concept of brute luck – the chance luck of happy or unhappy accident. Dworkin differentiated brute luck from earned, deserved luck – option luck as he called it – resulting in part from your own efforts. Brute luck, whether the good luck of being born privileged or the bad luck of being born with genes that dispose one towards ill-health, deserved either the taxation of inherited estates (inheritance tax – not a death tax but a we-share-in-your-good-luck tax) or compensation through collective insurance (social insurance or tax-financed public health systems). The option luck of your own efforts – the luck of the concert pianist or sportswoman who achieves success through working hard on their original talent – is their due desert.[3]

In 2015 the scale of income at the top and desperation at the bottom drives a coach and horses through any sense that the distribution is fair. This is brute luck in action. The average pay for the chief executives of Britain's top 100 companies has quadrupled in a generation. Few would argue that such a pay increase is proportional to their effort or to their economic contribution, or that it is deserved. During the New Labour years the gap between the bottom and the middle of the income parade narrowed a little, with significant improvements in the relative living standards of low-income families with children and of pensioners, but there was little attention to incomes at the top.[4] For twenty years the great British inequality machine has hurtled on, driven largely by the burgeoning incomes of this top 0.1 per cent – almost all of whom are directors, bankers or work in business services and real estate[5] – who captured the lion's share of any gains in real productivity. In 1995 they took 3.2 per cent of all income; by 2009 that had more than doubled to 6.5 per cent, falling back to 4.8 per cent in 2011 as bonuses fell during the recession. The other top 0.9 per cent were not slouches; together with the 0.1 per cent, the top 1.0 per cent saw its share rise from 10.8 to 15.4 per cent over the same period, then fall back to 12.9 per cent, impacted by the same cyclical effect on bonuses as the top 0.1 per cent. But 70 per of the rise of the income share of the top 1 per cent was driven by the top 0.1 per cent.[6]

What's merit got to do with it?

This growth in pay at the top has little to do with real merit. Top pay is much lower, for example, in mainland Europe and Japan – and even lower in the US, once adjusted for the size of the corporations under management. British executive pay is the highest in the world. British executives have had the brute good luck to be in post in a period when profits as a share of GDP are rising, unions are weak and an 'arms race' of executive pay has developed, propelled by ever more grandiose giveaways of shares justified by attempts to incentivise 'performance'. The quadrupling of executive remuneration has been propelled by the award of increasing proportions of pay in bonuses, deferred bonuses and long-term incentive plans linked to share-price performance, because the doctrine is that this will 'align' shareholders' interest in a higher share price with that of directors. At least three-quarters of total remuneration comes this way – increases in base pay have been much more modest.

French economist Thomas Piketty, in his book *Capital*, calls this the ideology of 'meritocratic extremism', the doctrine that extravagant pay is justified by the merit of performance. He considers it to have hardened into an Anglo-Saxon social norm. He is right. As I noted in the review on fair pay I undertook for the UK government, the way in which decisions are made as to how large bonuses and incentive plans should be is hardly scientific enough to argue that there is a robust link with performance. For example, bonuses of 200 per cent have become routine; but why do so many companies use such rough and ready round numbers – hardly a sign that anybody has thought carefully about what is needed to produce performance and much more like a pure bung – and then accompany them with requirements for their eligibility that are far from demanding and transparent? The truth is that remuneration committees are engaged in a pay arms race in which everyone is trying to ensure that their executive team is in the top quartile of pay – and what constitutes top-quartile pay is not some objective incentive, but a socially determined norm that is always on an upward ratchet.

For example, the Fair Pay Report noted that one of the best determinants of any CEO's pay in the US was the size of his or her social network. The more examples of highly paid members there were in one's network, the more generous a remuneration committee felt it had to be.[7] Boards in turn wanted to hire superstar CEOs, to signal they were performance oriented by paying in the top quartile, which by definition is impossible for everyone because in any ranking of 100 people only 25 can be in the top quartile. Boards themselves were social organisations vulnerable to the manipulation of a powerful or narcissistic CEO.[8]

'Super-salaries', as Piketty calls them, thus have almost nothing to do with carefully calibrated performance and everything to do with the attempts of CEOs and boards to keep up with each other in a status race substantially influenced by social and psychological rather than economic concerns. Bonuses and incentive plans, when distributed as shares, do not cost cash; for remuneration committees they seem like free money. They dilute existing shareholders' interests by such a tiny fraction that they will never notice, while keeping top executives happy.

In any case, executives like to argue that they are in effect entrepreneurs, the engine room of a capitalist society. But real entrepreneurs make fortunes on the back of genuine risk-taking, usually when they bet their assets and reputation on some innovation. They can also lose everything. But as companies have found their profits rising sharply, executives at the top have sold the unjustified proposition that it was because they too were entrepreneurial, rather than being lucky office holders at a time when profits were rising even if it had little to do with them – the real causes being weakened trade unions, globalisation or some combination of the two, together with the introduction of new technologies – so that they should too receive entrepreneurial returns. They might risk little, while expecting pay to rise on a permanent upward ratchet, and do not actually need reward on such scale – but they have been determined to have it, not least for its outward sign of worth.

In his *Theory of the Leisure Class*, a book published in 1899 when inequalities in wealth and income matched those of today, economist Thorstein Veblen captured this social dynamic well in his concept of conspicuous consumption. There is a logic to the need of the already very wealthy for more wealth: they show it off to demonstrate where they are in the social pecking order. Veblen writes that, while the livery worn by personal servants, the nature of pets and the grandeur of parties may seem to be economically irrational if not futile, to the very rich these are subtle, socially honed indicators of standing.

For example, rich men's wives at the end of the nineteenth century had a particularly important role, he argued, as highly visible 'ceremonial consumers of goods'. The sophistication of the household they ran, the quality of its furnishings and the extravagance of their clothes indicated the standing of their husbands. They had transmuted from being male chattels, said Veblen, to becoming lead players in driving conspicuous consumption. Economically irrational, certainly, but in social terms wholly comprehensible.

We now live in an era of 'conspicuous reward' – a notion understandable only as a social phenomenon because its extravagance has ceased to have any economic logic. Bonuses have become what wives' dresses and servants' livery were in the 1890s: signs of worth. Moreover, Veblen observed that the choice of what the rich conspicuously consumed was very important: one of the reasons sports such as shooting and yachting attracted such spending was that they were the best ways of acting in a peaceful way on predatory, aggressive, 'aristocratic' behaviour – character traits the very wealthy were anxious to show they possessed.

Similarly, the successful CEO today shows the predator instincts behind his success by doing something extravagantly but peacefully competitive – taking part in the America's Cup (Larry Ellison, CEO of Oracle), ballooning (Richard Branson) or racing at Le Mans. Owning an island in the Pacific (Ellison owns Lanai in Hawaii) or the Caribbean (Branson owns Necker Island in the West Indies) shows your need for extreme privacy and luxury – the quintessential expression of a natural aristocrat. Meanwhile, your exquisitely dressed partner – usually but not always a wife – runs an elegant mansion in Manhattan or central London. The sexes may have grown more equal between the 1890s and the 2010s, yet it is still women – as wives – who are typically leaders in 'ceremonial consumption'.

The problem is that these are no longer the harmless peccadilloes of the super-rich, presented as fundamental to incentivise performance. Rather, the US and British economies are increasingly being run in order to deliver these lifestyles, with disappointing wider economic results. In my chapter on inequality in *The State We're In* I lamented that the gap between low and high wages was then the widest since records began[9] – except that, twenty years later, it is higher. What is happening today is that executives, to deliver the share-price performance that will boost their bonuses and incentive plans, are turning organisations into payolas for executive pay.[10]

But there is an additional twist. One of the fastest ways of boosting profits in an era when trade unions are weak and union representation in much of the private sector has collapsed is to downgrade employees' terms of employment and working conditions, and reduce wages. Managements' bargaining power has been further increased by the threat – and sometimes the reality – of moving work offshore, and, since the accession to the European Union in 2004 of eight new members, which lifted inward migration levels from the EU by some 100,000 a year, by a larger pool of incoming migrant workers ready to work for keener wages. Trade unions were problematic in parts of the economy in the 1960s and 1970s – particularly in the printing and car industries – but as I argue later they did serve the purpose of keeping the wage share in GDP broadly constant, and acting as a countervailing power to sometimes rapacious managements. Cumulatively, over the last generation, the weakening of trade unions' countervailing market power has seen around 5.5 per cent of GDP being moved permanently from the workforce to shareholders.[11]

Average real wages at first stagnated and are now falling. Indeed between 2008 and the end of 2013, as an important study published by the National Institute for Economic and Social Research shows, real annual wages fell for the typical worker by 8 per cent, or £2000 – a fall the report describes as unprecedented. The falls for young people up to the age of 29 were even greater – 13 per cent for 25- to 29-year-olds, 14 per cent for 18- to 25-year-olds.[12] Part of the explanation is that the growth in productivity has become negligible. This is compounded by top, 'super managers' ensuring that whatever paltry gains that are made go not to workers but to profits, which then inflates the share price and, via related bonuses and incentives, those managers' own remuneration. Leading UK sport retailer Sports Direct, for example, employs 23,000 people: 20,000 are on zero-hour contracts with no holiday or pension entitlement, while in 2014 even shareholders revolted against a scheme to reward the executive team and senior managers by giving away more than 4 per cent of UK Sports Direct's shares as share options conditional on an increase in profits of more than 50 per cent up to 2019 – a target only attainable if the staff remain on zero-hour contracts. Shareholders' objection was not to the principle: rather it was to the extravagant but opaque generosity to the executive team, and to the founder and deputy chair Michael Ashley in particular, who would have picked up £73 million. In the event the shareholders finally caved in, while Ashley deferred receiving his bonus.

Meanwhile Swiss-based INEOS only agreed to keep the Grangemouth oil refinery and chemical plant open in October 2014 once the union had agreed to a three-year pay freeze, the closing of the company's defined benefit pension scheme to new entrants, and a union guarantee not to strike for three years. So it continues. There has been, as Guy Standing remarks in *The Precariat*, an orgy of regrading and redefining jobs as less skilled so that they qualify for lower wages; there has also been a growing confidence that employers do not need to pay higher wages in every annual wage round.

The weakening of trade unions has been central to this process; the popular view that the fall in wages is entirely because of immigration is wrong. It is true that immigration has had some impact in some areas, like semi-skilled and low-skilled service jobs in the period up to 2008.[13] UKIP is partly right, even if the benefits of immigration in opening up Britain to new skills, creativity and energy – the kind of capitalism this country needs to create – are submerged beneath a tidal wave of concern, misdirected at immigrants rather than at the proper villain, the deregulated labour market. The intensification and generalisation of the fall in wages after the recession in 2008, when net migration levels were falling, confirm the view that immigration can only be part of the story, and not a large one. The bigger picture is how the deregulated labour market has interacted with companies whose strategy is driven by shareholder value maximisation, and with the incentives offered to the super-managers. There are a few sectors where the impact of migration is being felt, but the main cause of stagnant or falling real wages is the new home-grown market in throwaway people. These raw trends are then exacerbated by the reduction of taxation on capital, companies and higher earners in the name of promoting incentives and 'wealth generation', and reducing social benefits in the name of capping the welfare bill and discouraging 'shirkers'. The cocktail is complete.

The result has been a stunning increase in inequality, the fastest in the OECD, so that Britain now ranks twenty-eighth out of thirty-four countries in the income equality 'league table'. It is almost entirely made at home. Simultaneously there has been a financial crisis, a subsequent weakening in the long-run growth rate, an incredible mountain of mortgage debt and labour productivity that in 2013 was an amazing 16 per cent below where it should have been given previous trends.[14]

Usually, these are understood as discrete phenomena with discrete explanations. Bankers, we are to understand, created the financial crisis by recklessly exploiting global imbalances and arguing for weak regulation in their own selfish interest. Productivity has fallen and is below trend because increasingly workers have inadequate skills or because they simply shirk. Mortgage debt has grown to absurd levels thanks to crazy house prices, driven by land shortages and the inability to build new homes. The low growth rate is because companies lack the confidence to invest.

All those explanations are partially true. But the bigger story is that all have common roots in inequality. Later in this chapter – and in Chapter 6 – I will explore in more detail the linkages between workers' struggle to maintain their living standards by borrowing and the build-up of insupportable levels of debt. And it should already be clear that directors' incentives, while producing great rewards for them, result in poor rewards for everyone else and do not develop high-investment, high-innovation companies. Indifference to the growing gap between rich and poor, in all its multiple dimensions, is the first-order category mistake of our times. No lasting solution to the socioeconomic crisis through which we are living is possible without addressing it. It is this twin perniciousness – the lack of fairness and plain economic dysfunction – that is combining to create the moment of metastasis. Britain's capitalist economy is not working effectively, even while inequality has surpassed the levels of Edwardian England.

Wealth inequality reinforces the process

Simply to own capital in a period when its returns are rising faster than economic growth is to find oneself wealthier through no effort of one's own. Two hundred years of data support this thesis, argues Thomas Piketty, and despite criticism of some of his calculations the weight of evidence is too overwhelming for the basic proposition not to hold. Piketty's contention is boosted by the fact that, since the 1970s, wealth in the UK has risen twice as fast as income.[15] Once the returns on capital – invested in anything from buy-to-let property to a new furniture factory – exceed the real growth of wages and output, as historically they always have done (excepting a few periods such as 1910 to 1950), then inevitably the stock of capital will rise disproportionately fast within the overall pattern of output. Wealth inequality rises exponentially.

The process is made worse by inheritance. Inequality of wealth in Europe and US is now broadly twice the inequality of income – the top 10 per cent have between 60 and 70 per cent of all wealth but merely 25 to 35 per cent of income. But this concentration of wealth is already at pre-First World War levels, and heading back to those of the late nineteenth century, when the brute luck of who might expect to inherit what was the dominant element in economic and social life. There is an iterative interaction between wealth and income: ultimately, great wealth adds unearned income to earned income, further ratcheting up the inequality process.

The extravagances and social tensions of Edwardian England, Belle Epoque France and robber-baron America seemed for ever left behind, but Piketty argues that the period between 1910 and 1950, when that inequality was reduced, was aberrant. It took war and depression to arrest the inequality dynamic, along with the need to introduce high taxes on high incomes – especially unearned incomes – in order to sustain social peace. Now the ineluctable process of blind capital multiplying faster in fewer hands is under way again, and on a global scale. The consequences, writes Piketty, are 'potentially terrifying'.[16]

For a start, almost no new entrepreneurs, except one or two spectacular Silicon Valley start-ups, can ever make sufficient new money to challenge the powerful concentrations of existing wealth. In this sense, the 'past devours the future'.[17] It is telling that the Duke of Westminster and the Earl of Cadogan are two of the richest men in Britain. This is entirely by virtue of the fields in Mayfair and Chelsea their families owned centuries ago and the unwillingness to clamp down on the loopholes in levying inheritance tax that allow the family estates to grow.

Anyone with the capacity to own capital in an era when the

returns exceed those of wages and output will quickly become disproportionately and progressively richer. The incentive is not to be a risk-taker, but rather to collect rents as a 'rentier' from the assets you hold – from property to patents: witness the explosion of buy-to-let. Our companies and our rich don't need to back frontier innovation, or even invest to produce; they just need to harvest their returns and tax breaks. Tax shelters and compound interest will do the rest.

Capitalist dynamism is undermined, but other forces join to wreck the system. The rich are effective at protecting their wealth from taxation, so that inevitably and progressively the proportion of the total tax burden shouldered by those on middle incomes has risen. In Britain, it may be true that the top 1 per cent pays a third of all income tax, but income tax constitutes only 25 per cent of tax revenue: 45 per cent comes from VAT, excise duties and national insurance paid by the mass of the population. The proportion of total tax contributed by inheritance tax, now a largely voluntary tax, has plummeted to £3 billion, or less than 0.5 per cent of all UK taxes, which even though it is now forecast to rise with increased house prices is still a sixth of the level immediately after the war. The wealthy have become ever savvier about hiding their wealth – and more capable, in an era of globalisation and free movement of capital, of doing it.

As a result, the burden of paying for public goods such as education, health and housing is increasingly shouldered by taxpayers on average incomes, who don't have the wherewithal to sustain them. Wealth inequality thus becomes a recipe for slowing, innovation-averse economies, tougher working conditions and degraded public services. Meanwhile, the rich get ever richer and more detached from the societies of which they are part; not by merit or hard work, but simply because they are lucky enough to be in command of capital which over time receives higher returns than wages. Our collective sense of justice is outraged.

The cascade of consequences is formidable. Workers, struggling to maintain their living standards, have borrowed extraordinary multiples of their income to make money in the only other certain way – through the housing market. Housing equity is now estimated by estate agents Savills to be worth £1.8 trillion in total; withdrawing this is the sole reliable route to sustaining living standards.[18] House prices have been bid up well beyond a sustainable relationship with wages. After being temporarily halted during the financial crisis, the process is now under way again.

None of this would be possible without credit. British banks have lent £1.2 trillion in mortgages. But if inequality has fuelled the demand for credit – whether through mortgages or payday loans – it has also helped drive the supply of credit and thus added further impetus to the creation of an extraordinary financial system biased to lend to property and not to enterprise. Recent statistics reveal that one in ten people over fifty-five now have assets worth £1 million or more, the consequence of owning property and pensions in a period of rising property and share prices – but which they had done nothing to earn.[19] Poorer wage earners left out of the boom have to rent, creating a new class of private sector landlords whose collective equity is now estimated to top £800 billion. There are 1.5 million buy-to-let mortgages, with historic returns exceeding 16 per cent, and good returns of 11 per cent are projected for the future.[20] Yet as a result owner occupation is falling. Your chance of getting on the housing ladder early or late in life is closely determined by the wealth of your parents: Shelter estimates that parents in aggregate give their children £2 billion a year to help them buy their first house. The brute luck of birth thus becomes essential to future housing wealth. Nobody would argue, I hope, that today's generation of young people 'deserve' the British housing market.

Bankers represented the occupation in the top 0.1 per cent whose incomes went up the fastest and furthest; an individual banker's contribution to profits is the most transparent of any sector, so the dynamic interaction between reward and corporate behaviour was the most pronounced. The faster and larger a bank could grow its lending, the higher its profits, and in the new world in which banking bureaucrats were paid as entrepreneurs, those profits fed straight through to bankers' bonuses. Bankers knew their balance sheets would in effect be guaranteed by the state. Regulation was weakened by the fashion for believing in free markets. Too much pay at the top of banks and too little pay in the middle and bottom became the structural cause of a financial system that by 2008 had become a predator on economy and society alike. Inequality, once again, had become the noxious catalyst promoting yet more economic dysfunction. We ignore it at our peril.

The 30/30/40 society twenty years on

Inequality is conceived principally as the scale of the gap between the best and worst paid, the richest and the poorest. Indeed I began Chapter 8 of *The State We're In* with the image of an income parade in which the entire British population walked past for an hour with their height representing their income. For the first quarter of an hour dwarves would walk by; it would only be after thirty-seven minutes that the first adult of average height would be seen, representing average earnings. After fifty-seven minutes we would see the first adults that were twelve feet tall – and in the last few seconds giants of ninety feet or more would appear. Today an income parade would be broadly similar: it would take a few minutes longer before we got beyond the dwarves and again to individuals of average height, and in the last seconds the ninety- foot giants would have grown to over 200 feet. In the final nanoseconds we would now see some King Kongs – walking skyscrapers.

But earnings were and are not the sole yardstick of well-being and of the degree to which an individual is exposed to life's hazards. One of the features of the 1980s and 1990s was a new insecurity that was overlaid on income inequality. To try and capture this I developed with Paul Gregg, then at the LSE, and drawing on the work of his colleague Jonathan Wadsworth, the concept of the 30/30/40 society, a categorisation that cut across the income parade by grouping workers' experience of risk, unpredictability and insecurity into three broad areas. They very generously reworked the numbers for today. The first 30 per cent were the *disadvantaged* – the men and women who were unemployed, economically inactive or could only find scraps of poorly paid work, typically 'on terms offering no protection or benefits and who are paid half or less of the average wage'. Thirty per cent was a stunningly large proportion of the adult workforce, much higher than the head-line unemployment number seen as the usual proxy for economic health.

The next 30 per cent were the *marginalised and insecure* – the struggling millions 'at the receiving end of the changes blowing through Britain's offices and factories'. The forty-hour week, complete with its benefits and protections, was under assault: but what again was extraordinary was how large the newly inse-cure segment of the workforce had quickly become. The numbers yet to be eligible for formal employment protection, the temporary and agency workers, and workers self-employed for less than two years ran into millions. They often worked uncertain, irregular hours, received no employment protection, and their eligibility for sickness, holiday and pension entitlements was increasingly qualified or non-existent. I also included in this category full-time employees earning half average earnings, whose low pay made their lives riskier, along with part-time workers who had worked less than five years (I excluded long-term part-time workers on the grounds that most of them were women and likely to come from secure two-income households). The definition broadly captured what Professor Guy Standing later in 2011 would call the precariat, the group of workers who were most exposed to managers' growing desire to reduce employment costs across the spectrum of occupations and skill types while simultaneously being able to reshape the firm at great speed, either hiring or shedding workers quickly. In sum, increasing numbers of jobs would be created that had less guaranteed remuneration and benefits but were contingent on demand and wider business circumstances. This was an exercise in displacing risk from the firm to the individual; understandable from firms' point of view, especially in a fast-moving, unpredictable economic climate, but disastrous for many of those who worked for them.

The last 40 per cent were the *advantaged* – employees who were tenured and/or represented by trade unions, in jobs offering thirty-five to forty hours a week. The availability of this kind of ordered, predictable work, whose image was so closely associated with the post-war working environment, had now shrunk so that only two in five of all workers enjoyed such jobs. If 55 per cent of the workforce had been in full-time tenured employment in 1975, by 1995 the proportion had alarmingly dropped to 35 per cent; the 5 per cent balance to arrive at 40 per cent was made up of the long-term self-employed and long-term part-timers. Some of the advantaged might earn less than average earnings, but wherever their position in the income parade, at least their incomes were predictable and relatively secure. These were the workers with access to privileged assets like defined benefit pension schemes or profit-sharing arrangements. They could take on mortgage and debt with relative ease, could bring up families, and tended to hold their marriages together.

The insight – revelation even – was not only that more than half the UK working population earned less than average earnings but that they were also at growing risk. The 30/30/40 society was casting a long if unremarked shadow over Britain. Indeed Tony Blair used the notion in his 1996 speech to the Labour party conference to telling electoral effect, although he or his writers confused the categories: it was thirty not forty per cent who were at risk and struggling. Even in the mid-1990s it was already apparent that whatever the gains in employment from Britain's new-look labour market, there were substantial social costs. I noted that, once in the bottom two categories of 30 per cent, escape was very hard; two-thirds of all jobs offered to the unemployed were part-time or temporary, and only one in ten of the 30 per cent in the insecure category moved to full-time employment. The social ramifications of this low-income, high-risk trap were huge: the new labour market was intruding into every nook and cranny of British life, whether it was young women finding that there were fewer and fewer men capable of taking on the commitment of marriage and so opting for single parenthood, or just the strains leading to divorce.

Twenty years on, the trends driving the 30/30/40 society are no less pronounced even as overall employment has risen. The big plus of Britain's labour market, with its huge bias to promote work on terms agreeable to employers, is that it encourages the hiring of workers; the protracted recession that lasted from 2008 to 2014 saw many fewer job losses than might otherwise have been expected. The unemployment rate peaked at 8.1 per cent; the employment rate never fell below 70 per cent. But the headline numbers hide the deep social fissures in terms of ever more unequal wages, lowered career expectations, unpredictability of income, diminished opportunity, squeezed living standards and sheer risk to which British workers are exposed. The big trends over the last twenty years have been to more self-employment and contingent work, a weakening in the advantages of full-time employment, a growth in the numbers of over-fifties in work, ever tougher conditions for the young, and the increasing scarcity of work in occupations which promise steady, rising wages.

For millions it is a grim fight for survival, with the knowledge that it will be even tougher for their children. Small wonder that the first response has been to borrow in order, either to be part of the only certain route to more security – rising house prices – or, defensively, to maintain living standards to stay alive, in the worst case using payday lenders and loan sharks. Writing twenty years ago I noted that the biggest case load for Citizens' Advice Bureaus was employment issues. Today it is questions about the tough qualification tests for employment and support allowance – which replaced incapacity benefit – and about debt.[21]

The 30/30/40 society, in short, lives on, although because the employment rate has risen compared with twenty years ago, proportionately more people work either in secure or insecure work – and fewer are either unemployed or economically inactive. But secure work has less advantages than it used to – for example the headlong decline of the good defined benefit pension – and insecure jobs are if anything even risker – witness the rise of zero-hour contracts. As for the marginalised 30 per cent, twenty years of toughening the criteria to qualify for job seeker's allowance, the promotion of job search and now the redefining of incapacity benefit have succeeded in reducing the numbers on benefits. But the experience of those at the bottom is as it was twenty years ago. Very few move from benefits to anything other than high-risk, low-paid, contingent work – and almost none move from that to securer, more advantaged forms of employment.

Self-employment continues to boom. It has now climbed to 15 per cent of all employment, a proportion that has trebled over forty years. Around 30 per cent of the self-employed are older, cushioned from interruptions to their income with equity in their homes and accrued pension rights, and prepared to take a chance, albeit at much lower remuneration, at selling their skills, often to the organisations that used to offer them full-time employment. Many prefer that to the pressures and whims of organisational life; after all, many large companies – ownerless, lacking a core purpose and treating their people as disposable commodities – are hardly attractive places to work Nonetheless the self-employed are completely at the mercy of wider economic forces with no structures to mitigate risk. There are advantages and disadvantages to self-employment: twenty years ago my definition was that if you were self-employed for more than two years then you could be regarded as part of the advantaged 40 per cent; if you had worked for less than two years or were working less than sixteen hours a week then you were insecure. By that yardstick four million people today fall into the insecure 30 per cent.

The proportion in tenured, full-time employment has risen slightly from 40 to 42 per cent. It is true that workers have the right to request extended maternity, paternity and adoption leave up to twelve months – but after six months that is very largely at their own expense. Beyond that, the story is of firms' benefits being scaled back and more risk being inserted into the employment contract. The most significant loss is that the promise of a decent, assured pension in retirement has evaporated. In 1995 there were five million members of defined benefit, final salary pension schemes offering a guaranteed pension proportional to the number of years worked and one's final salary. Today only 841 schemes remain open, covering less than half a million workers.[22] In their place employees can expect to be automatically enrolled in so-called stakeholder pension schemes: their employers will be obliged only to contribute 3 per cent of their wages to a pension fund that the holder may or may not use to buy a pension when he or she reaches retirement age. Pension risk has been transferred lock, stock and two smoking barrels from the company to the individual. Most pensions in a generation's time will be a fraction of those paid today, even though the country is very much richer.

On top, the right to claim unfair dismissal or seek the intervention of an employment tribunal is now only available after two years' continuous working with an employer, thus matching the qualifying period for the right to statutory redundancy. Add the fall of union representation to 14.4 per cent of the private-sector workforce, and full-time, tenured employment in the private sector is much less advantaged than it was.[23]

Age cuts across the trends – better for those over fifty, worse for those under thirty. Twenty years ago the over-fifties took the brunt of the reshaping of Britain's companies, but the long period of growth up to 2008 together with a recession characterised by relatively fewer job losses has seen a transformation in their standing. Using the same definition as in *The State We're In*, 1.8 million more over-fifties are in secure forms of employment than they were in 1994; another 800,000 are working in forms of insecure employment. Even allowing for the rise in

the working population, it means that today there has been a
rise of one in eight of those over fifty in work compared with
1994. In part this is a return to the pattern before the 1980s;
this is partly because it is much more expensive to make over-
fifties redundant now that most pension schemes – which were
used to sweeten the pill of taking early retirement – are much
meaner; and partly because over-fifties have knowledge, skills
and networks that employers value highly in a knowledge-
based, service economy.

The flipside is the much tougher world for the young.
Three-quarters of a million more 18- to 29-year-olds work in
part-time, temporary or short-term self-employed jobs than
they did twenty years ago; two in five young people now work
in these 'precariat' jobs. Moreover, as remarked earlier, real
wages for 18- to 25-year-olds have dived 14 per cent since 2008
and for 25- to 29-year-olds by 11 per cent.[24] On top, more young
people over eighteen are studying in higher education – a jump
from three-quarters of a million to 1.1 million. It is good for
them and society that they will be equipped with degrees or
the equivalent; but under the new system of financing they
will leave higher education with debts of more than £40,000,
facing a labour market where real wages for the first ten years
of their working lives have on average retreated to pre-2000
levels. To become an adult in 2015 is to make your way in a
world that demands more skills while offering fewer rewards,
besets you with more risks, confronts you with more debt and
makes you wait until your mid-thirties before you have a
chance to buy your own home. My generation has not served
its children well. Indeed that is hardly a surprise: if it is not prepared vigilantly to defend the values and principles of a social
contract for itself, it is hardly likely to be concerned about its
children. Justice, to echo the refrain from Chapter 2, is in
eclipse.

The intensification of the forces at work

Writing twenty years ago I was dismayed that the economic liberals in charge of economic and social policy – so anxious to reduce what they saw as the 'serfdom' induced by the state and to promote the trinity of 'more choice, more efficiency and more individual responsibility'[25] – were indiscriminately superimposing upon the 30/30/40 society the same market principles in every dimension of society, from housing to pensions, education to health – even if more layers of inequality would ineluctably follow in their wake. We knew the socially and psychologically destructive effects of too much inequality; I quoted Richard Wilkinson, whose research – prefiguring *The Spirit Level*, which he was to write with Kate Pickett fourteen years later and which built a much more complete and damning case – then showed that inequality impacted on life expectancy and even on young men's suicide rates.

Human beings associate in society and build public and social institutions that represent their collective aims, social purposes and human ambition, while sharing risks – not least in an effort to counter brute bad luck, share brute good luck and show empathy one to another. We have sentiments and emotions; we feel for and look out for each other. We compare and rank ourselves with others. We flourish in a complex interaction of our individual actions and the social institutions which shape them. Yet all of this was to be relegated to the realm of the 'private'; the public domain that expressed such non-market values was to be throttled back and diminished. The British were to live in a market society. A social contract that expressed reciprocity of obligation, equalised life chances, offered protection against life's many hazards and risks, and above all drove justice into society was to be recast as a minimal safety net – superimposed upon the widening fissures of the 30/30/40 society.

Britain was particularly susceptible to such a programme. Democracy was and is expressed through pre-democratic institutions that were biased to top-down discretionary government rather than the expression of a social contract and the sustenance of strong public institutions held in common over time, a bias entrenched by long-standing cultural tinder suspicious of anything other than self-help and reinforced by an overwhelmingly right-wing media. Now the Thatcherite liberals would exploit these biases to transform Britain – in my view for the worse.

This does not, and did not, mean I wanted to freeze British social institutions as they were, or had a misty-eyed view of some utopia Britain had left behind. My argument was, and is, that societies and effective capitalism itself need trust; that trust springs from social capital; and that social capital is produced necessarily by institutions and processes that represent non-market values. These institutions and processes will need renewing, redesigning and investing in as economy and society change to keep the social contract relevant and effective; what is wrong is to abandon the entire perspective.

It was little short of astonishing in May 2014 when no less a figure than the Governor of the Bank of England, Mark Carney, weighed in with his support when he argued for a social contract based on a 'trinity of distributive justice, social equity and inter-generational equity' to deliver more relative equality that was good for growth and personal well-being, while fulfilling an essential human need for justice. But he acknowledged the social contract had been disregarded. The business and financial elite were in thrall to the god of the market, and so disregarded their obligations to the wider system:

Capitalism loses its sense of moderation when the belief in
the power of the market enters the realm of faith. In the
decades prior to the crisis such radicalism came to dominate
economic ideas and became a pattern of social behaviour . . .
Just as any revolution eats its children, unchecked market
fundamentalism can devour the social capital essential for
the long-term dynamism of capitalism itself. To counteract
this tendency, individuals and their firms must have a sense
of their responsibilities for the broader system. . . . Prosperity
requires not just investment in economic capital but investment in social capital.[26]

His particular concern was the impact on the integrity of the
financial system. Amen to that – in essence it was the case
made in *The State We're In*.

Looking back, my warnings in 1995 about the impact of mar-
ketising society and shredding the social contract now seem
self-evident. Of course the wanton sale of council houses without replacing them would lead to cherry-picking of the best
properties, leaving behind concentrations of the disadvantaged
into ghettoes of the worst, rising long-term homelessness and an
explosive rise in the housing benefit bill as ever more tenants
were forced to rent privately (at increasingly extortionate rents),
so that more of Britain's population receive cash allowances to
pay their rents than any other in the OECD.[27] Property and
land is distributed ever more unequally.[28]

Of course driving the market principle into the NHS would
lead to a retreat from the provision of universal services in
every part of the country and to a tiered health service, while
opening the door to privatisation; of course private providers
would again cherry-pick the best, most profitable and easiest
parts of health care to leave the public system with the expensive and intractable. No other outcome was possible.

Of course privatising and individualising pension provision would lead to an orgy of commission-hungry mis-selling and then the degradation of incomes in retirement, as they became dependent upon the vagaries of the stock market and annuity rates. The state, I wrote, 'was doing all it can to wash its hands of responsibility for future generations of old people … they don't know it yet but the old age they face will be remarkably less affluent than that their parents enjoyed'.[29]

Of course a decent state pension, properly indexed to the growth of wages instead of being allowed to wither away, had to be the cornerstone of retirement income – a recognition finally conceded, albeit at a very low rate, with proper indexation to begin in 2015 – twenty years after I called for it. Of course allowing private schools to recruit 7 per cent of the school population solely on their parents' capacity to pay fees that for boarders exceeded most people's yearly earnings created an educational apartheid, undermined the public system, and diminished equality of opportunity. As the State of the Nation Report on child poverty and social mobility years later was to observe, 'nearly a quarter of university vice-chancellors, one-third of MPs, more than half of senior medical consultants, FTSE chief executives and top journalists, and 70 per cent of High Court judges went to independent schools, though only seven per cent of the total population do so'.[30] It is both unfair and a scandalous waste of talent, highlighted by the fact that, according to the Sutton Trust, 37 per cent of medal winners in the 2012 London Olympic Games came from private schools, reflecting the disproportionate representation of the privately educated in Team UK. Who believes that the genes and capacity to compete at international level in sport are disproportionately given to the children of those who can pay for their education?

But perhaps worst:

The private school system becomes not only the hothouse of a privileged caste but also of an ideology that justifies its position. Its alumni necessarily believe in the primacy of voluntarism and choice. They do not think of themselves as stakeholders in a wider society, not only because they have set themselves apart from any commonly supported social structures in the quest for their own advancement, but because the justification for doing so is that stakeholding in the wider society is not important. This is why the voices reciting that the prime obligation of the firm is to its share-holders and the state has no business to intervene tend to speak in the modulated tones of the privately educated.[31]

A social contract, the trinity of 'distributive justice, social equity and inter-generational equity', and the case for inclu-sive, stakeholder capitalism is less likely to be part of the DNA of the privately educated. They have to argue that critics of pri-vate education are 'social engineers' who do not respect choice or parents' proper concerns for their children – even if private education, as Social Mobility Commissioner Alan Milburn declares, is social engineering on 'a grand scale'. The larger argument – as true for society and capitalism in the round as it is for private education – that individual choices lead to sys-temic and deleterious consequences cannot be accepted because to do so would be to run up the white flag. Yet to eat what you kill, the core philosophy behind the readiness to accommodate the organisation of an enormous part of the edu-cation system around individual families' capacity to pay, is not a philosophy that can bind society together.

This is not an iron law: some survive the private education system and become citizens mindful that there is a social con-tract with wider and reciprocal obligations. But Britain is fundamentally disabled because it does not have a critical mass of elite members who understand in their hearts, and whose interests allow them to accept, the arguments that Mark Carney – or I for that matter – put forward.

Many parents are fundamentally decent, aware of the invidiousness of private education, but feel they have no other option given the alleged (and often overblown) deficiencies of the state system. Trapped in a mass version of the prisoner's dilemma – compelled to betray the state system because they fear everyone else will betray it, and wanting to do the best for their children – they join the social opters-out, and therefore feel compelled to speak against the very values that are needed to hold the country together. For others the private school where they educate their children is another dimension of status rivalry and conspicuous consumption. With motives like these propelling the parents, even Britain's very good state schools cannot compete against schools whose resources are absurdly extravagant, benefiting from world-class infrastructure, small classes and elite teachers. Thus the elite is co-opted to the march to a 30/30/40 market society, an enfeebled social contract, a denuded public realm and dog-eat-dog transactional capitalism.

New Labour?

New Labour's landslide election victory in 1997 was my generation's chance. The mandate was clear. The electorate wanted a government that would address the obvious deficiencies of Thatcherism by providing a more just economy and society with less inequality and less outright poverty, underpinned by renewed, improved and responsive public services – without throwing away what it saw as Mrs Thatcher's achievements, notably the reduction of trade union power and the creation of a more dynamic economy. The country had had enough of rolling back the state, paring back health and education spending, privatisation and the drive towards a market society. It wanted to turn the page and reassert a value system with justice at its core but which was not traditional Labourism.

The kindest thing that can be said about the New Labour years was that after implementing the reforming legacy commitments of Labour leader John Smith, who had prematurely died in 1994, on devolution and the minimum wage, New Labour made some good but transient progress in improving health, education and reducing poverty. The tougher assessment is that the opportunity was squandered. The government had the resources and mandate to remake the country and establish itself as the default governing party, replacing the Conservatives. It never attempted the task.

In essence New Labour, and Tony Blair in particular, did not want to interpret the mandate in these terms. Vaingloriously he thought it was an endorsement instead of what he was trying to do to the Labour party – to remove the substantive elements of socialism within its thinking and reinvent it as a soft, pro-business, liberal social democratic party under the vapid banner of the 'third way' – closer to liberal conservatism than to the labour tradition.

The reform of private sector institutions, from the City through to business more generally, to engineer better performance and longer-term thinking was not on Blair's agenda. Nor was the building of institutions in general. He did not understand that, having won the trust of the electorate, he was expected nonetheless to have sufficient progressive instincts to launch a non-socialist but reformist Attlee-type government. Instead what the electorate got was a continuation of the Thatcherite settlement, if with a preference for using the rising tax revenues from an unsustainable economic

boom on improved public services and the reduction of child
and pensioner poverty rather than tax cuts – although even
here too much capital spending was organised around the ill-
fated private finance initiative artificially to keep public debt
down. Under this scheme private contractors owned and built
public assets like hospitals, leasing them back to the government at a fat price along with accompanying (usually very
high) charges for services like maintenance and catering. In
the NHS alone this meant that the taxpayer now cumulatively
owes £121.4 billion to pay for infrastructure that is only valued
at £52.9 billion, with increasingly burdensome obligations with
respect to debt servicing and running costs.[32] The idea was
that risk would be transferred to the private sector along with
debt: the reality was that it was a triumph of rentier capitalism,
extension of corporate welfare and exploitation of the
taxpayer.

Business and finance were left broadly untouched, and the
Thatcherite labour market reforms were left substantively
intact. In this respect the more important election in Labour's
history was the one it lost in 1992: Labour leaders' confidence
that they could win a mandate even for moderately liberal left
economic and social reform was shattered. That could only be
achieved by stealth, if at all – a judgement made not only by
Blair but by his colleague in arms, Gordon Brown. The Scots
might vote for such a programme; the conservative English
never would.

In mitigation, 1997 was when the market fundamentalist
tide was flowing at its strongest, beginning to transmute into
what Mark Carney calls a faith. US President Bill Clinton was
gearing up to make what we know now was the fatal mistake in
1998 of abolishing the New Deal legislation – the Glass-
Steagall Act – separating investment and commercial banking.
The new markets in allegedly 'innovative' securitised debt

instruments and private insurance contracts were exploding. The seeds of the crash of 2008 were being sown. The financial and business elite in Britain and the US believed that the future was about the success of private markets, a project endorsed even by the pro-market reform programme of the Chinese government. Regulation should be light touch; interference minimal; finance was at the centre of creative innovation; the market could be presumed never to make mistakes. Concerns about the weaknesses of capitalism and the lack of interest of unreformed PLCs in investment and innovation were those of a minority; with the economy recovering the neoliberals had won the economic argument.

Before the 1997 election Blair and his immediate circle, including in particular David Miliband and even Alastair Campbell, were mildly sympathetic to the thrust of the arguments in *The State We're In*. They could see that in a modified way these could be the basis of a new post-socialist coalition – hence the favourable references to stakeholder capitalism in Blair's January 1996 speech in Singapore and, later that year, to the 30/30/40 society in the speech to his party conference. But the left of his party told him they had not come into politics to create stakeholder capitalism; Gordon Brown and Peter Mandelson meanwhile, already bitterly at odds, were united in their belief that the agenda would be portrayed as anti-business and corporatist and that Labour could not risk derailing what promised to be a successful election campaign by allowing its policies to be seen to be overly influenced by one 'left-wing' writer/journalist/intellectual.

A convinced leader would have knocked heads together and brokered a consensus, but Blair was happy to retreat to the broad-brush generalisations of the unanchored third way. In the climate of the late 1990s and early 2000s it would have taken a government with very strong social democratic convictions, shared among all its senior members, along with a smart policy agenda, to strike out in a different direction contesting market fundamentalism. New Labour was not that government.

Thus what followed. During its first term, when the government had the country at its feet, it did little or nothing – with two honourable exceptions. It introduced the minimum wage, despite Conservative warnings that it would cost more than a million jobs. Today Chancellor George Osborne has acknowledged that the argument was wrong: the minimum wage is firmly established as a cornerstone of the British labour market – perhaps the only enduring achievement of the Blair years in terms of establishing significant economic and social institutions, and one he would not have introduced if his party had not insisted on honouring John Smith's commitment. New Labour also launched major constitutional change, creating devolved government in Scotland, Wales and London – again initiatives to which Smith was committed and which will in future only be deepened and extended. Scottish government after the referendum is now a non-negotiable constitutional reality; nor will any government abolish the post of London mayor. But beyond that, New Labour's achievements would not survive the arrival of the Coalition government.

New Labour did keep part of its electoral contract, as highlighted by the LSE in an important report appraising its social policy between 1997 and 2010. Over those thirteen years public spending rose by around 8 per cent of GDP, which was what the public voted for. The spending produced startlingly good results, even if unacknowledged both at the time and now. Hospital waiting lists were eliminated. Three and a half thousand Sure Start centres were established, offering near-universal pre-school education for the first time. Forty-eight thousand extra full-time equivalent teaching posts were created, and the proportion of children with five good GCSEs rose from 45 to 76 per cent – a rise that cannot be accounted for by grade inflation alone. Ninety per cent of social housing was brought up to a 'decent homes' standard. The numbers of children and pensioners in poverty declined by around a million each. And although, as described earlier, income inequality overall rose, the impact of the minimum wage and growth of in-work benefits to support the working poor was to reduce inequality within the bottom half of the working population.[33] Beyond traditional public services there was an important investment in Britain's science base. There were significant commitments on climate change and the reduction of carbon emissions. Given its assets, New Labour should have achieved more: but at the same time it should be recognised that there were achievements.

But there was nothing like the political payback there should have been – mainly because the government was too embarrassed to shout about what it was achieving with its spending. It did not want to portray itself as a great reforming government, improving the lot of ordinary people as part of a wider challenge to the deformed institutions of contemporary British capitalism. It preferred to do what it could under the radar and not frighten the capitalist horses. After all, the economy seemed to be working as free market theory said it would. Reform required political bravery, a willingness to take on powerful vested interests, conviction that they needed reform and a readiness to risk being called anti-business.

New Labour had no appetite for any of that. It was brave only in taking on its own, exemplified by the near-joyful way it overrode what we now know to be the correct objections to the Iraq war. The government blithely endorsed the growth of a banking system that was to crash in 2008, evaded addressing the shortcomings of the financial, ownership and corporate governorship system and watched elite pay, especially in finance, go through the roof. It fiercely resisted any suggestion that it should have an industrial policy or create new public economic institutions, like a Knowledge Bank, to deal with the obvious market failings in the supply of risk capital and debt to the burgeoning high-tech, knowledge sector. I canvassed the idea to the then secretary of the Department of Trade and Industry (DTI, to become the Department of Business in 2007), Stephen Byers, who wanted to put it into the Labour manifesto nationally, and later I supported the Welsh Labour party's efforts to do in Wales what its big brother in Westminster would not. Gordon Brown went to enormous lengths to prevent both. Wales ended up with Finance Wales, a pale version of what was proposed. Britain ended up with nothing.

One story reveals the extent of New Labour's cravenness, and in particular Brown's, over the building of progressive business institutions. In 1997 Margaret Beckett, the new secretary of state at the DTI, established a review of company law under the de facto chairmanship of a leading expert in corporate law, Professor John Parkinson. Its brief was to examine reform, including how and if stakeholder principles could be introduced into company law. Number 10 insisted it could progress only by unanimity and ensured that a blocking minority of banks, accountancy firms and institutional investors was present on the steering group. The committee worked for six years and despite the obstructive efforts of Downing Street, finally produced a blueprint that would have been an important step in changing the constitution of British firms. In particular it called for the publication of companies' annual and report accounts to be accompanied by a statutory Operating and Financial Review (OFR) that would give all stakeholders a rounded view of the company, its business purpose and how it was achieving it.

Blair vetoed the introduction of the Companies Act that would implement the OFR in both the 2003 and 2004 Queen's

Speeches, terrified that even this would be portrayed by the right-wing press and some lobby organisations as 'anti-business'. But there was no longer any reason to block it in the autumn of 2005 after a third election victory. Finally, after eight years' work and hard-won unanimity, a progressive piece of business legislation would reach the statute book. Except Mr Brown needed something 'pro-business' to say to the CBI annual conference in the December of that year. Without prior consultation with the DTI, he unilaterally declared that the 'gold plating' of legislation going through the House of Commons to establish the OFR would be withdrawn to save £35 million of regulatory costs on business. He even hinted that the impulse for the legislation had come from the EU. The permanent secretary at the DTI, Sir Richard Mottram, formally placed on record before other permanent secretaries at their regular Wednesday meeting that the Chancellor's protestation that he had consulted with the department was not true. This was unprecedented for a leading civil servant.

For a tepid round of applause at the CBI annual conference, and in an attempt to show he was 'pro-business', Brown had publicly trashed the carefully constructed consensus case for change made by his own government while trying to cover his tracks with at best cynical manipulation, at worst duplicity. Brown's actions foreshadowed the debacle of his prime ministership. It would take the imminent success of the Yes vote in the Scottish referendum eight years later for this tortured politician to recover his beliefs – on this occasion union with England – and with them the conviction and force that had originally propelled him to the front line of British politics. His tragedy is that he could have been a powerful force for good; too much temporisation laid him low.

It was the financial crisis and the evident collapse of New Labour's economic model that forced a reappraisal of

New Labour's stance. Peter – now Lord – Mandelson, returned to government as business secretary and launched the New Industry, New Jobs programme (full declaration – I was a pro bono adviser). Labour was finally to adopt an industrial strategy to rebalance the economy away from excessive reliance on financial services. There was a billion-pound strategic investment fund; attempts to improve the flow of finance to business; investment in advanced manufacturing; and a skills audit with the promise of following through with public investment in skills.

There was even, weeks before the general election in 2010 (and as advocated in *The State We're In*), a conversion to the notion that Britain should create a network of public/private institutes, modelled on the German Fraunhofer Institutes, consecrated to driving new technologies into the business sector. Twelve years earlier the concept would have been decried as an unnecessary obstruction of market forces and as representing failed industrial policies, and would likely have been depicted as corporatist, or worse, as stakeholder capitalism in practice. It was a sea change – and in this area at least, the Coalition government under business secretary Vince Cable has built on New Labour's foundations. Britain now has a much more coherent industrial and innovation strategy (as described in Chapter 6).

But it was too little too late. New Labour had not built a progressive coalition. Even the elites it might have expected to support it in the trade union and public sector were disillusioned, and business and finance regressed to the comfort zone of the Conservative party and its familiar gentlemanly capitalists. It had no record of successful institution building in the private sector to which it could point as evidence of a successful social democratic approach to shaping capitalism. It was embarrassed by its public spending and so could not boast about the good it was doing. It had no theory of its purpose and how that purpose related to any progressive tradition. The Iraq war was an ineradicable stain.

It was a lost party and a lost movement. The Coalition quickly hung around its neck the sobriquet of being the author of excessive, wasteful public spending despite the huge gains it had brought along with a high budget deficit – extraordinarily, according to that narrative, not the consequence of the financial crisis but one of its causes. Within a few short years the Coalition had shredded most of New Labour's thin legacy by rolling back the public spending that supported it, with the Labour opposition unwilling even here to defend its record. With one or two exceptions – devolution and the minimum wage – it was as if it had never been. There was no political credit even for the industrial policy it had launched. But the times are a-changing. There may be a second chance, but this time round there can be no mistakes.

5
What Is to Be Done?

The problems in the British economy and society have profound roots. Put at its rawest, our private institutions provide insufficient widespread social or public good to justify their continuing unreformed autonomy. On top, the willingness and indeed the capability of our democracy to challenge, change and reform has been undermined by the new neoliberal consensus that such deep intervention is inadmissible because it will interfere with essential liberties. Our private institutions, notably the way our organisations are owned, financed and managed, are in this worldview depicted as the result of free, private decisions made by individuals on the basis of rational preferences independent of social influence. Only if the system is on the point of collapse, as in the banking crisis, is there any reason for systemic public action. No public good can come from designing markets and institutions to behave differently, because the way they behave is the way they choose, which must be optimal. After all, wealth has to be generated before it can be distributed. The state has no business either in promoting justice or in imposing its morality on free business decision-making. Its role is to stay as small and as minimalist as it can.

This book is based on a very different political economy. A democracy has both the right and the duty to ask tough questions of the effectiveness of all its institutions, public and private: moreover there is a public realm and public interest that can only be represented by public institutions with public values. To insist that the reform of private institutions can in essence only take place if they provenly fail, and that public institutions must as far as possible simulate private ones, is to accept that the only good order is private. But if there are no networks of reciprocal obligation, and no acknowledgement that human beings associate in a society they can construct, redesign and reform around those principles, then we are all reduced to atomistic consumers and workers – serfs who are no more than notations in the spreadsheets of companies and public bodies alike. Our politicians are turned into journeymen with no great purpose, and into the vacuum pour nationalists, populists and the weird. We can do better.

Wealth generation is not some magic left to business, enterprise and individuals in their low-taxed private garden: it reflects how companies are owned, financed and incentivised within a framework of public law – and thus what risks are run and what innovation and investment undertaken. Business is healthier, the healthier the society in which it trades: it cannot be blind to social obligations. There is of necessity an inter-relationship with the democratic state. What follows in this chapter are thus proposals for deep change in the way wealth generation is approached: substantive reforms in the ways companies are owned and financed – the heart of the matter economically – along with suggestions as to how public action can capitalise on those reforms to enlarge the scope for innovation and investment. Importantly, to argue for reform of capitalist enterprise should not be interpreted as anti-business: rather it is to be anti-dysfunctional business. In the next chapter I turn

my attention to the institutions that constitute the social settlement, and then in the Conclusion to the institutions of
democracy and state. I am keenly aware of the scale of the task,
and how hard it is to carry out in any one western country.
There are a plethora of articles, books and commission reports
that deplore the impact of the great neoliberal experiment,
pointing to its intellectual wrongheadedness and disastrous
practical consequences. So far they have done little to arrest its
progress.

An important explanation – one often disregarded – is that
all great movements of ideas, values and policies are rarely
home-grown alone; they develop across borders as part of a
shared zeitgeist, whether the Renaissance and Reformation of
earlier centuries or, closer to our times, the New Deal of the
1930s and 1940s. The rise of neoliberalism today is similarly
international, and the most important locus of all is the US.
That country remains in the grip of current orthodoxies, typi-
fied by the strength of the Tea Party movement. If the greatest
economic and political power on earth marginalises creative
thinking about how to prosecute capitalism more fairly, innov-
atively and productively, continuing to propagate asinine
propositions that superior economic and social organisation
should be based solely on semi-divine free market principles
and an individualism carried to libertarian extremes, then the
task of developing a new consensus is made very much harder.

Nonetheless the US does have an industrial policy, does
allow its company boards some shelter from greedy footloose
shareholders, does have a decentralised banking system that
engages with entrepreneurial business, and does advantage
many industries with formal and informal protection. All the
General Purpose Technologies the US developed in the twentieth century, as I noted in Chapter 1, have come courtesy of
strong support from the US government. American passion for

neoliberalism is more observed in the breach. But instead of the British copying what the Americans do rather than what they preach, the British are true believers in doctrines that are inoperable in the real world. Our officials, anxious to prove their free market credentials, are reliably obstructive to anything but free market ideas while the new elite, as I have argued in the earlier chapters, profit so handsomely from the current arrangement that it is proof positive in their eyes that the system is working very well. Striking out in a new direction thus requires both considerable confidence that a new set of arrangements is possible and the nerve to take on the current beneficiaries. It is a combination that so far has eluded putative reformers – along with creating new channels of persuasion outside the traditional media that advances and polices the neoliberal consensus so effectively. China's propaganda machine could hardly do better. It is a tough challenge, but two preconditions are essential – an intellectual road map and a programme of feasible action. So here goes, beginning with the foundation of any capitalism: how it is owned.[1]

Making stakeholder capitalism real – the PLC

No reimagining of contemporary British capitalism is possible without the reimagination of how companies are owned, in particular asserting obligations of ownership alongside the rights and privileges of incorporation. Companies are, after all, the central economic actors in the market economy – the investors, the innovators and employers. They give any capitalism its particular character and dynamic. Britain's 30/30/40 society and the character of its labour market, with the emergence of so many contingent low-wage jobs, is inextricably intertwined with how its companies behave. So is the weakness of exports, investment and innovation. My contention is that limited liability companies, having certain formal privileges and status, should not be the private playthings of transient owners interested only in their own immediate self-enrichment, caring little how profits are made. Rather they should be organisational structures of potential genius that allow humanity to innovate and then produce to meet the great challenges of any era: in this context profits are made by delivering a noble, moral business purpose, integral to the wider legitimacy of the enterprise.

Of course in the hurly-burly of business and organisational life, nobility and integrity of purpose get qualified, but they are nonetheless at the heart of any just and sustainable economic and social order. In the second decade of the twenty-first century the idea of the company has lost its way: it has been redefined as an organisational casino chip or a constituent in an investment portfolio – a convenient means for private equity partners to get very rich very quickly by loading up the company under their ownership with debt before selling on their bauble to some other greater fool, or for directors to arrive at the same destination of self-enrichment by means of share options. So carelessly are ownership obligations regarded that Britain has a vigorous if opaque market in shareholders lending their shares to others. Companies are only incidentally seen as the vehicle for the marshalling and stewarding of human, physical and knowledge assets in the service of humankind. Yet it is for that reason society offers them privileges. It is not unreasonable to want to see the terms of the bargain reciprocated; indeed it lies at the heart of a just relationship between business and society.

Companies are currently conceived not as vehicles for the expression of business purpose and values that earn trust, loyalty and commitment, but as legal entities whose very existence is temporary and contingent on immediate financial gain.

This is starkly revealed in how easy takeovers are to carry out in Britain as compared with other countries: it is much easier to take over ownerless companies because all that concerns shareholders is the immediate share price. For decades Britain's relaxed approach to takeover seemed justified: British companies spent many more billions on overseas takeovers than foreign companies did in Britain. But since 2004 the trend has sharply reversed, The value of British company acquisitions by foreign companies has generally outstripped UK acquisitions overseas, and now stands at a cumulative £170 billion deficit (in total £440 billion of British companies have been sold abroad in this period). Only in 2011 was the trend reversed, re-establishing itself in 2013.[2]

Moreover the value of takeovers in relation to GDP is higher in Britain than anywhere else. Between 1998 and 2005, writes Jonathan Ford in the *Financial Times*, the value of all mergers and acquisitions in the USA – no slouch as deal-makers – amounted to some 10.7 per cent of GDP. Over the same period, the value of UK takeovers climbed to an 'astonishing 21.8 per cent of its GDP'. Britons are in addition 'much more prepared to see companies sold from under boards' noses without consent. Between 1991 and 2005, unfriendly bids for UK companies enjoyed a success rate of 61 per cent – far higher than anywhere else in the developed world.'[3] There has been no let-up since.

Yet there is a wealth of evidence that takeovers consistently fail to create value for the companies that do the acquiring: a glance at the Kay Review or KPMG's annual surveys, for example, shows that only around 30 per cent succeed. Any wider benefits are tenuous, and gains are hard to evaluate against the destructive proclivities of the system as a whole. For above all takeovers are a means of enforcing the particular values of British capitalism across all companies: if you don't conform to

the norm of extreme focus on high short-term financial prof-
itability, expect to be taken over. As I wrote in *The State We're In*,
'Takeover reduces the critical mass of the industry; reduces the
level of competition; and sends signals to the remaining companies that they must make do with less investment and
training in order to boost immediate dividends.'[4] Excessive
takeovers are both an expression of a business environment in
which every company's existence is contingent on financial performance, and a means of ensuring that financial contingency is
the dominant business value. The structure of Britain's PLCs
means that they have become 'rent extraction vehicles for the
shortest-term shareholders'. The threat of takeover is a means
of holding all other shareholders to ransom, so that companies
have become organisations without principles, no longer fundamentally caring about their consumers or employees.[5]

Nor are shareholder and public interest the same thing, an
argument made forcibly by Professor Chris Higson of the
London Business School, and brought into sharp relief by the
consequences of foreign takeover. The UK, he writes, has a
robust framework for assessing the public interest in foreign
takeovers, if it chose to use it – the one it has developed for
assessing requests for industrial support. Employment and
R&D, and in particular the impact on intangibles, are all eval-
uated when deciding on whether to make grants. Of course
there is a high degree of uncertainty in such public judgements; but uncertainty exists for all the decision makers
whether private or public. In particular he notes that companies have a bias to favour their own country of origin – a 'home
bias' effect – which he believes should be part of the calculus
when assessing the impact of take-overs. For example, 88 per
cent of the CEOs of the global top 500 companies and 85 per
cent of their management teams are nationals of the country
where the company is headquartered.[6] Headquarters are

important: they generate jobs with high added value, recruit
and groom the business's leaders and are the locus for the creation of intangibles – which are fundamental to business
success in the twenty-first century. In this environment Britain
needs all the home bias it can get.[7] Indulging and favouring
excessive foreign takeover is a form of unilateral business dis-
armament, however fabulous are the fees of the investment
bankers who arrange the deals.

In the late nineteenth century and the first half of the twentieth, the left correctly regarded challenging unalloyed private
ownership as the precondition for the enfranchisement of the
mass of citizens and workers. It drew the wrong conclusion
that wholesale monopoly public ownership, especially of
the commanding heights of the economy, was the answer.
Nationalisation did not work as hoped; it was too much of a sta-
tist monoculture and its designers gave too little thought to
how nationalised industries would perform, change their business model and innovate. Even so, it worked less badly than its
many detractors insist. For example the organisation of the
electricity grid by the Central Electricity Generating Board,
along with the long-term planning of energy need and thus
power station construction, now looks more of a golden era of
rationality than the current system, on the verge of having
insufficient capacity and the lights going out. The left critique
was essentially right. The character of private ownership does
need to be friendly towards society, investment, worker and
innovation alike. Ownership should resume its place at the
heart of the left's concerns, and thus become part of the wider
public conversation. Public ownership certainly had deficiencies but they could have been redressed rather than
concluding that any form of private ownership must be better,
and which itself could not be reformed or improved. Indeed it
is an imperative that it is improved. Equally we need to create

better forms through which enterprise can, where appropriate, achieve wholly public objectives.

The reform of private ownership

The cornerstone of a new approach to ownership should be a Companies Act for the twenty-first century, designed to create purposeful companies with a more just relationship between themselves and the wider society, capable of fostering the trust relationships that are at the heart of high-innovation and high-performance workplaces. Companies will be required to declare their business purpose on incorporation: they should incorporate to deliver particular goods and services that serve a societal or economic need and will need particular capabilities and skills. It is through delivery of their purpose that they should seek to make profits. Most great companies have this purpose at their heart already, even if informally. Unilever famously exists to make the best everyday things for everyday folk; Boeing to build planes that fly furthest safest; the owners of the Guardian Media Group, the Scott Trust, pledge to ensure that the *Guardian* is edited as it has been 'heretofore'.

 The objective is to put business purpose at the heart of every enterprise and make it something for whose delivery directors are held to account – to create a societal obligation to match the privileges of incorporation. This will not be a weasely commitment to 'have regard to' the delivery of business purpose, echoing the current Section 172 of the 2006 Companies Act.

It will be a statutory obligation. Directors will have a 'safe harbour' provision, so they are legally protected from investors who want to change the business purpose merely to the maximisation of profit or the share price, the latter very important in contested takeovers. Directors need to be under no obligation ever to recommend a bid to current shareholders if they have reason to believe that the predator company will not carry forward the victim company's business purpose. Directors will have to produce, along the lines of the Operating and Financial Review so casually scrapped by Chancellor Gordon Brown, an annual account of their stewardship of the company, of which today's financial reporting will be but one element. There will also be an account of investment, innovation, research and development, human capital development, pay scales, executive pay in relation to median pay and supply-chain relations, along with an account of the company's wider commitments on the environment and bribery.

There will be two categories of non-executive director. One will sit on the operational management board, as now, to offer advice and hold directors to account for the company's operational performance. The other will be trustees of the business purpose, either sitting on the same board or on an independent board of trustees. Their task will be to see that the organisation cleaves to its stated purpose, and to build engaged relationships with long-term shareholders. One such trustee would be elected by the workforce, representing the employee stake created via the employee share ownership scheme that all companies would be required to offer their workforce.

Investors will thus buy shares in purposed companies, reflecting a new compact between the company and its investors. The asset-management industry has quadrupled in size over the last thirty years, so that, as I observed in Chapter 3, 41 per cent of the shares of British companies are now held overseas, typically by a global asset-management group: British pension funds own a mere 5.1 per cent of all shares and British insurance companies 8.6 per cent. British companies willy-nilly will find that a significant part of their shareholder base is held by global asset managers supported by a vast network of

supportive intermediaries and agents all taking fees and commissions. Some are engaged long-term investors; some are
passive investors whose portfolios track the stock market
indices; some buy and sell their shares frenetically.

No UK government can reform the global asset-management
industry unilaterally, but it can frame the terms on which British
shares are owned. It can demand, for example, that all investors
in British companies sign and comply with a tougher
Stewardship Code, which currently sets out milk-and-water
obligations to monitor investee companies, exercise votes,
steward companies and act with other investors if necessary. It
is better than nothing, but essentially minimalist. The Code
should be greatly stiffened. It should set a cap on the annual
turnover of portfolios under asset managers' direction at 30 per
cent (following the recommendation of the LSE's Paul
Woolley); not pay performance fees; and insist on total transparency on strategies, costs, leverage and trading. One of the
features of the asset-management industry is that not only does
it not support enterprise, innovation and investment, it is
organised as a system of wealth transfer from the ultimate
savers to the stage army of intermediaries – some of it very
opaque. For example, one recent report from the Financial
Conduct Authority (FCA) castigated the market-makers, intermediaries, banks and investment banks who take orders to buy
and sell shares for not working hard enough to secure the best
price for their customers, and, worse, charging both the buyer
and seller a commission, so-called 'payments for order flow'.
This was a blatant conflict of interest, but was nonetheless
widespread and continued despite the FCA's advice it should
stop.[8] The benefit of such a toughened stewardship code is
that it will both create more engaged investors and reduce such
practices, so potentially increasing returns to the ultimate
savers by up to 2–3 per cent per annum.[9] A win-win all round.

The proposed new Companies Act will set out a new legal framework that will privilege long-term, engaged investment. Thus the basic voting share will continue as now, but it will attract more votes the longer it is held. If shares are lent, voting rights will be forgone. A share held for five years will attract 50 per cent more votes, doubling once it is held for ten years. Alternatively shareholders can contract to hold shares for pre-determined periods, thus attracting greater voting rights immediately.[10] Capital gains tax paid on selling shares will reduce on a sliding scale that reflects the period over which shares are held. Those investors – hedge funds and day traders – who are primarily short-term traders and do not want to accept stewardship responsibilities or sign the Stewardship Code should be able to buy non-voting shares. Equally any owner who does not want to disclose their identity will lose voting rights automatically. Stock Exchange listing rules should be relaxed to allow such non-voting shares to be readily traded. These will receive dividends and can be lent to others, but they will attract no votes; gains will attract capital gains tax whatever the character of the holder – pension funds as much as hedge funds.

This will strike many in London as a bridge too far – an anathema, a dagger at the heart of British capitalism. But when Google floated, its founders Sergey Brin and Larry Page issued two classes of shares, with Class A shares having ten times more votes attached than Class B – so Brin and Page ended up with 37.6 per cent of the votes for 3.7 per cent of the shares. As they said in the letter accompanying the initial public offering, 'we have set up a corporate structure that will make it much harder for outside parties to take over or influence Google. This structure will also make it easier for our management team to follow the long term, innovative approach.'[11] Ten years on from the flotation, who can say they were wrong? LinkedIn offered its original long-term shareholders ten times the votes when it floated in 2011, and the Glazers floated Manchester United in New York rather than London because American rules allowed the family shares to have ten times as many votes. Owners in mainland Europe – from the Wallenbergs in Sweden, who have holdings in most of Sweden's top companies, to the Piech family, part-owners of Porsche – use similar devices. Where there is business success and innovation, look for non-British corporate structures.

The new Companies Act will also provide for the creation of not-for-profit mutuals whose sole purpose is to aggregate the proxy votes of those investing institutions who are essentially passive investors and who do not want or do not have the resources to become committed, contracted long-term shareholders. Shareholders will be compelled to exercise their vote, either directly or through the new proxy mutuals.[12] These mutuals, expanded versions of how Hermes (owned by the BT pension fund) acts as an active, responsible investor on behalf of many funds under its management alongside the core BT fund, will thus take their place in a new ecology of shareholders. There will be contracted shareholders with a long-term engagement who may have more votes; there will be shareholders exercising voting privileges through proxy mutuals; and there will be non-voting shares that are essentially casino chips. This trinity – business purpose, trusteeship and a range of committed shareholders – will be the foundation for the creation of purposeful companies, freed to behave like long-term trusts rather than dance to the tune of peripatetic day traders. They will be value creators rather than rent extractors. It would be stakeholder capitalism in practice.

These proposals must be supported by a new takeover regime. Director teams will already have their position against hostile takeover strengthened by the 'safe harbour' provision

outlined above. In addition predator companies should be
obliged to ask their own shareholders whether the bid
conforms with their own business purpose and to pay the fees
of the defending company in any circumstances. If a bid is not
recommended by the defending board, then predators will
need a two-thirds majority of those shares held on the day the
bid was launched to win control, rather than any old transient
speculator buying shares after the bid to make a quick buck.
The government should refer bids that create public interest
concerns – regarding employment, R&D, taxation intentions,
location of headquarters – to an independent adjudicator,
which can use the same public interest criteria to inform its
decisions that the government uses when deciding on industrial grants and subsidy applications. There should be more
aggressive use of the Competition and Markets Authority, so
that concerns about future market dynamics with a monopolistic merged entity should be as relevant to adjudications as
current market shares; what is likely to happen in five years is
surely as significant as excessive market power in the here and
now. In short, takeovers, especially hostile takeovers, should be
the exception rather than the rule of British business life.

Social and public ownership

Around this flagship policy on PLCs – after all, it is the larger
companies in any economy that necessarily are the most influential in forming its dominant business culture – Britain can
then build a web of supporting policies similarly to reform
other kinds of ownership so as to deliver better stewardship,
more engagement and creativity. The more diversity, the
better – from the ownership of football clubs to that of mainstream medium-sized companies. We need to turn round the

steady drift to a monoculture of public companies and instead create a richer ecology within which many forms and types of ownership can flourish.

Let us start with mutuals – organisations owned in common by their customers or policy holders. The ease with which many building societies demutualised in the 1990s, a practice largely aimed at enriching their incumbent management teams, is still shocking. Within a decade almost the entire building society movement had reinvented itself as 'go-go' banks, tapping the wholesale money markets and as a result offering mortgage debt on an unprecedented, unchecked and, as we now know, disastrous scale. It was a demutualised building society, Northern Rock, with its vastly overstretched balance sheet that was the trigger of the financial crisis in September 2007. It was another, the demutualised Halifax, which following the same business model merged with the Bank of Scotland to create HBOS, that ranked alongside the effectively bankrupt RBS as twin epicentres of the crisis in the early autumn of 2008. If the building societies had remained in mutual ownership, and had bank PLCs been owned in the way advocated above, it is hard to believe that so much credit would have been advanced, underwritten by so little capital, in such a short time. The financial crisis, when it came, would have been markedly less severe. It might even, as in Canada, have been relatively mild.

Mutualisation, from worker co-operatives to consumer-owned mutuals like building societies or even football clubs, must represent an irrevocable ownership choice. The capital built up over generations of stewardship is not there to be flipped into different forms of ownership. As a country and a society we want mutuals to be a permanent feature of our ownership landscape – another way of approaching the relationship of an organisation to its workers, members and customers. Mutuals will have their ups and downs over the decades, sometimes looking rather old-fashioned as they did temporarily in the 1990s and sometimes looking voguish as they do today. They are an organisational form that, as we now know, shows its worth over decades. Every other European country requires that once assets are mutually owned they must stay mutually owned, being transferable only if a mutual is failing or its business model is changing to another mutual under a provision called 'disinterested distribution' – in other words the assets are not distributed for gain except to the mutual. If Britain had had a similar provision, the demutualisation of the 1990s would have been prohibited. Such a provision should now become part of British law. Equally, all the obstacles to mutuals attracting the long-term capital they need for expansion – often imposed with the intent of doing no more than protect non-mutuals from allegedly unfair competition – should simply be scrapped. The excuse for demutualisation, that it provides access to otherwise unavailable capital, would thus be closed down. Suddenly, for example, it would become possible to create football clubs, as in Germany, that are permanently owned by their supporters but which could tap public bond markets for extra capital. There is no need for all our top football clubs to be owned by foreign oligarchs, bought and sold as casino chips like every other trading asset. They could be embedded in our communities, investing in local footballers and in the game itself.

The lack of interest in these apparently arcane questions is but more evidence of how unserious and lackadaisical Britain has been and is about ownership. We never cared about demutualisation – or indeed about the bankrupt constitution of our biggest mutual, the Co-operative, which allowed such severe mismanagement in the 2000s culminating in the stunning £2.5 billion loss reported in April 2014 – the highest in its history. In effect the Co-operative had become an ownerless mutual with a diffuse set of oversight committees and councils that allowed no proper stewardship of its assets: intriguingly, the much-resisted reforms proposed by Lord Paul Myners, and agreed in August 2014, were in effect designed to ensure that the members properly owned the mutual.

The same insouciance infects the lack of care over who owns not only our football clubs, but our television companies and newspapers. The constitutional protections demanded when Rupert Murdoch bought *The Times* in 1981 were valueless in protecting its editorial independence; but then no constitutional template existed for a company in which they could be made to work. Equally David Abrahams pointed out in his 2014 MacTaggart Lecture at the 2014 Edinburgh television festival that there was a 'gold rush' of American companies buying up UK TV production houses and channels, so easy to buy is every company in Britain. Yet it was the free-to-air public service broadcasters (the BBC, Channel 4 and ITV) who spent £1.7 billion on new commissions, 80 per cent of all such spending – while BSkyB returned £700 million to its shareholders.[13] ITV, a British PLC with public service broadcast obligations, was and is being stalked by US mogul John Malone, chair of Liberty Global. Without regulatory or ownership protection it too would eventually fall into US hands, as part of a strategy to create content for global pay TV – hardly much help for British creativity or British culture. It is time to think of better ways of doing ownership that express public and social dimensions.

Professor Colin Mayer advocates the introduction of the public benefit company. This would be a particular class of company delivering public benefits, one that would retain private ownership but under more demanding obligations than even the reformed PLC. There would be compensating privileges. Companies delivering goods and services of fundamental public or social importance – say in banking, insurance, the utilities, defence or the media – would incorporate by going beyond the declaration of business purpose required in the new Companies Act. Instead they would receive a licence to operate by incorporating with a charter, setting out along the lines of the BBC's charter the detailed terms under which they would do business. This would represent an overt bargain between the company and the wider community, recognising that whether in defence, media, financial services or the utilities the attitude of the government is of existential importance to the business model. The charter would set out the objects of the public benefit company, the terms of its governance and constitution of its board, the contract with public or private shareholders, how it would hold itself to account for the delivery of its public benefit services, its approach to executive remuneration, its policies on innovation and training, how it would recognise employees' voice and the priorities it would have in allocating any surpluses. The charter would be subject to periodic review, say every ten or fifteen years. In return the public benefit company would enjoy tax advantages, reflecting its status along with guaranteed autonomy and independence. It would be a non-public body, free to borrow without that borrowing being categorised as public sector debt.

The public benefit company would represent a major corporate innovation, crystallising the new deal on ownership advocated in this chapter. Such an approach already exists: the BBC is a form of public benefit company run according to its charter, even though it is wholly owned by the public through the licence fee and its borrowings count as public debt. Channel 4 is a not-for-profit public corporation, investing all its surplus in programmes; it would find life easier as a public benefit company. The Guardian Media Group, owned by the Scott Trust, is more clearly a public benefit company: it is privately owned but explicitly run for the public benefit of maintaining the *Guardian* (and the *Observer*). 3is, before its owner banks cashed out, turning it into a PLC – since when its role in supporting the financing of small and medium-sized firms has become much less effective – was also a form of public benefit company with its origins in the Industrial and Commercial Finance Corporation established by the Bank of England in 1947. All had or have guaranteed autonomy and all operated or operate either explicitly or implicitly under a charter. All have been very successful. The proposition is that this form of ownership should be more broadly extended by creating a formal legal template for its widespread adoption.

There is even a case – whisper it softly – for outright public ownership of companies carrying out those economic activities which conform to four key tests: that they constitute a natural monopoly, that the good or service they provide must be universally supplied because it is fundamental to life, that the good or service must be fairly available to every citizen and that their trading legitimacy requires an ongoing dialogue with citizen consumers to ensure that the pricing and access to the service is not being abused. So, for example, all the country's varying national networks would meet these tests. The rail network is a natural monopoly (it is absurd to have more than one railway line between one destination and another); it must connect all major population centres; it must be fairly accessible; and to ensure legitimately that the network is as safe and as modern as possible requires ongoing dialogue with citizen passengers.

Despite its initial privatisation as Railtrack, the rail network has ended up under the control and direction of Network Rail, a not-for-dividend statutory company limited by guarantee and accountable to the government of the day. Its creation was forced in 2004 when Railtrack was overwhelmed with debts and New Labour, anxious not to be tarred with the sobriquet of nationalisation, came up with an organisational form that it hoped would achieve public ends without representing nationalisation. In effect the solution was to try to invent Railtrack as a public benefit company, but with no proper template. In 2014 its debts were reclassified as public debts; it is in effect a publicly owned company, which given the lack of private shareholders was inevitable.

Turning monopoly networks like the National Grid, the mobile telephone network, the money transmission system, the optical fibre and fixed line telephone network, and the water collection, distribution and sewer system into public corporations would plainly be expensive and contentious. Some networks, like the money transmission system, have never been in public ownership anyway. But there is value in signalling to the owners of such networks that continuing private ownership is conditional; that it needs to simulate the best of public ownership if it is to be sustainable, indicating the criteria that pass a public ownership test. They should create public value, as I discuss in the Conclusion. Any new network infrastructure, such as the Thames supersewer built with government guarantees, should at the very least be owned by a public benefit company subsidiary within the host company to be given sufficient autonomy to conform to its charter. Ownership is not carte blanche to do whatever the owner wants irrespective of the claims of society. It is a reciprocal relationship, most particularly when there is a powerful public interest in the outcome. A readiness to sustain the principle of publicly owned companies, creating new ones where there is the opportunity, is a forcible reminder of that reality.

Readers will be surprised to read that Britain does possess an organisation – the Shareholder Executive – that holds all the public's remaining shareholdings in the last non-privatised assets like the Post Office (UK Financial Investments holds the government stakes in RBS and Lloyds). The Shareholder Executive could be a means of expressing such a public interest. Yet its ethos is neither to be engaged, nor to influence decision making if there are public interest implications. Rather it is where the government corrals its assets before their unthinking disposal to the private sector, deemed to be automatically better, with none of the issues raised in this chapter ever addressed. It was the Shareholder Executive, for example, that organised the privatisation of the Royal Mail as a PLC, never putting forward other options like its recreation as a public benefit trust. UK Financial Investments, disposing of part of the government's stake in Lloyds, is similarly disengaged and arm's-length.

The contrast with Singapore's Temasek, the country's strategic wealth fund, could hardly be more marked. Success for the Shareholder Executive (and for UK Financial Investments) would be the disposal of all its public shareholdings and the government's complete disengagement from business investment; success for Temasek is to be a strategic long-term investor in key Singaporean enterprise, anchoring companies with its long-term stakes for public interest outcomes, and building up a flow of growing dividends that will support the government's finances. It is also becoming a global force.

In the currency of Anglo-Saxon neoliberalism there can be no philosophical or economic justification for an organisation like Temasek; only global asset managers are deemed to be legitimate and effective, and the Shareholder Executive is right to plot its own disappearance. In reality the opposite is the case. The Shareholder Executive should become the foundation of a British sovereign wealth fund – symbolic of a purposeful, value creating, long-term British capitalism. It should work alongside a revived Industrial and Commercial

Finance Corporation, that for decades worked well as a provider of equity and debt to small and medium-sized business – taking risks its commercial bank owners would not take themselves. The very proposition is of course far-fetched; but the fact that it is so shows just how far Britain has to travel if it is ever to become more productive and innovative, building companies with real scale and impact.

The financial system

If business and society rest on a reciprocal bargain, so, more emphatically, does finance – however much many financiers try to deny it. In the decades before the financial crisis the doctrine was that society could enjoy the costless efficiency of financial markets, and ride fancy-free on the coat-tails of a credit boom generated by the bankers. The scale of the credit could not be a problem because financial markets were efficient and designed to maximise profit. No bank would willingly and self-consciously make mistakes. We should be delighted at the liquidity and many 'innovative' financial instruments to hedge risks that the bankers were creating. These were public goods being spontaneously produced by markets, just as neoliberal economists proclaimed. Nobody needed to worry their heads about potential conflicts of interest within banks, clashes between the public and private interest, or whether society was being offered a fair deal. The long years of prosperity, low inflation and rising house prices provided their own answer. Britain had an inestimable jewel: the City of London.

Nobody would repeat that with the same conviction in 2015; if they tried they would be howled down. In the aftermath of the bailout, amounting to more than £1 trillion, that followed the financial crisis it became routine to accuse bankers of wanting to privatise profits and socialise losses – and the statement captured an important truth. In fact the direct costs of the bailout are likely eventually to be repaid. It is the wider costs, in terms of cumulative lost output, squeezed real wages and the collapse of business investment, that raise more fundamental questions. The Office for Budget Responsibility, for example, says that output in 2018/19 will be 16 per cent below what it would otherwise have been had pre-crisis trends been extrapolated.[14] The growth model of the twenty-five years before 2007/8 had been predicated on credit growing two or three times faster than the rate of nominal GDP. Suddenly that has come to a halt. Consumers, households and many businesses are overburdened with debt. Households in particular could not borrow significantly more even if the banks wanted to lend at their former rate.

Banks, we have always known, have the capacity to create credit apparently out of nothing: because not all their depositors will ask for their cash simultaneously, banks – unless they are prevented by a legal requirement to keep their reserves 100 per cent in cash – will lend a fraction of their deposits to other borrowers, who will redeposit some of the cash for the process to be repeated. It is called fractional reserve banking. What we have relearned is that the resulting credit-creation process is too important to be left to bankers; this is why we had the varying regulations and requirements that were relaxed or abolished in the run-up to the crisis. But banks don't regulate themselves. No individual bank can protect itself from credit explosions or implosions. The system has its own momentum. Banks don't only need society when things go wrong; society cannot afford to leave them to their own devices when things seem to be going right. The aftermath of excessive debt will take many years to clear up. If Britain needs to reframe the terms on which business incorporates, it needs a parallel reframing of the terms on which banks create money.

The central pivot of this relationship is the Bank of England. The way it banks to the banking system, the privileges it affords when it supplies liquidity – cash – and the reciprocal demands it makes on the banks dictate the financial system's incentives and momentum. Essentially from the early 1970s the Bank led forty years of disengagement and deregulation. Restraints on the credit-creation process were dismantled across the board: reserve requirements, liquidity requirements, capital requirements and prudential requirements were all relaxed or abolished. The way the Bank intervened to set interest rates became as minimalist as possible, simply operating on the shortest money market rates of all. I thought at the time such a policy was inadvisable, even deranged; I wrote a paper in 1991 called 'Good Housekeeping: How to Manage Credit and Debt' in which I recommended instead retaining and developing this panoply of interventionist instruments, repeating the argument in varying newspaper articles and later in *The State We're In*.[15] It was obvious that the ability of the banking system to create credit had embedded within it a proclivity to generate asset-price bubbles and destabilise the economy, and interest-rate hikes alone could never prevent the dynamic from running away with itself once it was under way. But that was not the prevailing spirit of the times; the Bank of England's chief economist, Mervyn King, wrote to me personally to explain how wrong-headed I was. Interest rates would do the job alone, he patiently explained. The regulatory and prudential framework to which I was so attached inhibited 'banking efficiency'.

The neoliberal snake oil was very attractive at many levels. Looking back, the Bank's stance not only conformed to the increasingly dominant nostrums of free market economics, it was also de facto an industrial policy promoting the growth of the City of London and making it attractive as an international financial centre. Industrial policy was not permissible for industry, but it could be carried out to promote the interests of Britain's gentlemanly capitalists. As more and more international banks crowded into London to take advantage of its freedoms and light-touch regulation – for more than a decade Big Bang allowed American banks to engage in both investment and commercial banking in London, a coupling prohibited in the US by the Glass-Steagall legislation until its repeal in 1998 – the City's financial markets grew deeper and many more banks joined their British competitors in concentrating their lending to support the buying of residential and commercial property. The London wholesale money markets in which all the banks participated seemed like the ocean, an ineluctable fact of life on which any individual bank could rely. That they might seize up in panic as they did in 2007 and 2008 seemed impossible.

The good news is that the Bank of England, whose balance sheet is now bigger in relation to GDP than it was during the Second World War, has firmly got the message that it was wrong – as have the political class. The British state has only so much financial firepower; it cannot regularly mount £1 trillion-plus support packages for its banking system. The Bank's balance sheet could not double again. Not only would the reputation of the banking system and the City of London not survive a second major crisis, it would be inadmissible for the wider economy to suffer a second prolonged economic contraction. The clamour for wholesale recasting of the City, along with outright nationalisation of parts of its activities, would become irresistible.

These realities have forced significant reform and retreat from the follies of the pre-2007/8 era. The Vickers Commission's recommendations, discussed in Chapter 3, are being implemented,

albeit only by 2019. The Bank of England has established the
Financial Policy Committee to ensure financial stability, and
since responsibility for what is called 'macro-prudential'
supervision has been transferred to it from the abolished
Financial Services Authority, it has a potential array of instruments – resurrected from those it once abolished – under its
direct control with which to act. It can require banks to hold
proportionally more capital against property lending at different stages of the property price cycle; it can require
affordability tests for new borrowers; it can set limits to the
multiples of borrowers' incomes that are admissible for mortgage lending; it can set maximum proportions of the value of a
property against which a bank is allowed to lend; it can recommend changes in the government's Help to Buy scheme. It
can be more forensic about which categories of loans it is prepared to help finance under its Funding for Lending
programme, recently favouring loans to small and medium-
sized enterprises.

Recently, and extraordinarily, it caught up with the practice
of central banks in other advanced countries when in January
2014 Governor Mark Carney declared that the Bank would
accept as collateral for its lending not just no-risk government
securities, its policy for three hundred years, but loans made to
business. The Bank's refusal for centuries to underwrite any
lending risk whatsoever had been one of the most important
signals to the British banking community not to make long-
term loans to business and only to lend against property
collateral, giving British banking its distinctive bias against
business engagement. Suddenly the injunction has been
removed. The Bank has even proposed that, from January
2015, it should be possible to claw back bonuses paid to
bankers for up to six years if malpractice or simply commercial
misjudgement is proved. Together with the injection of

£375 billion of cash into the banking system's balance sheet by buying government bonds off it – so-called quantitative easing – the Bank's stance represents perhaps the most complete policy volte-face of modern times. Although only a beginning, it is long overdue and very welcome.

The problem is that the Bank has yet to acknowledge to the wider public the profundity of what it is doing, and thus to trigger discussion about and support for the radical recasting of the relationship between finance and society on which it is embarking. Rather it describes itself as technically trying to fix a broken banking system, trying to make sure there is no repeat and trying to head off another destabilising and damaging house-price boom – and being willing to use novel instruments technically to achieve its ends. All well and good. But as a growing number of economists argue, what we are living through is much more than the consequences of technically broken banks and a technical house-price bubble. For example, in his powerful book *The Shifts and the Shocks*, leading economic commentator Martin Wolf warns that the western financial system is too little reformed, that the structural causes of the 2008 crisis remain and that there is every prospect of another financial crisis. Britain's difficulties, though similar in character to those of other economies, go even deeper, as I argued in earlier chapters. In essence overlaid on the global problems Wolf describes, Britain's ownerless banks have exploited the more aggressive dropping of controls on the fractional reserve banking system to create credit on a vast scale whose final destination, emphasising Britain's biases, has been almost entirely residential and commercial property – underwriting their activity with ever less capital and paying directors and executives extravagantly for their alleged business acumen.

Research by three leading economists, Oscar Jordá, Moritz Schularick and Alan Taylor, shows that the banking systems of no less than seventeen advanced countries have been increasingly focused on lending against property. Historically, they write, 'with very few exceptions, the banks' primary business consisted of non-mortgage lending to companies, both in 1928 and 1970.' But, they continue, 'By 2007, banks in most countries had turned primarily into real estate lenders.'[16] Approaching 60 per cent of bank loans, on average in these countries, were to real estate. It has been reckoned that in Britain the figure is approaching 85 per cent, with only 15 per cent of lending identifiably non-real estate.[17] Britain was thus a more acute outlier of a general trend – fractional reserve banking systems, aided and abetted by the emergence of a vast offshore shadow banking sector, were and to an extent still are creating money out of money and directing it at property, an asset that is in relative fixed supply. Because the credit drives up property prices, that seems to make the lending and borrowing more rational still. In Britain the cocktail is completed by ownerless corporations who reward their management teams even more richly than elsewhere for apparently risk-free profits growth. Residential mortgages alone constitute 64 per cent of all lending.[18]

The task is thus to reform the real estate/fractional reserve banking system axis, and move the financial system away from its fixation with property and onto a new basis in which it supports more consumption, innovation and business investment. This is the project I advocated in *The State We're In*, and it is even more urgent in 2015 than it was twenty years ago. Then it was an opportunity forgone. It is good that the Bank of England has now acquired some of the appropriate tools that I urged then, and which would have certainly mitigated the force of the financial crisis. But success will require determination in using them, a willingness to insist on parallel and supporting reforms that go beyond the Bank's purview into areas such as property taxation, ownership structures and the creation of publicly funded financial entities and networks that are fit for purpose and have the capability to do what is necessary.

Reforming banks and banking

First the Bank of England should throw its weight unambiguously behind the ownership reforms proposed earlier in this chapter. We need purposeful banks with committed owners who want to co-create great, high-trust banking institutions that in turn want to support enterprise, investment and innovation. There should be no temporising with the Vickers reforms in the face of bankers' warnings that they constitute too much regulation and will impair lending; rather we need bank capital to underwrite not investment-banking risk but lending risk to the non-property sector. Investment banking must be undertaken separately in ring-fenced investment-banking arms, as Vickers recommends. Indeed there is a case not only for a ring fence but for full separation, with the government requiring that the commercial arms of banks incorporate under charter to operate as public benefit banks. Banks in any case should be required to hold more capital. Some economists argue that every £100 of lending should be supported by £20 of capital as a way of both building in a buffer against calamity and slowing the capacity of a fractional reserve system to create money.[19] Critics argue that the transition to such a well-capitalised banking system will at the very least temporarily – and perhaps permanently – slow down lending levels, even in high-priority sectors. It is a legitimate concern, but misses the wider point: Britain cannot allow a fractional reserve banking system to create credit as indiscriminately as it has in the past – the risks and wider costs are just too great. In any case it is always open to the authorities to compensate for any shortfalls in private credit by creating compensating public credit through variants of quantitative easing, pumping government-created cash back into the system as required. Only in the failed imagined world, in which all enterprise must be private, credit can only be created privately and there is neither need nor utility in public initiative, is there no role whatsoever for government. In the new context even the creation of credit can and should be sponsored by government if necessary.

The Bank should use all its new powers, especially the power to demand that lenders adhere to loan-to-income multiples, to damp down the excessive flow of mortgage credit to overvalued property. In addition it should operate a regime in which it adjusts upwards and downwards the amount of cash that banks hold in their balance sheets. In the upswing phase of the economic cycle the central bank should hoover cash out of the system by requiring the banks to hold more cash with the Bank as cash-reserve requirements; in the downturn phase it should inject cash by lowering the cash-reserve requirements. This will reinforce the tightening and relaxing of capital requirements demanded to support both lending on property, and other forms of lending. Britain will start to develop mechanisms that damp down the economic cycle rather than magnify it.

Corporate borrowing is tax-deductible; building up equity in companies is not. Debt should no longer be privileged by the tax system; either a means should be introduced for equity to be sheltered from tax, or the tax deductibility of debt interest should be progressively disallowed. One way or another the tax system should not favour debt over equity. Property, in particular residential property, should be taxed properly. Residential property values have absurdly not been revalued for council tax purposes since 1991; the refusal to accept short-term unpopularity to achieve an unarguably rational objective shows our politicians at their most callow. A revaluation must take place in 2015, otherwise the whole system of property taxation will fall into complete disrepute. At the very least there must be more council tax bands above the current maximum of £320,000. Better still council tax should be replaced by a system close to the old rates, in which homeowners paid a rate reflecting the current value of the property. Legal title to property should only be confirmed if owners disclose their identity, rather than hiding on the property register behind anonymous offshore companies. Failure to pay tax should mean they lose the legal title to their property. The *Financial Times* estimates that the total value of the assets of all unidentified property owners now exceeds £100 billion, and that their anonymity is designed largely to avoid and evade tax. Apart from the moral offence, it is another way of giving incentives for credit to flow into property as in effect an onshore tax shelter. It is extraordinary that Britain allows this to continue.

The banking system itself needs more diversity. Challenger banks would be very welcome if they challenged incumbent banks for non-real estate lending; in fact they are almost entirely focused on lending to buy to let and property, as I wrote in Chapter 3. They intensify the system's biases. The US-owned Silicon Valley Bank, rapidly expanding in Britain but still small, is one of the few banks that lends to innovative business models rather than property. The banking system will only focus on non-property lending at scale, develop smarter lending vehicles and promote more competition, if there is a range of public interventions, in particular putting public capital behind new banking institutions and using the public balance sheet to guarantee desired flows of new bank lending. A timorous starting point has already been made by the Coalition government with its Green Bank and Business Bank, although both are constituted more as pretend banks than the real thing to assuage the Treasury. Rather than establishing a jumbo National Investment Bank, as the Labour party is proposing at the time of writing, I would develop these two banks as proper public benefit banking corporations with particular business models, clear mandates and well understood strategic aims. Thus the Green Bank is a green bank, and so it should remain; but it needs to receive capital so it can behave as a bank, rather than as the unsatisfactory hybrid it now is – an agency investing government grants, often to promote matched funding, only doing deals on the same commercial basis as the private sector and offering advice rather than driving forward the development of Britain's green economy by lending at real scale and undertaking genuine risk.

The Business Bank, as proposed little more than a one-stop shop marshalling under one organisational window all the schemes and advice offered by the government, suffers from the same weakness; rather it should be at the centre of a massive effort, in partnership with existing banks, to reduce risk in business lending by offering guarantees and insurance through new instruments. For example, many small business loans could be given a government guarantee so that bankers were only at risk for the first 10 or 15 per cent of the losses in any loan, and then the underwritten loans could be aggregated into one single 'securitised' bond: these would be very attractive to investors, and the vigorous new market in business loan bonds would trigger massive new lending to business.[20] This is securitisation for public benefit. In addition the character of much British business lending has scarcely changed since the nineteenth century: for example 'income-contingent' loans, like those students repay to the Student Loans Company, which fluctuate with the borrowers' salary, should be developed for small and medium-sized businesses. Business borrowers would be empowered to pay loans back earlier without charge when their fortunes went better than planned, or to defer payment automatically if trading was worse than expected.[21] The Business Bank should be required to develop imaginative initiatives of this type, and it would also house or work closely alongside the revived Industrial and Commercial Finance Corporation. The government should exercise its ownership privileges in RBS and Lloyds for the public interest and instead of calculating when it can sell its stakes at the first opportunity, with the banks reverting to business as usual, it should encourage them to redirect their business models away from lending on property and towards value-creating businesses. Infrastructure UK, a unit within the Treasury, should be split out to become the cornerstone of an infrastructure bank that issues bonds to finance infrastructure spending, supporting a massive programme of infrastructure investment.[22] All these proposals are aimed at creating a diverse, safer, long-term, engaged, purposeful banking system catalysed by new public banks and new insurance tools to take more risk and drive lending forward in the economy other than the current dysfunctional obsession with real estate and property.

All this of course supposes that there are more non-property borrowers and more genuine innovators to whom the banking system can redirect its lending. To create them requires a third prong of reform: society needs to forge a new bargain with its innovators, taking and sharing the risks, in order to trigger an innovation revolution.

The innovation bargain

Innovation is the transcendent driver of economic growth. The reinvention of how and what we do increases productivity, transforms the productive base and continually reframes how we work and live with reimagined goods and services. It happens best in open societies that invest in the creation and free diffusion of knowledge where the new is a matter of celebration. But there is a second reality. Innovation is risky, and it needs paying for. Many more innovations fail than succeed.

The neoliberal doctrine is that innovation will happen if there is no state involvement and if it is left to individuals having light-bulb moments, taking risks in free markets in the pursuit of bonanza profits. In Chapter 1 I suggested that the number of general purpose technologies would double in the twenty-first century, presenting enormous innovative opportunity – but I also noted that all GPTs in the past five hundred years have one way or another been catalysed and developed by the state. The risk and the financial consequence of potential failure is beyond any one company or any single venture capitalist to bear, which is why, contrary to the avalanche of praise for individual risk-taking, in reality business and banks do not take much risk. Instead the job of frontier, game-changing innovation is one way or another catalysed by the state.

Sometimes this is a visionary act; sometimes accidental; sometimes the by-product of war or straightforward corporate lobbying. But unless the state gets out there and takes what may seem to be foolish risks, not much innovation is going to take place. Britain is an open society with a knowledge infrastructure that is bursting with ideas. This precondition for innovation is met. But its capacity to translate that into innovative capability and growing companies has been undermined by a stubborn refusal to recognise the obvious. Only grudgingly and in niggardly fashion does the state take any role in driving innovation. This is even more important now that intangible investment, fundamental to the economy of the future, is more important than tangible investment – but lagging behind levels in the US and Japan.

To correct the imbalance we need the state to transform its relationship to innovation. It must adopt some audacious, national innovative goals, find the wherewithal to back them and then self-consciously design an ecosystem of imaginative new institutions designed to nurture the companies that translate innovative conceptions into goods and services. But this cannot be a straight copy of how, say, the South Korean, Singaporean or even Brazilian governments have driven innovation through top-down initiatives supported by state development banks and wealth funds – successful though those initiatives have been – or even an imitation of the closet American developmental state built around institutions like DARPA.[23] In the twenty-first century there is already so much scientific and technological complexity that it is easy to make expensive mistakes and go down blind alleys; any actor, business, government or university research laboratory has continually to test what it is doing and proposing by being in a permanent, iterative, open relationship with similar institutions. The new model certainly entails purposeful state behaviour, but this needs to be carried out in close collaboration with universities and businesses as 'co-creators' of innovative action. It is less that the state should lead from the front, its own officials coming up with top-down plans, processes and proposals as in the various iterations of innovation policy since the Second World War (first science, then technology, then knowledge transfer policy[24]); it is more to reconceive the state – itself made over into less top-down structures, as I argue in the Conclusion – as the equal partner of business, finance and universities in a dense network of interactions, sharing, co-creating and co-funding.

This is the core proposition of the Big Innovation Centre (an innovation hub cum think tank that I chair). Innovation has always been about trial and error; in the twenty-first century trial and error has to take place across an evolving ecosystem of co-created innovative institutions, and then, crucially, the skills of the people within them must be empowered, incentivised and developed.

Importantly, some of the foundations exist, as I indicated in Chapter 1 – and more interestingly are being expanded in ways very different to those of the free market. This is not a greenfield site. Britain has great research universities. Imperial and Cambridge University rank joint second in world rankings; Oxford and UCL are joint fifth. Overall the UK has 29 universities in the top 200 globally, so that per head of population we are the world leader; only the US with 51 does better in absolute numbers.[25] There is a considerable science base, producing 14 per cent of the most cited 1 per cent of papers globally – second only to the US.[26] There is the autonomous Innovate UK (formerly the Technology Strategy Board), set up by New Labour and backed by the Coalition, and a growing network of knowledge transfer and business stimulus centres, the Catapults. The government has created eleven Industry Councils to bring industrial leaders together, identify weaknesses or areas of strength and co-ordinate their responses. Thus the Automotive Council for the car industry has secured £500 million of government funding, which the industry will match, for a £1 billion Advanced Propulsion Centre. The Aerospace Council has similarly created a £2 billion Aerospace Technology Institute. All this is cross-cut with backing eight 'great technologies', identified by former science minister David Willetts (big data, robotics, space, life sciences, agri-science, regenerative medicine, advanced materials, and energy), in which the government wants to prioritise and accelerate investment.[27] Thus £61 million has been committed to build the National Graphene Institute at the University of Manchester, where this light but diamond-hard material was discovered by two scientists who are now Nobel laureates – Sir Andre Geim and Sir Kostyo Novoselov. There are, notwithstanding their weaknesses, the Business and Green Banks – institutions that can be developed. There is the network of Local Enterprise Partnerships, even if they are poorly resourced. The Intellectual Property Office is creating a more liberal, open stance on patenting and copyright consistent with diffusing the gains from new innovations rather than allowing patent to be a way of locking up discovery so it is unusable by anyone else. The Department of Business talks of an industrial strategy, and of creating an innovation ecosystem. Policy is moving in the right direction.

But it has been done almost by stealth – largely by unpublicised moves beneath the radar of free market orthodoxies. What is missing is the overt admission that the state must act purposefully and take the lead if there is to be any significant change in the pace of innovation; it must stimulate and jointly create an accompanying vision of where the country might go; and it must ensure sufficient mobilisation of resources to achieve that end. So here is my stab at what such a vision could be. Britain should aim to be the world's leading smart society, an aim underwritten by its status as the world's leading open innovation hub, a magnet for scientific endeavour worldwide and a creator of public knowledge. It already has the capability, with sufficient new investment, to be the global health hub in fields ranging from antibiotics to new gene technologies and regenerative medicine. It could also be the master co-innovator in big data, and the world centre for the co-creation of new materials. It should aim to be a leader in the green, sustainable and energy revolutions and to be at the forefront of global aviation and space technology. All this is within our grasp.

This ambition cannot come from government alone; it has to be shared by all those involved in making it happen – and then owned as a shared mission. One obvious implication is that spending on R&D must increase: currently it stands at 1.7 per cent of GDP, below the EU average of 2.06 per cent, of which around 60 per cent is carried out by the business sector.[28] In 1980 Britain was one of the most R&D-intensive countries in the world: now it has slipped to be one of the least. Any recovery must see a reversal of this trend, which for all the reasons identified in this and earlier chapters has seen business R&D fall away faster than government R&D spending – a fact that makes the ownership and finance reforms advocated here the precondition for change.[29] Some point to the collapse of the great business research laboratories, notably at GEC and ICI, who before their demise as ownerless corporations driven by shareholder value were two of the great centres of UK industrial R&D.[30] The paucity of the business response to a British invention such as graphene underlines the hollowing out of the country's indigenous industrial and R&D base, along with the capability to capitalise upon invention, over the last thirty years. Britain has taken out just over fifty patents on graphene use; the US 1700 and China 2200.[31]

Business and government alike must raise their game, but the relationship must be transparent and based on mutually shared goals. Above all, if the government were to double its R&D spend to £16 billion in an effort to trigger an overall increase in R&D spending to 3 per cent of GDP – the precondition for any transition to a smart society – by making further frontier investments, say, in the eight great technologies identified by David Willetts, then there have to be better ways of ensuring it gets a financial payback. There must be a sense of a continuing, jointly created effort – not a stream of one-way grants and tax reliefs. For example the government has been right to insist on matched funding for the Advanced Propulsion Centre and Aerospace Technology Institute. But it can go further. All the UK companies it backs should undertake as a precondition of support to pay the appropriate UK tax on the profit streams so generated; the British taxpayer cannot be expected to be a huge high-tech venture investor only to find that its partners – in what would be essentially a parasitical relationship – sequester the resulting profit streams in offshore tax havens.[32] Innovate UK and the Shareholder Executive need to work in tandem, taking appropriate stakes in new companies and joint ventures – a British variant of Temasek!

The public commissioning of original research needs a root-and-branch overhaul. Our great universities are constrained by cash limits, hoping their teams will deliver breakthroughs that can be patented to deliver rich returns, while the research councils reinforce this approach with ever tighter terms for research grants. A revolutionary new approach is needed. Universities need to be freed from the suffocating requirement to create patents and copyrights for themselves through go-it-alone research, which often means – in areas where, in any case, the chance of success are small – they replicate each other's work. Instead, they should become transformative, open innovation hubs aiming to create knowledge as a public good, and taking a much more permissive approach to the subsequent co-creation of business models along with new goods and services. An important survey of 200 businesses showed that while there were good contact points with universities, the next step – co-creating innovation – worked much less well.[33] One model for the future is the Structural Genomics Consortium at Oxford, host to eight leading drug companies that are together funding frontier research that none could do on their own, with Britain's GSK the leading instigator. This has already achieved more in two years than any single company could have achieved in ten.

Our intellectual property regime needs to be reorganised to favour open innovation, experimentation, sharing and cheap licensing. The Intellectual Property Office is moving towards less restrictive patenting with built-in obligations to license; it should be encouraged to go further, faster. The aim should be to create spaces where data can be freely shared, with the presumption that, unless otherwise stated, data is opted in for fair use – but with protections for how the data is used publicly and firewalls for the protection of anonymity. If all or even most of this data is to be held by restrictive patents and copyrights providing for the enforcement of exclusive rights, then the leaps and cross-fertilisation between varying forms of content and data that the technology enables will simply not take place. Tim Berners-Lee, credited with inventing the world wide web, talks evangelically of rich data rather than big data: by giving people ownership of their own data they will be able to merge it with other data to gain more insight into their lives.[34] The aim is to move from a world in which government and companies spy on people's data to a world in which there is sufficient trust, proper ownership and a liberal intellectual property rights regime for data to be fairly used and shared. After all the next phase in the digital revolution is now palpably about transmission of content, whether as individuals having real-time access to their health condition or companies having multiple sources of information about their customers' preferences – all of which is digitised. There is going to be a mountain of data; already, in 2014, 90 per cent of all data had been created in the last two years. Ultimately the enfranchisement must come from below. There is already a rapidly growing sharing economy, where people share assets, cars, houses; with the right framework of protections and rights over personal data, there will be a sharing data revolution. The only question is when.

Of course intellectual property is valuable; the problem is

that there is no systematic means of valuing it. Research by the Big Innovation Centre shows that innovative firms grow faster, but also have 74 per cent more intangible assets and intellectual property on their balance sheets than firms that grow less quickly.[35] Start-ups and innovative firms in the early years of growth find it incredibly difficult to gain the credit that will enable them to expand; the so-called valley of death – the transition from a tiny to a medium-sized company – is even harder for high-tech, innovative, capital-hungry firms to cross than a firm growing more slowly. Their intellectual property does not appear to have a value beyond the firm's business model. Typically by the time they have reached £2 million of turnover, the owners in desperation have sold majority control to external investors, meaning their fate is no longer in their hands – the point made by ARM's CEO, Simon Segars. They sell out to a larger company, usually overseas.[36]

Professor Birgitte Andersen proposes an Innovation Bank to fill the gap. Essentially the Innovation Bank will create markets in intellectual property rights, so securing valuations that would not otherwise be available, and will offer to insure these. Thus it will enable other lenders to finance an intangible asset as though it was a tangible asset.[37] According to one survey, half the owners of patents cannot assess their value, while almost as many find problems enforcing their rights. A quarter do not know who is even using their patents.[38] One task of the Innovation Bank will be to solve this problem by creating a platform that will allow intellectual property properly to be traded and valued. In a world where ideas will become as attractive to finance as real estate, these reforms are imperative. The Innovation Bank will take its place alongside the reshaped banking system with its new banks, strengthened Innovate UK and Catapult network, rising R&D and new ownership framework to spearhead the growth of an innovative, vigorous

British small and medium-sized business sector. Together these measures will address the scale-up crisis identified in Chapter 1 – as well as invigorating business performance over a company's entire life-cycle. Thus will Britain challenge the much-vaunted German 'Mittelstand', the innovative medium-sized companies that form the backbone of the German economy. A recognisable and distinctive British innovation ecosystem will finally exist.

Better ownership, better finance and open innovation are thus mutually reinforcing – key ingredients of a new capitalism. The growing companies that result will want continued access to Europe's single market if they are to grow to substantial scale – and competition law will need to be vigorous to protect them from the incumbents they challenge. Put aside grim austerity and mindless cutting of the public deficit; it is the road to nowhere. Britain must set out to become a leading centre of global innovation and strain every muscle to pull it off. It is the only conceivable future.

6
How Smart We Can Be

Britain must aim to be the smartest economy it can be – it is the only route to prosperity in the decades ahead. The propositions in the previous chapter will lay the crucial economic foundations, but a smart economy needs roots and a culture beyond the solely economic. Necessarily those are rooted in a smart society populated by smart people. Such an economy cannot successfully be built to any scale on the deepening fissures of the 30/30/40 society and dysfunctional, undernourished, ailing social institutions that do not allow the mass of people the opportunity to realise their potential – to show themselves and those around them what they can do and what they have to offer. The smart economy and the smart society are two sides of the same coin. Equality, justice and enfranchisement are not merely nice to have, the preoccupation of inveterate liberals and leftist social movements. They are the cornerstone of the good economy.

For this smart future cannot be constructed without enfranchised citizens, intelligent, risk-taking consumers and equally intelligent, reflexive, creative employees. They are the investors, workers and consumers in the better-owned, better-financed and more innovative enterprises that we need to create as the core of a great economy. I borrow the notion of mass flourishing from Nobel Prize-winning economist Professor Edmund Phelps. Flourishing, he writes, is 'the heart of prospering – engagement, meeting challenges, self-expression and personal growth'. He continues that 'a person's flourishing comes from the experience of the new: new situations, new problems, new insights and new ideas to develop and share. Similarly, prosperity on a national scale – mass flourishing – comes from broad involvement of people in the processes of innovation; the conception, development and spread of new methods and products – indigenous innovation down to the grass roots.'[1] Amen to that.

Put in my terms, the smart economy, resting on innovation, is coterminous with a society that ceaselessly and restlessly sponsors mass flourishing: they are indispensable and interdependent concepts. This was the heart of the Enlightenment – makers, inventors and philosophers all interconnected, daring to think, to understand and to challenge old boundaries, infecting each other with the enthusiasm for the new while being part of a great social awakening that affected everyone. This spirit imbued every branch of British economic and social life in the late eighteenth century; it was this as much as cheap labour, water mills and Europe's first single national market that triggered the Industrial Revolution.[2] Every age is different, but what is not different are the interdependencies between the economic and social that animate and lift the human spirit.

This is a world of sentient adults trying to live their lives as well as they can, doing what they need to do as individuals while at the same time recognising their obligations to support, help and associate with others. Please don't raise your eyes to the ceiling as you read the next line, but the object is to live virtuously in the very broadest sense. Instead, the injunction of the last thirty years has been that virtue lies in the sovereign individual expressing his or her choices, ambitious for self-betterment, and the devil take the hindmost. 'There is no such thing as society,' in Lady Thatcher's telling phrase, 'only individual men and women and their families.'[3] They shouldn't look for handouts from the state as entitlements without accepting obligations, she continued. But that obligation was to look after yourself and stand on your own two feet. The enemy of the piece was government that undermined individual effort.

This is an enervating and desiccated creed. There is no virtue in living merely as a sovereign individual enriching oneself, however much the virtuous individual should look after herself: virtue also lies in recognising and discharging the obligations to others intrinsic to sharing the same street, town, country, in a much broader and generous conception of society than ever imagined by Lady Thatcher. The polarity is not between individuals and their families and government. Rather there is participation in a network of intermediate civic, social and political institutions that stand between the individual and the state.

A genuine Big Society needs a smart state

Mr Cameron was right to argue in the run-up to the 2010 general election that Britain needs a denser network of middle-ranking, intermediate, non-state institutions that stand between the state and the individual: what he called the Big Society, in his short-lived attempt to dissociate himself from Thatcherism. However, he was wrong to think it could be achieved by charitable voluntarism, inevitably short of cash, uneven in character and haphazardly located in varying parts of the country. Instead we need more creative and substantive building of institutions that incorporate civic and public values, so as to reproduce in society what the proposed reforms in Chapter 5 will produce in the economy. It will require sometimes building on what we have, sometimes building anew, actively using public initiative and, where necessary, public funding – but decentralised away from Westminster and Whitehall in the new federalist constitutional structure that Britain must develop.

The state may shape, design and even finance these institutions, but they must have a life of their own beyond government. They are created by and create flourishing adults, and the healthier they are, the healthier will society be and the more the mass of people will flourish. My contention is that contemporary Britain has woefully neglected this matrix of institutions in the name of the sovereign individual and a mean, narrow definition of economic efficiency. We are more than shoppers. Trade unions in the workplace, self-government in the neighbourhood, co-operatively, mutually owned firms are as important to our society as vigorous charities, strong self-standing schools, caring hospitals, mission-driven housing associations and spiritual places of worship – even prisons that seek to release prisoners better than they arrived through imaginative rehabilitation. All are essential to our capacity to be treated as adults, to have a stake and to be enabled to grow.

Similarly the neglect of the institutions of justice, as I described in Chapter 2, has signalled how low a priority that is now given. We care about order so that the individual can be untroubled by disorder. We downplay justice, fairness and rehabilitation – the possibility of a second chance. A good, virtuous life has become harder to live. Everyone is the poorer.

This requires a wholesale reorientation in the way we think

and what we do. Just consider the workplace, where we spend most of our waking time. Lady Thatcher's doctrines were spun out of the propositions of classical free market economics. These state that the sole propellant of economic activity is the monetary incentives that drive us to work more. Wages are what persuade us to give up delightful leisure. There are no values or ethics in these statements, just bald assertions of what seems incontrovertible fact. Forget worries about inequality and justice; they simply don't intrude into the economic, arithmetic calculus that drives economic decision making. Indeed fundamentalist economics goes beyond that. It argues that anything that gets in the way of pure incentivisation and the operation of markets will be economically and indeed morally harmful because markets thus organised will always deliver the best outcome.

But suppose the purpose of economic and social organisation were instead to provide the mass of people with the opportunity to do challenging work that engages all their capabilities – and thus build a smart, innovative economy. What follows from that reconception is a wholesale overturning of the received wisdom and its complacent assumptions. It turns out that my interest in being part of a smart society means I must also care about your successful membership, and that will mean that it is in my interest that you are best equipped to participate. Suddenly inequality matters a lot. If inequality becomes so embedded that millions cannot take part, for no good reason except that they began life with disadvantage and that there are too few supports for them to overcome that disadvantage, then we are all worse off. Mass flourishing can only happen in more equal societies animated by a sense of justice that equips every citizen with the opportunity for self-realisation and self-expression. After all, network theorists propose that the larger the network, the greater the returns.[4]

The same theorem applies to creating a good society: the more smart people, the smarter the society and the richer and more prosperous – in the generous definition offered by Phelps – more of us will be. Suddenly the concern to see justice more hardwired into our affairs is no longer simply a moral concern but of existential economic and social importance.

The neo-classical economics of the free market is based on the opposite hypothesis. It is far from reality, condensed into the abstract theorems of fundamentalists who – to quote Governor of the Bank of England, Mark Carney, again (so good it deserves a second outing!) – have reduced their discipline to no more than a faith. The real justification of markets is not that they are always 100 per cent efficient and spontaneously create prosperity. They do not. Rather it is that they give the mass of people the chance to experiment, express themselves, rise to challenges and innovate. But to do that, markets have continually to be shaped, designed, framed and energised by constantly reinvented intermediate economic, political and social institutions that allow the new to be expressed and support the multiple ways that individuals need to be equipped to play a full part if only their capabilities have been unleashed.

This opens up a very different role for the state. For a generation we have been inculcated with the view that the state needs to be as small as possible, not concerning itself with the operation of business and markets because they will regulate themselves to the best outcomes, and that taxation is a necessary evil and should be as low as possible. Those that disagree are depicted as Fabian apologists for big government, the friends of top-down solutions that always fail. In *The Blunders of our Governments*, Professors Anthony King and Ivor Crewe set out a litany of thirty years of governmental errors, ranging from the Child Support Agency to the public–private partnership (PPP) that was to run the London Underground – and many more. Centre–right politicians would also include in any such list governmental efforts at supporting companies, picking winners, or nationalisation. Many officials themselves have become convinced of the inevitability of public failure: markets and business will fail less often, and cost the taxpayer less.

Yet these failures are less in the nature of the state but more in the nature of the utter lack of deliberative capacity of the British government to consider, to experiment and to feel its way to the best outcomes. We need, King and Crewe say, a more deliberative state that thinks before it acts. I would add that many of the failures come from trying to introduce neoliberal ideological simplicities into areas where they do not belong. The fiasco of rail privatisation, the Coalition government's fatuous health reforms or the disaster of PPP in the London Underground all occurred because politicians, with little accountability, tried to drive the market principle into areas where its failure was inevitable. This was government trying unsuccessfully to abolish the public nature of activity that must lie within the public sector – a rail network or the provision of public health.

It is also an unwillingness to focus on what government can do well; to build and shape institutions for the wider good. British universities, the BBC, Innovate UK, the judicial system, the Bank of England, academy schools and NHS trusts are all examples of British institutions that work moderately or even rather well. In the economic domain too little attention has been paid to the institution of the company, the bank, and how the innovation system is to be institutionally populated. The same can be said of too many of our social institutions. Government is above all the builder and custodian of our institutions. It is a job it does inadvertently or not at all.

The larger point is that public action, and public resources, are indispensable. We have to ask whether our power-hoarding, centralised state is fit to carry out what we need it do. We also have to ask whether our democracy encourages sufficient deliberation. And whether taxation should be depicted as pernicious: without resources there is no state – and if we want innovation, effective infrastructure, functioning public services, a decrease in inequality and any kind of social settlement, ultimately they can only be achieved by a comparatively well-resourced state. There must be taxation; it is a badge of citizenship and belonging, and without it there can be no investment in what creates mass flourishing. To build a smart society in which the mass of people can flourish requires us wholesale to turn our backs on the economic and political nostrums of the last thirty years. The conservatism that promulgates the opposite is as bankrupt and useless as socialism once was.

The crisis of trade union decline

One of the most marked changes of the last twenty years is the changing attitude towards inequality. Essentially there is growing recognition that it matters. The International Monetary Fund takes prides in its hard-headedness, but here is its current managing director, Christine Lagarde, speaking at a speech at the Inclusive Capitalism conference in May 2014 in London. Excessive inequality, she declared, 'makes capitalism less inclusive. It hinders people from participating fully and developing their potential. Disparity brings division.'[5] Inequality, she continued, erodes the principles of solidarity and reciprocity, and great concentrations of wealth – if unchecked – 'even undermine the principles of meritocracy and democracy'. It should not be a surprise that IMF research, she said, 'finds that more unequal societies tend to have lower and less durable economic growth'. Change had to happen.

She then listed a cocktail of possible remedial interventions – more progressive tax systems, more property tax, better in-work social benefits and improved education and skills – that would have been almost heretical twenty years ago. No less heretical was her criticism of how deregulated finance had become 'extractive rather than inclusive', with big banks holding society to ransom. Mrs Lagarde is but another leader joining the swelling ranks of dissidents from the orthodoxy.

Central bankers and financial regulators' concern about inequality is not brought about because of their sudden conversion to being warm-hearted. It is because there is growing evidence that its interaction with the deregulation of finance was one of the chief reasons for the explosion of debt and the resultant fragility of the banking system. Bankers certainly wanted to lend money, but they had a ready market in the mass of the workforce who were trying to defend their living standards as inequality bore down on the growth of their real wages. Raghuram Rajan, former chief economist of the IMF and now governor of the Bank of India, makes this point, as of course does Lord Adair Turner, quoted earlier.[6] The explosion of private debt bought time, but the extent of debt and the consequent financial fragility means the amount of debt cannot continue to grow – nor should it. Indeed, it is now becoming obvious that the Thatcherite policy mix – which simultaneously emasculated union power and removed controls from fractional reserve banking – was a first-order disaster whose baleful consequences go beyond even Turner's and Rajan's tough critiques.

The rise of inequality is plainly in the first instance a labour market phenomenon, as I discussed in Chapter 4 – and the usual explanation for the squeeze in living standards is the rising importance of skills and growing competition as globalisation has accelerated. Those are important forces, certainly, but they neglect the greater explanation: the assault on weakening trade unions and thus on collective bargaining power, which is very much home-made. An important IMF working paper with the less than catchy title 'Income Inequality and Current Account Imbalances' locates the rise in inequality precisely in the decline of collective bargaining, and spells out the disastrous consequences by economically modelling how the process might work, comparing it with what happened in practice. The decline in workers' collective bargaining power over the eighteen years of Conservative government (1979 to 1997) had measurable consequences on real wages. The paper hypothesised that a cumulative decline in collective bargaining power of 10 per cent over an eighteen-year period would lead to a 7 per cent decline in real wages and a 3 per cent rise in the return on capital. This, eerily, is what happened: the fall in union density (the proportion of the workforce who are members of trade unions) was associated with a cumulative decline in real wages 7 per cent below what they would otherwise have been.

The IMF team then hypothesised the reaction. As a result of such a decline, workers would try to protect their living standards by borrowing – easy to do as the controls were removed from now deregulated banks. They theorised that worker debt (expressed as a percentage of GDP) would rise cumulatively from 60 per cent to 170 per cent over thirty years as the deregulated banks quickly responded to the demand for more credit. But of course, as the cost of servicing so much more debt rose, it would further reduce workers' disposable incomes.

Meanwhile the incomes of the top 5 per cent would rise, along with their spending, which would jump 50 per cent. Imports would be sucked in from abroad as debt-financed consumption departed from underlying production, so the IMF team anticipated a rise in the trade deficit. Again reality fitted their model with eerie precision. The rise in worker debt grew to almost the exact levels predicted, while the entire deterioration of the UK current account between 1980 and 2007, they say, can be explained by the interaction between banking liberalisation and the weakening of workers' bargaining power.[7] Put more bluntly, Mrs Thatcher's assault on the collective bargaining power of trade unions may have increased UK employment – but it has led to a country with rock-bottom levels of productivity, squeezed living standards for the mass of the population, has driven huge levels of personal debt and prompted a dramatic weakening of Britain's international accounts. Worse, the process became the principal cause of a financial crisis the consequences of which will last decades. For this she was afforded a quasi-state funeral.

Britain's labour market is certainly brutal, as I observed in Chapter 1. To recap briefly, too much work is transactional. Trust relationships between managements and workforces are typically lacking. Real hourly wages are only forecast to regain their 2008 level by the end of 2016, the longest period of stagnating wages for more than a century.[8] Wages for those under thirty, as I wrote in Chapter 4, have fallen by double-digit percentages since 2007. Productivity is 'abysmal', reports the National Institute of Economic and Social Research, again predicting a recovery to pre-recession levels only in 2017, which – as I also wrote in Chapter 4 – will still leave it enormously below where it should be.[9] The labour market throws up enormous and growing inequality. Business secretary Vince Cable, reflecting the changing consensus, pondered out loud in a speech at the Resolution Foundation in May 2014 whether Britain's flexible labour market has become too flexible, entrenching low wages and removing the incentive to invest.[10] Its saving grace is that it creates jobs – but nobody would describe the British labour market as the handmaiden of any mass flourishing.

Vince Cable is more right than he knows. The neoliberal story is that there are only benefits from what is known as 'labour market flexibility'. The choice of the word flexibility to describe the near-elimination of the role of trade unions in the private sector workplace, accompanied by the parallel empowerment of management to near-imperial standing and the removal of nearly all restraints on hiring and firing, while making any form of income support conditional on a constant search for jobs, is neatly done: who could be against flexibility any more than apple pie and motherhood? The weakening of trade unions may have contributed to the 30/30/40 society, concede the policy's apologists, but that ignores the great gains. The resilience of employment during the Great Recession and its rise by 1.8 million since 2010 to a rate of over 73 per cent in the summer of 2014 seems proof positive that flexibility works. Nobody in their right mind would want to re-empower trade unions. After all, the only part of the economy where the unions remain strong is in the public sector, where they represent more than half the workforce: London's commuters can testify to the cavalier way the RMT calls strikes on the London Underground over apparently trivial issues, imposing disproportionate suffering on millions. Society should make such strikes harder, not easier, argue the proponents of flexibility. Unions, for example, should have to achieve a 50 per cent threshold of all their members in any vote for strike action as a requirement made in no other part of British democracy: key public sector workers should sign no-strike agreements as part of their terms of employment.

The unions' retort is rarely heard, but it is crucially important: strikes are weapons of last resort – acts of desperation when all else has failed, and for which it is very hard to achieve majority support from workers in any ballot, let alone achieve the current threshold for participation of 40 per cent. They are also an internationally agreed basic human right. Trade unions are defending terms and conditions of work that, although they do not use the words, are how their members flourish.

For example, Unison care workers in Doncaster engaged in one of the longest-ever strikes in the NHS in the spring and summer of 2014 in an attempt to resist cuts in wages of more than 30 per cent imposed by Care UK, a company majority-owned by the private equity firm Bridgepoint. These workers are in the front line of the battle against remorseless cuts in the living standards and working conditions of skilled British workers – and want to protect a conception of public service provision. It is legitimate for the RMT to want to phase in the change to automated stations and robotic, unmanned ticketing; it is autocratic management that wants to set an unrealistic timetable that is to blame. The INEOS workers in Grangemouth, involved in the bitter dispute mentioned earlier, were equally trying to defend wages and pensions. More importantly, public sector unions, for all their detractors, do an effective job. They have succeeded in maintaining real wages in the public sector despite the unprecedented cuts in current public spending: unadjusted for skills and size of employer (public sector workers are more highly skilled and work in larger organisations, which tend to pay more even in the private sector), hourly earnings in the public sector in 2013 were £16.28 an hour compared with £14.16 in the private sector.[11] But wages reflect skills and the size of the organisation; broadly higher skills in bigger organisations leads to higher wages. The public sector tends to be higher-skilled and work in larger organisations: but even allowing for this, public sector workers are only paid fractionally less than their private sector counterparts. The union effect works for the mass of workers, and it is not necessarily obvious that a decade-long freeze on real wages when the union effect is absent is as brilliant as the economic consensus argues.

But strengthening trade unions and redesigning collective bargaining are not on the list of remedies for inequality. Mrs Lagarde would not go that far. Unions are seen as a toxic force. For that, trade unionism itself bears some responsibility, notwithstanding the demonisation of unions by our press. Contemporary trade unionism urgently needs to reinvent itself as part of the new solution rather than being a remnant of the old problem – but reinvention is not something which comes readily to British trade unionism, forged in the great struggles of the late nineteenth and early twentieth century. As the economy moved on, unions did not. Industry-wide collective bargaining agreements were never strong in Britain, and those that did exist were already beginning to weaken from the mid-1950s, with the responsibility for wage bargaining migrating to individual firms – so that long before the Thatcher reforms of the 1980s, unions were strategically conceding one of their major sources of strength.[12] Nor had they capitalised on the opportunities of the 1970s to reinvent their role. They were unable to coalesce around the proposals by Sir Alan Bullock to establish worker directors on the boards of all private companies, which would have taken the unions in the direction of German co-determination and reinvented themselves as business partners. Despite the TUC's active support, too many in the union movement – unaware of what was to hit them in the 1980s – clung on to oppositional collective bargaining, by now plainly decaying, as the best way to influence companies.[13] Companies were equally dismayed that they might have to compromise managerial autonomy and the priority they gave to the maximisation of shareholder value. There was no deal.

Today there is a second opportunity. Christine Lagarde knows she will not be shouted down when she makes a speech decrying inequality as she did. There is a groundswell of intellectual, business and political support for the notion that we cannot go on as we are. The British *are* chafing at current levels of inequality, *are* dismayed at what is happening in their wage packets, *hate* the unwarranted remuneration paid to top executives and want to work in workplaces where they are trusted and respected. Business itself can no longer argue that managerial autonomy and the maximisation of shareholder value are the sole criteria on which to organise companies. But there is no love of trade unions; the popular memory – fanned, often unfairly, by conservative ideologues who only portray one side of the argument – is wary nonetheless of the world of closed shops, secondary picketing and the tens of millions of working days lost through strikes in the 1970s and early 1980s, compared with a million or less today. Equally the labour market cannot carry on as it is. What to do?

Reinventing unions to save them

Campaigners for strengthening trade unions – a rare and doughty breed – argue that unions need saving from above: the state should stop chipping away at collective bargaining and instead act to oblige companies to recognise unions and to bargain with them to set wages collectively across businesses and sectors. The anti-union legislation of the last thirty years should be unwound. If the state once undermined these great social institutions, it should now build them up.[14] But politically this is a dead letter: there is no constituency in support of what would be seen as a return to the past. Instead unions need to discover a role that has popular support in the economy of the here and now, building momentum and on this basis winning legislative support for their strengthening – but as very different institutions to those they are today.

The starting point must be that unions are the societal institutions above any other that can take responsibility for two giant social needs – lowering inequality and re-enfranchising workers in order to create mass flourishing. Of course they must cleave to their traditional role as defenders of the underdog and champions of workplace justice. But they should also talk incessantly of their willingness to be partners in enterprise, to experiment with new forms of workplace organisation, to be involved urgently in the exploration of public sector reform and of how they want to be champions of mass flourishing. They need both to be pioneers in the reinvention of the public sector that is newly responsive to citizen preferences and to take part in the reinvention of British capitalism around the inclusive forms of ownership proposed here, while also being active instigators of a genuine Big Society.

Trade unions should be central to such an effort. They are intermediate social institutions with both an economic and social role: they are value driven, and they are present throughout the country. Already this is acknowledged, if grudgingly. Unions have key roles in the Low Pay Commission, the Health and Safety Executive, the Equal and Human Rights Commission, the Commission for Employment and Skills, employment tribunals and ACAS. These are all established features of the British landscape, but the union position on each should be bolder and more strongly rooted in the network of ideas embedded in the idea of mass flourishing. Unions should be prepared to proselytise about skills, employment rights, the benefits of workplace consultation and the miseries of low pay. To an extent they always have; now the public is readier to listen.

The aim is to build legitimacy. Unions need to be more like guilds, guarantors of skills and fair wages, than confrontational representatives of a shrinking working class. So, for example, unions are properly concerned about zero-hour contracts and workplace insecurity. They should campaign for change. But they should create employment arms of their own – employee mutuals – run by the union on good work principles, hiring out to other employers (who in turn pay the mutual for labour services) on flexible terms appropriately skilled workers paid by the mutual but whose ultimate employer is the union. Unions should pioneer profit sharing and employee share ownership schemes. Unions should be the avenue to better pension advice, coaches in the creation of programmes of lifelong learning in general and skills development in particular. The union should provide skilled pension fund trustees to represent workforces, skilled remuneration directors to sit on company remuneration committees to determine executive pay packages, and potentially skilled non-executive directors as trustees for corporate purpose under the new Companies Act. In all these examples, managements will find that union contributions legitimise and generate more trust – from executive pay to the development of training programmes.

Unions themselves want to convince managements that to sit down with union representatives and negotiate firm-wide wage deals or consult over a major change – a takeover, a redundancy or hiring programme, a relocation, co-ordination on a multi-billion-pound infrastructure project – will seem less a ceding of managerial sovereignty, and more a way of achieving a high-trust outcome. There may be conflict and tension, but a commitment to 'good faith' bargaining – entailing transparency on both sides and an understanding that deals, once struck, will be adhered to – will reinforce relationships of trust. This is a means of offering workers a voice and influence within a bounded framework of reciprocal partnership.[15]

If all this seems a pipedream, consider the Social Covenant signed in July 2014 by EDF Energy and four unions – GMB, Prospect, UCATT and Unite – to create a common framework

for 'just pay, industrial relations, recruitment, health and welfare, skills development and workforce communications' for
the up to £24 billion nuclear construction site at Hinkley Point
C, in what will be the largest infrastructure project in Europe
today. Kevin Coyne of Unite welcomed its 'astonishing ambition', while Vincent de Rivaz, EDF Energy's CEO, said how
he had wanted 'a different kind of culture from the established
national agreements and some of the entrenched positions that
were underpinning them' and praised the 'collective creation'
of a new partnership approach replacing collective bargaining
as confrontation. He called it 'Project Solidarity'.[16] BT, for its
part, has struck a three-year pay deal running from 2014 with
its two chief unions – CWU and Prospect – to give both sides
financial certainty over three years of ongoing economic difficulty: on top BT has invested many millions in developing the
leadership skills of over 100 frontline and union middle managers, not only to help them contribute to developing a
common purpose and culture within BT but to drive similar
vital change into their own unions. In short, constructive union
management dialogue can be done.

The approach will lead to higher real wages, more skilled
workforces, more modest executive pay and ultimately to mass
flourishing – but this is what is wanted, and it is impossible
without unions operating as a trusted intermediary. In this conception the unions do not fight capitalism; they continually
reshape and reconfigure it. As this new economic and social
purpose evolves, so it can be legislatively reinforced by, say,
requiring employers to offer new employees a choice of unions
to join: employers will be required automatically to enrol workers in the union of their choice, deducting a small proportion of
their wages as a membership fee. Unions will have been seen
to have earned the right to public support because they create
public good. In the manner of guilds and mutuals, these new-

look unions will have more power to actively set minimum wage rates, but will also enfranchise workers to flourish. An important building block in reducing inequality will have been created. It will need to be supplemented by a renewed and invigorated social contract, but workers at last will have at least one social institution unambiguously on their side.

Let's invest in ourselves

Around 750,000 babies are born every year in Britain. Any society should want to ensure that every one of them will flourish – especially a society that aims to be smart. Britain's system does not do that. Around 50,000 will be educated privately, with all the privileges that entails. But 230,000 (31 per cent in 2014) will not achieve five good GCSEs between A* and C – a substantial improvement on the rate twenty-five years ago when some 55 per cent failed to meet that threshold, but still far from good enough. For today it is even more marked that we live in a knowledge economy, and are ambitious to become a smart economy and society. It cannot be done when so many do not even reach the starting blocks.

The story is well known. Many of those babies, around a third of all those born in any year, will have the brute bad luck to be born into disadvantaged homes whose parents will be the among the 10 million British with annual incomes of £15,000 or less. Their lives will be blighted from the start. The gap will have opened up even before they start school; pre-school kids whose parents read and talk to them are able to extend their vocabulary, and already show more cognitive and emotional development than their peers who do not enjoy the same advantages.[17] So it goes on. The disadvantaged quarter of a million in any year will suffer more from family breakdown, and from all the emotional and financial distress that ensues in its wake. As Britain divides into more segregated neighbour-hoods of rich and poor, the chances for the poor to break out of an area of self-reinforcing disadvantage declines. Their homes will have few books, little space for study and no online capa-bility with a dedicated laptop or PC. Their local peer group will not value education, not least because so few of their elder brothers and sisters will have attained qualifications and bene-fited from them. Shamingly, according to the OECD, family background has greater influence on educational outcomes in England than in any other country.[18]

As formal academic education fails this group, the training system as an alternative is Britain's permanent Cinderella – a bewildering alphabet soup of diplomas offered by colleges that do their very best but are beset by structural difficulties. They are starved of resources; professional standards are not high; and few local employers offer apprenticeships on which they can build. The Commission for Employment and Skills reports that just 29 per cent of employers offer work experience oppor-tunities and only 15 per cent apprenticeships. In addition, it has found that only 27 per cent of employers said they recruited young people directly from school or college.[19] The interaction of poor education and an indifferent skills training system is devastating by international comparison; Britain alone of any OECD country has more literate and numerate people approaching retirement than young adults. Eight and a half mil-lion people have only a very primitive understanding of arithmetic.

Even those kids from disadvantaged backgrounds who show more academic prowess do not fare well. In raw numbers, 11,695 students from advantaged backgrounds entered the top thirteen universities in 2013, but only 1232 from the most disadvantaged backgrounds – an almost tenfold difference.

The ratio drops to just over seven times for the thirty most selective universities. For the entire university sector, the difference in 2013 stood at 2.8.[20] This is a massive squandering of talent; 80,000 fifteen-year-olds receive free school meals: only 20 go on to be admitted to Oxford. The Sutton Trust reports that four private schools and one state sixth-form college in Cambridge send as many students to Oxbridge as nearly 2000 state schools. Are we to believe that native academic ability is uniquely concentrated in the children of parents rich enough to afford to pay the fees (or to live in the catchment area of Cambridge's state-funded Hills Road sixth-form college – an excellent institution whose success underlines that in the right economic and social circumstances the state can compete with private schools)?

The differences even come through in the personal statements that accompany university applications. Taking students with the same grades, 70 per cent of those from private schools are generally admitted to top universities, compared with 50 per cent from state schools. And the key difference is personal statements, which testify to vast differences in cultural capital and experience: for example, the difference conveyed by accounts of work experience that involve a Saturday job or a school visit to a business from those that include work with a local radio station, with a City law firm, a designer, or events planning in a five-star hotel.[21] None of the kids at the receiving end of this systemic disadvantage can be said to have deserved it: they just had the brute bad luck to be born to the wrong family in a country that does less to remedy that disadvantage than almost any other. This is unfairness in neon. Everyone knows it; too few act. Mr Michael Gove, former education secretary, for all his ideological weaknesses, was right to be a zealot trying to reform the system. Self-governing academy schools free to set educational objectives themselves are certainly part of the solution.

In 2014 too little had changed compared with twenty years ago; indeed, if anything the grip of private schools has intensified and training structures, despite much huffing and puffing, have grown weaker – largely because so few employers engage with or want to take on the cost of offering apprenticeships, and the government is not prepared to find the resources to compensate for the shortcomings. But then too few British companies are owned in ways that allow them to make long-term investment in training any more than any other long-term investment. It is much better in a laissez-faire universe, where the share price is all, to let others bear the cost, and then raid them for the young men and women who have been trained. It is time for an across-the-board mobilisation and a new bargain.

Britain needs to spend serious money on education, biasing any new spending towards disadvantaged schools. Ratios of staff to students in these schools should be progressively reduced to the same level as those of the top 100 private schools, and their teachers rewarded appropriately. The young, idealistic graduates who spend a couple of years teaching in disadvantaged schools via the excellent Teach First initiative know how tough and emotionally demanding it is; those who make a career in it should be paid properly and celebrated for their dedication. Similar if less urgent moves must be made across the state sector. Simultaneously the unfair impact of the private school system must be reduced by insisting that private schools' formal educational licence is conditional on opening them up to a high proportion – certainly no less than a third – of non-fee-paying students. Attempts to make private schools do this voluntarily have been a lamentable failure. The only option now is legislation.

The days of paying lip service to supporting training need to end. There must be a well-understood, generously funded training ecosystem in which companies take responsibility for

training and offering apprenticeships, government for ensuring
there is proper funding by levying companies for training costs,
and a codified system of vocational qualifications and diplomas
which are linked both to academic qualifications and to on-the-
job experience. Adults should be able readily to update their
qualifications across their lifetime – lifetime learning – and the
training system should be organised on that basis. A smart society requires continual reinvestment in personal skills. The UK
Commission on Employment and Skills should be accorded
the power to become the catalyst for a training revolution.

Access to university is improving, but desperately slowly.
One of the worries about the £9000 per annum fee regime was
that it would deter applications overall, disproportionately
affecting disadvantaged students. It has certainly devastated
part-time higher education, where most students came from
moderate and low-income homes, and where there are now
over 100,000 fewer students. Numbers of mature students are
also well down. But application rates from eighteen-year-olds
to English, Welsh and Northern Irish universities for full-time
education are all up on 2010. Part of the reason is the recognition of the value of higher education; but part is that repayment
of £45,000 of student debt – the most expensive system in the
world for the general student – seems very distant in faraway
adulthood, and anyway there is the reassurance that repayment
will only begin when salaries are higher than £21,000, which for
many seems a large amount of money. The reality – a large
debt, owed at high real interest rates, which with the effect of
compound interest will grow bewilderingly quickly – only sets
in after university. As the experience bites, the news of the
onerousness of the new system will start to spread.

It is already hitting those taking second degrees. Few can
undertake the expense of a doctorate or master's, increasingly
important in today's knowledge economy labour market, unless

they have additional support – and such support is shrinking. There has to be relief. One obvious means to persuade more kids from poorer homes to apply to university would be to universalise and standardise the patchwork quilt of access agreement rebates into a standard lower fee for disadvantaged applicants of, say, £3000. Such a skewed fee regime would help, but the truth is that differential university applications reflect the desperately unequal and unfair society Britain has become. The education and training system cannot offer redress on their own. Inequality has to be tackled too.

A social contract for the twenty-first century

To state the obvious: the poor don't have any money and don't own much. Stronger trade unions and better education and training will offer some redress, but attempts at self-betterment are infinitely harder when you have little or no hard cash. For the poorly paid or those unable to work, taking a bus, finding the deposit for a rented flat or eating healthily may be beyond their means. Living a life they have reason to value, being in one way or another participants in the smart society and economy, even relaunching themselves with different skills and in a different place, are impossibly expensive. The poor are obviously diminished thereby; but, less obviously, so are those who are better off.

I wrote in Chapter 2 that Britain's fraying social contract was in peril before the indifference to justice and punitive attitude towards the poor driven by the new harsh individualism. William Beveridge in his famous 1942 report proposed a social security system based on the insurance principle: everybody paid in, and everybody would draw on the fund when they experienced one of life's hazards – sickness, disability, unemployment, old age. The availability of help was not to be at the discretion of power-hoarding politicians at the centre, to be withdrawn and pared down with every scare story in the populist press. It was to be one's due as a member of a national insurance system. Everyone drew out according to their need, in proportion to what they had paid in. This was fairness for all at its purest.

But the contribution principle has been allowed to wither: it is just a second 'stoppage' on one's pay slip, with governments wanting the discretion to pay what they determine in benefits rather than have levels pre-set by the insurance fund. The principle is just about alive with the state pension, where thirty qualifying years of payments are required for the full state pension to be paid; but elsewhere it is meaningless. Chancellor George Osborne floated the idea of merging the national insurance and tax system into one (even commissioning a Treasury consultation in 2011) because the distinction retains so little meaning, and by so doing he hoped – when workers could see the true scale of their deductions – the Conservative party would build a bigger constituency both for reducing taxes and shrinking the state. Only the technical complexity of uniting two different computer systems deterred him.

Beveridge was right, just as was Roosevelt, quoted in Chapter 2, in insisting that social security should be paid for by hypothecated taxes. The only way to legitimise social security so that it stops being regarded as a series of morally sapping handouts to the undeserving poor is to make everyone pay in to a common fund to receive common benefits. Economists and technocrats may think that targeting such spending on the needy is more technically efficient, which is self-evident. But, like so much in economics, it abstracts values and motivation from human conduct. The problem is to sustain the system, given there will always be a minority of the needy who game it, from the collective shout that the taxpayer is indulging benefit cheats and fostering a dependency culture. Only universal benefits to which everyone contributes and which everyone deservedly receives have a chance of survival – especially in today's right-wing climate when those collective shouts have become hysterical.

There needs to be a new social bargain that the majority will accept, one which conforms to economic logic and is resilient to attack from those for whom any kind of social contract is anathema. It needs to take into account the fact that in today's fast-moving economy, employers need to be able to reshape workforces quickly, both upward and downward; in most sectors business models are so under threat that employers will not hire unless they know they can quickly fire. But that introduces even more risk and uncertainty into the workplace. The social contract has to compensate.

First, as the quid pro quo for retaining the hire-and-fire element of the contemporary labour market, employers must accept the proposed skills revolution, a commitment to train and provide lifelong learning – and the accompanying financial commitment. This will empower workers with greater skills, making them more employable. But in a fast-moving economy making rapid readjustments to its workforces, all but the very privileged will experience periods of unemployment. All should pay into a strong system of national insurance; all should receive for six months unemployment benefit that is between half and two-thirds of what they earned in the year before the unemployment disaster – but as an entitlement for which they have paid by being a member of the national insurance system. Supplements above the core benefit would be paid the more a recipient looked for work, but today's penal system of making niggardly benefit conditional on immediate job search, with recipients having to wait seven days for payment after one of the most unpleasant events in their lives – being made redundant – would stop. Lastly, the government would step in as the employer of last resort, offering the guarantee of a job or training for twelve months after an unsuccessful six months of search.

It is a system, in short, of 'flexicurity'. A term originally coined by the Danish Prime Minister Poul Rasmussen in the 1990s and then fleshed out more fully by Dutch economist Ton Wilthagen, it is a bargain for the smart economy and society of the twenty-first century.[22] The Danes saw it as a 'golden triangle' of active labour market policies to promote employment, of generous benefits in the period of transition between one job and another, and of the acceptance by unions – and of business, agreeing mandatory training as their part of the deal – that businesses could lose workers without too much expense when circumstances changed. In essence employers retain the vital freedoms to adjust their business by making workers redundant without too much expense in fast-moving global markets and under the pressure of constantly evolving new technologies. But they do so within the context of a new social settlement, accepting reciprocal responsibilities to train, to hire apprentices, to recognise trade unions who themselves accept the bargain, and to operate a system of lifelong learning. The state builds an unemployment benefit system whose aim is not to punish the unemployed, but to support them with a decent income, one they have earned and which is their right. The government's promise of work and training underwrites the deal to ensure there will be no losers.

It is practical, realistic, fair and generous – a Beveridge approach for the twenty-first century – and it will be popular. Within this framework and together with a realistic minimum wage the government can build income support for those in work to make work even more attractive if it chooses, but if the flexicurity system is well designed there will be little need. There will be no invidious distinction between the deserving and undeserving poor.

One of the most disabling features of poverty is the inability to escape it at the moment it is most possible – early in one's life. To move to another town to start an apprenticeship, to find the down payment to rent a flat, even to fund the travel to a different city requires access to a small pot of capital that can be transformatory. The children of middle-class parents turn to the bank of Mum and Dad; the children of the poor have no such recourse. They are trapped.

The Labour government created child trust funds into which the government made two small £250 contributions (£500 for low-income families) at entry into the scheme and at the age of seven, and which the family and friends of the child could top up. As the friendly society the Children's Mutual said, 'In terms of changing people's behaviour this is the most successful product there has ever been.'[23] It allowed the creation of a small nest-egg that an eighteen-year-old could deploy to support his or her ambition for self-betterment, to unlock the door to his or her potential flourishing.

The Coalition government shut it as soon as it took office. It was seen as typical New Labour wastefulness that produced no worthwhile asset and encouraged state dependency. It was, of course, the opposite. Yet nobody came to its defence – testimony to the extraordinary bias in our media and political system. Too few know what it means to be poor, and there are no rewards, only brickbats, from trying to empathise. The child trust fund should be reinstated – and made more ambitious.

How the great 'cashing out' completed the shrivelling of Britain's social contract

A social contract is not only about income and assets; it also encompasses housing, health, pensions, public transport, education, training, and access to art, culture and sport. But here too the story has been one of shrinkage, privatisation and displacement of risk from the state and large organisations on to the individual. Year by year the effects often go unnoticed. Cumulatively the impact is shocking.

For example the sale of council houses. Since the policy was launched in the early 1980s the stock of council houses has fallen from 6.5 million to 1.7 million in 2013.[24] The impact has been partially offset by the 2.3 million dwellings now provided by housing associations, but nonetheless this is an extraordinary cull. Many councils report that a third of their former council houses, up to one and a half million in all, are now owned by private landlords who charge significantly higher rents, many of them as buy-to-let rentals.[25] It is a thoughtless enrichment of the incumbent generation, who have been allowed to cash out at great personal gain – and then to hand on the economic and social consequences to the next. In this respect its rationale is very similar to the demutualisation of building societies in the 1990s – cashing out to the advantage of incumbent depositors and managements, but with disastrous medium-term consequences. As a self-defeating policy this has few rivals.

A similar if more subtle process has been under way in the NHS. New Labour's public spending on health certainly improved health outcomes, but that good was undermined by allowing too many hospitals to be built via the private finance initiative (PFI). Apart from the astonishing financial burden described earlier, a no less important factor for health policy is that the thirty-year PFI contracts allow no flexibility of provision without the payment of onerous break clauses. It was bonkers – a craven surrender to the notion that private is always best and that any form of public debt is toxic. It was part of a wider programme that allowed yet another public asset to be cashed out for private gain in the name of diversity of provision and greater (if dubious) private sector efficiency.

Yet the NHS, for all the ideological criticism levelled at it for being closed, suspicious of competition and monopolistic, is the cheapest system in the world producing the best health results across a range of key indicators. The New York-based Commonwealth Fund recently ranked eleven advanced countries' health systems for cost and health outcomes. Britain spends $3404 (£2000) per head on health each year compared with the $8508 (£5001) spent by the open-to-new-entrants, market-based US system, with the other nine countries in between. Yet on measures of effectiveness, safety, patient centredness, co-ordination, quality and access, Britain scores number one.[26] The NHS may have problems, but it is not in crisis. It faces an ageing population and more expensive treatments, but from the best starting point. What it needs to do is to retain its public character and universality of provision, offer operational autonomy to decentralised units as it is doing, benchmark efficiency against private providers and above all spend the necessary money to achieve the health outcomes we need. What it does not need is the attention of endless reformers who see as the answer to its alleged problems the cashing out of a public asset and the adoption of the market principle – actions likely to make it as inefficient and expensive as the US system, while rendering it a honey pot for risk-free profits from private contractors.

It is the same story with transport. The privatisation and break-up of the rail system was cashing out taken to an absurd degree. An irrational and inoperable structure was created with the railway track owned by one private company, the operating companies by others and the rolling stock by others again. The strategic intelligence so crucial to ensuring the co-ordination and complexities of a rail network was thus lost; the aim was rather to allow this public asset to be cashed out. I wrote in the previous chapter that the privately owned Railtrack soon collapsed following the Hatfield rail disaster, allowing the impact of privatisation to be partially remedied by the creation in 2002 of Network Rail, a not-for-dividend statutory corporation limited by guarantee – an elaborate organisational con to avoid the dread words 'public company' and 'nationalisation', even though it is 100 per cent owned by the state. Thus structured it has been able to borrow more than £30 billion to finance the infrastructure spending needed to modernise the network, which would have been impossible as a private company. Meanwhile the private operating companies have driven British rail fares to the highest per passenger mile in Europe; a further 24 per cent rise is in prospect by 2018 as grants to the rail industry are withdrawn as part of the cumulative £80 billion of spending cuts planned between now and then. This is a poll tax on wheels, an unavoidable impost that must be paid at the same rate by rich and poor alike, even though rail transport is an indispensable public service.

The Labour government's ill-fated attempt to finance the modernisation of the London Underground through a public–private partnership with two private contractors running the trains ended in a parallel disaster; it was only, again, when the public utility of the transport system was recognised by bringing the Underground back under the direction of Transport for London in 2010 that a more rational system of financing the infrastructure and organising the integrity of the system was created. By that time, the PPP 'blunder' cost UK taxpayers 'not less than about £2.5 billion and probably far, far more, possibly in the region of £20–30 billion'.[27] This is taking cashing out to new levels of extremity. Nor was it difficult to anticipate; I co-authored a report for then London mayor Ken Livingstone warning of the disaster ahead. Metronet and

Tubelines, the two proposed private operators, had far too little capital and could not finance the massive spending and borrowing that was being asked of them, the report warned; no system of contracts could capture all future eventualities; and it would obviously be cheaper for the government to borrow for investment unless there were hard, tangible benefits from the PPP arrangement that would offset the higher costs – and the proposed tests for those were far too lax.[28] Reality far outdid my worst fears.

After twenty years it is possible to make a considered judgement. Where transport is under public ownership and direction – TfL in London, Network Rail and the East Coast Mainline – it works. But the more it is privatised and corresponds to a market, the more it does not work, with deregulated bus transport the most complete example. Thus bus services in London, run and controlled by TfL, have seen fares rise broadly by the rate of inflation between 1995 and 2013: outside London, where services are deregulated and many services have become de facto monopolies, fares have climbed in real terms by 34 per cent over the same period. Over the last twenty-five years passenger volumes have doubled in London, cutting public subsidies, while passenger volumes elsewhere have declined by around a third, forcing higher subsidies. It is a mini-laboratory demonstrating the futility of applying deregulation in inappropriate markets.[29] Similarly Directly Operated Railways is the 100 per cent publicly owned company that took over the East Coast Mainline when the incompetent private operator walked away from its obligations in 2009. After five years of public ownership it is now the best-run and most efficient operator of all, making a net surplus of £16 million for the taxpayer. Its reward is to be privatised again. Meanwhile two of the three companies that own the rolling stock leased to the train-operating companies are owned in Jersey, the third is owned in Luxembourg. None shows any interest in supporting rolling-stock manufacture in the country they so casually pillage. The ultimate owners of Virgin Trains are Branson's family trusts in the Virgin Islands. All in all rail (and bus) privatisation is a salutary tale – an object lesson in how the categories into which so much thought and policy has been organised in the last thirty years are thoroughly counter-productive.

The privatisation of public space goes on apace. Gated communities and privatised shopping malls mushroom while public parks, school sports fields and recreational sports grounds are cashed out. Our museums and galleries remain free, but television and film are increasingly framed by US ownership and the demands of US audiences. The great cashing out is transforming British TV, as I trailed in Chapter 5. Almost every large British independent television producer is in foreign ownership; ITV is under threat. David Abraham, the CEO of Channel 4, told his audience in the same James MacTaggart Lecture I cited earlier that 'TV is clearly now a combat vehicle for tech and mobile companies and platforms to compete with each other rather than a sovereign industry in its own right.' American media goliaths dwarf Britain's public service broadcasters. Yet the system had 'created the best conditions for creative programme-making on the planet'. It was now in peril. British creativity risked being sacrificed for a great cashing out, at the same time as the risk capital, via the static BBC licence fee and a pressurised Channel 4, to support original British programme making was continually shrinking. Channel 5 had gone to the US, as had the former British TV production company, All3Media. 'This special landscape of ours did not happen by accident,' Abraham said. 'So we should not assume that, left purely to the market, it will continue to thrive. If you care about creativity, speak up and speak up now.

Stay silent and our special system may wither. Once gone, it will never come back.'[30]

Who has any confidence that his cry for action from our regulators and politicians will be heeded? I was concerned enough in *The State We're In*, but with the BBC now deciding that all in-house production can be contracted out, and little prospect of anything other but the income from the licence fee falling in real terms, the march to ending comprehensive public service television is all but irreversible. Indeed the Conservative party's proposal to decriminalise the non-payment of the licence fee, apparently innocent, will cost the BBC a further lost £200 million and is another nail in its coffin. Dismemberment, scaling back and partial privatisation are the next steps. British TV is set to become a variant of the US system – but, as with council house sales and building society demutualisation, this generation of producer-entrepreneurs will have made some very fat killings as public service broadcasting shrinks before our eyes.

It was equally obvious what was going to happen to pensions. 'More than ever people are on their own – left to the tender mercies of the scarcely regulated labour, capital, annuity and pension markets', I wrote in *The State We're In*.[31] Risk was being displaced from organisations capable of bearing it on to the shoulders of ordinary people who only had their own resources and little good advice. The state pension, not indexed to the growth of wages, was being allowed to become 'nugatory', as the then chief secretary to the Treasury Michael Portillo put it, so relieving pressure on state finances. In its place commission-hungry salespeople were selling indifferent, barely regulated pension saving plans that would create an indifferent fund which would buy an indifferent annuity, while little was being done to stop companies, because of the alleged expense, walking away from good defined benefit schemes that promised pensions calculably related to salaries. Anticipating what I would write twenty years later in Chapter 4 of this book, 'They don't know it yet – but the old age they face will be remarkably less affluent than that which their parents they enjoyed. For that they can thank Britain's gentlemanly capitalists and their New Right accomplices in government.'[32] It was a unilateral rewriting of Britain's social contract with the elderly.

So it has come to pass. The withering of the state pension continued until the Turner Commission on pension reform in 2005 which, brave, independently minded and with powerful analysis, proposed that it should again be indexed to the growth of real wages as a core element of everyone's retirement income – a suggestion strongly opposed by the then Chancellor Gordon Brown, who wanted to retain means-tested targeting. With great reluctance, the link to earnings was agreed but its introduction was deferred until 2012, which the incoming Coalition government (aware that older voters vote Conservative) then expanded to the so-called triple lock – that the state pension would rise by at least 2.5 per cent or either by the same amount as the CPI or earnings index, whichever was higher. At £113.10 a week in 2014 it was now barely more than nugatory, and could hardly have got much lower without pauperising the old. The Treasury would only reluctantly accept the deal if the age at which the pension would start reflected longer life expectancy – progressively raising the age threshold for eligibility for both men and women to sixty-six in 2020, sixty-seven in 2028 and sixty-eight in 2044. This was a more than reasonable demand, given the improvement in life expectancy, if it had been accompanied by a commitment to a significantly better state pension as the quid pro quo. The current arrangement, certainly better than what preceded it, is the very least the Treasury could get away with.

There were over five million adult members of defined

benefit pension schemes in the mid-1990s, and most such schemes were open to new members. Even then I was worried the system was creaking; today only two million adults are enrolled and only a fraction are open to new members, as I remarked earlier. Meanwhile the average pension pot available to buy an annuity is a tiny £35,000. Old age is going to be very much less affluent for the generation retiring after 2020. Only at the last gasp in 2014 did the government propose anything creative to stem companies' generation-long march away from supporting their former workers' pensions. It floated the possibility of creating a new form of defined benefit-scheme which would essentially allow companies to vary the promised pension downward if investment returns were to prove disappointing. This, or something similar, could have been done at any time in the last twenty years to save the company pension fund. At one stroke the great pension fund deficits, which have haunted so many companies, charities and universities as growing liabilities exceeded poorly performing assets, could have been eliminated, and workers would have had a little more certainty about their retirement incomes. In the event it proved a false dawn. Companies did not like even this watered-down idea, and it has been allowed quietly to die.

This is the opportunity for new trade unions, engaging with companies newly empowered by company law reform, to take a rounder view of their responsibilities beyond the share price. It will require both pressure from unions and a new readiness from the companies themselves to create such 'risk-sharing' pensions, but I hope if the reforms proposed in these pages were implemented that would become more likely. The cultural assumption of most management teams is that in today's labour market they don't need to offer such schemes to attract and retain workers; all the power resides with sovereign management, and escaping pension obligations has helped to boost profits, cash flow, share prices and directors' remuneration. Left to themselves in an unreformed universe, be sure that most companies will offer the cheapest pension deal they can.

It is true that life expectancy is lengthening and that investment returns have been disappointing, but a country richer than it was a generation ago is offering its elderly a much worse deal – and a deal only stopped from being much worse again by the prospect of a social crisis for the elderly. Without the intellectual courage of Adair Turner in 2005 the deal would be even worse. Alleged unaffordability has trumped inter-generational justice; the lowering of taxes has been prioritised over obligations to the retired; a know-nothing individualism and kowtowing to business have been put before any conception of a social contract. Imaginative proposals to preserve the security of retirement incomes – for example allowing companies to pay pensions later, at sixty-six or sixty-seven, in order to save the defined-benefit scheme – have been conspicuous by their absence. The managerial, financial and political establishments have simply colluded in making old people in the future relatively poorer, a grave betrayal of their duty of care. Nor can this be blamed on the European Union or foreigners. The great cashing out and the displacement of risk onto ordinary citizens is firmly home-made, a failure of our political system and of the wider public culture which allowed it to happen. So, on to the Conclusion – an examination of why our system works as it does and an assessment of the prospects for change.

Three Crises and a Conclusion

There will be no re-energising of Britain without a complete makeover of the state. It has to change from being a directive sovereign over us to a co-creator with us. Top-down directives and control from Westminster and Whitehall never did work well, but they work even less well in the wired, digitised, networked world of today. The state will continue to strategise and enable, but it will have to work through revitalised or newly invented social and public institutions that fire up the networks and occupy the territory between it and the individual. In areas like education and training or innovation, government's role is to be a co-creator with business, finance, training institutions, unions and universities of the public/private hubs and networks that will drive so much forward in the future, rather than a top-down instigator of predetermined plans. Crucially it will have to devolve power to city and local government, where this co-creation can be done more effectively, but it must also open itself up at all levels so its decision making becomes more iterative and deliberative. Just as companies are increasingly resorting to open innovation in order to minimise the chance of making costly mistakes and maximise the chance of uncovering opportunity, so government must become more open and two-way so that it is more surefooted in winning continued consent and legitimacy for its actions.

If this is one pole on which the metamorphosis must take place, another is the constant reality testing of the 'publicness' – that is to say the public character – of its actions. Government exists to create public goods which have public value for citizens. The more open and devolved the government, the more successful delivery of these goods will be, but they also must have a clear public character. Transferring public services to the private sector, either by wholesale privatisation or through contracting its delivery out to private providers, all lightly regulated to prevent overt abuse, has so much become the default model for public activity that society has almost forgotten why some functions were ever in the public sector in the first place. There needs to be a renewal of the very idea of the public domain and what are public interest outcomes, and crystal-clear clarity about the public value that government creates. After all, the public realm, and the good government that goes with it, are indispensable components of our civilisation.

There are functions and services so fundamental that society has to ensure their provision. What defines their publicness is a trinity of qualities: they must be available to all, fair to all and accountable to all, because taxation is levied to pay for them. Thus, for example, health, education, policing, trains, buses and the utilities are all by this definition public services. But there is also a public interest in, say, the universal and fair provision of news, in sharing the risks of innovation to ensure there is more of it or in creating a training ecosystem that permits mass flourishing. Thus public service broadcasting, the creation of institutions like Innovate UK and the Catapult network or the business–government–training ecosystem I proposed in Chapter 5. These all create public interest out-comes from which every citizen benefits, to which all contribute and to which all can expect access or opportunity.

This metamorphosed British state has to put the creation of public value at the heart of what it does. The process is delib-erative democracy in action. Public officials must enter a deliberative, educative discussion with citizens about their pri-orities and what they value, which a public agency – or a social institution – then tries to deliver.[1] It could involve reconfigur-ing the function of a library so it becomes a youth club as well as a library because teenagers are using the library after school; it could be the reprioritisation of what the police do; it could be rescheduling the timing of refuse collection. In each case, as the Work Foundation characterises it, the public managers seek authorisation from the public for what they are doing, measure it and then deliver it. At its most sophisticated the public agency will constantly be reality-testing what it is doing to ensure it is delivering public satisfaction. Germany's most successful football club, Bayern Munich, checks back regu-larly along these lines with its fans to decide its spending priorities, as does the German Federal Employment Agency its clients.

In Britain there was some interest in public value generation in the more creative years of the New Labour government between 2002 and Blair's resignation; so, for example, the BBC's current charter contains a commitment to create public value in its broadcasting using the methodology developed by the Work Foundation. Polls showed that if public value could be demonstrated, a majority of the public would be ready to pay an even higher licence fee.[2] But although the BBC talked the talk, and even used some of the methodology to measure the impact of varying services, it was wary that the results of deliberative democracy might differ from the choices of its commissioning editors. It never systematically used the approach to decide on what programmes its audiences preferred, or to justify the choices it made. Before the ongoing ideological onslaught – despite its excellence and the high regard in which it is held by audiences – it has constantly been on the back foot without any systematic defence. Today it is running up the white flag and disbanding its in-house content-production capability, as I remarked in the last chapter, along with all the training that went with it. It is certainly not fighting for public service broadcasting via a public value test. It was a lost opportunity.

For if public bodies do not dare to show they are generating public value, the game is up. It is imperative to ensure that the public agree such bodies are discharging activity that it considers properly public. It will also make it more certain that they are doing the right thing as effectively and efficiently as possible.[3] This was always vital, but it is even more so in today's atmosphere, in which the cultural assumption is that the state is bound to cock it up, a belief fanned by conservatives anxious to shrink the state as a matter of principle. On top there is the populist writing off of politicians as self-interested charlatans – a belief inflamed by the expenses scandal. In this atmosphere notions of the public interest and public service are always set back. Middle-class dinner tables take it as a starting point that taxes surrendered to government can be better spent by the taxed individuals or companies; avoiding taxes thus becomes a duty and evading taxes morally understandable.

Scepticism about government runs deep. When given the chance to vote for mayors or regional government, or even a more representative voting system, most voters have been at best apathetic or at worst actively hostile. It was remarkable that Londoners voted three to one in favour in the referendum to establish a London mayor in 1998; almost every subsequent referendum proposing constitutional change, from regional government in 2004 to a more proportional voting system in 2012, has been lost. Only two cities – Bristol and Liverpool – of the twelve invited voted for the principle of mayor in 2012. A programme like that set out in Chapters 5 and 6 is very much harder to initiate because the state that will launch it is so distrusted. Which is why successful reform must be predicated on ensuring that the state delivering that reform is as smart, responsive and alert to creating public value as possible.

This is a huge challenge in Britain, cursed as it is with state structures that are essentially monarchical in character and which politicians, once elected, essentially take over and run in the same discretionary, centralised power-hoarding way as a monarch. As I wrote in *The State We're In*, Britain has never had a comprehensive discussion about how it is governed or set down the principles in a written constitution. It has just grown up over the centuries, making, as Tom Paine famously argued, adaptations of the monarchical state created by the Normans in 1066.[4] Control the House of Commons and elected politicians control the state *in toto*. They control the executive, the legislature, every administrative component of the country and to a degree the judiciary, rather as William the Conqueror did. The House of Commons is a cipher; the role of the average backbench MP is to be lobby fodder in the hope of preferment or to live a life of political disappointment. These powerful governments make everyone wary and apprehensive. They can exercise their discretionary power to do daft things because there is too little requirement for ideas to be challenged, discussed and road-tested before they are launched. Thus, for example, Andrew Lansley's now widely derided health reforms, opening the door for systemic cherry-picking of the NHS by large corporations, or the Department of Work and Pensions' commitment to introducing the inoperable universal

credit – and before them New Labour's attachment to the economically irrational private finance initiative, or its commitment
to a self-defeating war in Iraq that the public, if not the fawning
courtiers adorning Tony Blair's sofa, knew was ill-founded and
could only go wrong. There is no countervailing power, apart
from criticism from the opposition, within the state. Yet democratically elected politicians want to take initiatives because
that shows they are governing, advancing their narrative, justifying being elected, and hopefully being re-elected and
appeasing a media that is hungry for every offence, large and
small, to be immediately redressed. The people are properly
suspicious.

But, paradoxically, all this power avails the centre less than it
should. Precisely because there are no formal mechanisms for
co-creation, iteration and sharing of power that might force
deliberation, the system has developed mechanisms for self-
protection – a form of passive but nonetheless effective
defensiveness. Departments are run as organisational monarchical fiefdoms that are practised at making the implementation of
every centralised proposal they don't like as difficult as possible.
Civil servants feel they have to be custodians of an impartial
public interest because it is palpably obvious that their ministers,
responding to the dictates of day-to-day party management, are
not – a state of affairs that creates frustration and distrust on
both sides. In any case, to get anything substantive done
requires cross-departmental dialogue, and the assent of both the
Treasury and Number 10; as every insider testifies, getting
everything into line is time-consuming and often proves impossible. The whole process is patrolled by an under-resourced but
over-mighty Treasury with high staff turnover (its officials are
thirty-two years old on average), which has seen so many blunders that its scepticism over public spending, especially on
capital projects, has become pathological.[5] Thus the British

state – underinvesting, over-centralised, blundering and too little capable of creating public value. It is a state structure that makes advancing the public interest close to impossible.

Exploiting three crises to revive the public realm

There needs to be a wholesale structural and democratic over-haul of the state. The outlines are fairly obvious. New life has to be breathed into our democracy by reasserting the importance and value of public activity, and thus the importance of citizens' voices and votes in what takes place. In turn, public activity at local and central level has to re-earn its legitimacy by overtly and continuously committing to create public value, which itself will open up new avenues for citizens to express themselves and vote. This new culture must inform central government, especially the Treasury – which is the over-powerful heart of the centralised state and needs to be broken up. There must be a new deal for our nations, cities, counties and towns so they are accorded the competence to govern themselves.

All this depends on establishing a new legitimacy for the concept of taxation, and a more rational and fair design for the tax system. If citizens are to play a more active role in a society of mass flourishing, then they need to be equipped with infor-mation they can trust. Our media has to be held to account for misinformation and falsehood. The makeover of the public domain must include ensuring the accountability of all its actors – from the humblest local government official to the loftiest editor.

There is support to build on. Amid the distrust of the public sector there is also grudging acceptance of its role. The NHS, as I reported in the last chapter, is the most efficient health

organisation among countries with health services of parallel
size; this is understood, and the institution is loved – recall
Danny Boyle's celebrated tribute to the NHS in the opening
ceremony of the 2012 Olympic Games. HMRC costs eighty
pence for every £100 of tax raised – an astonishingly low ratio.[6]
Public health programmes have reduced the incidence of
infectious disease and without the timely intervention of the
state, Rolls-Royce in the early 1970s and the banking system
more recently would have gone bust. The public knows this. In
general it has little trust in the media for news and information,
but it does exempt the BBC. And while politicians are held in
near-contempt, turnout in general elections though falling consistently is still remarkably high – and the trend capable of
being turned round. When a politician comes along who looks
genuine, the public are ready to believe her or him. There is
still a revivable view that politics is a noble art; we don't want
to hold our politicians in such low esteem. We would like to
have a different relationship with those we elect.

But it is crises that propel change; and in the late 1990s
crises seemed theoretical rather than real. Today few would say
that. First, there is the rise of the SNP and UKIP. Scotland did
vote to remain part of the UK, with 55 per cent voting No in
the historic 18 September 2014 referendum, but at times
during the campaign it looked a close-run thing – with one
opinion poll ten days beforehand even registering a narrow
lead for the Yes campaign. Unless the country moves to a
proper federal structure, breaking up the monarchical state and
devolving democracy in all its manifestations to its constituent
parts, the next vote will be lost. Scotland must be a country
within a federal Britain: no more – no less. Equally the rise of
UKIP, coming first in the European elections of 2014, and
following through with remarkably high voting shares in a
succession of by-elections, is tapping a well of discontent and

disaffection from those parts of the country that the current economic and political order so palpably neglects. Britain has to find a better way of doing democracy, of creating wealth and sharing it around the country more equally and of organising its social settlement, otherwise it will not only leave the EU, it will find itself repudiating so much of what so many hold dear in the name of a right-wing populism.

Second, the Conservative party's exploitation of the legacy of the banking crisis to impose centralised spending cuts of an unprecedented degree, while refusing to redesign the tax system, widen the tax base or increase rates, has raised fundamental questions about the state's capacity to deliver public goods, justice and equity. Third, there is a collapse of trust. Neither the state, with a growing apparatus consecrated to unaccountable surveillance of the individual, nor the unaccountable media, too freely manipulating information, unfairly reporting and disregarding privacy, inspire confidence that we live in a society founded on respect. Each is creating a crisis. But each is creating an accompanying opportunity.

Crisis one – Scotland forces a new federalism

Britain accords less decision-making and less tax-raising power to authorities beyond the centre than any other leading advanced country. A miserable, token 5 per cent of total taxation is raised locally.[7] Seventy per cent of all public spending is controlled by central government, and local government has almost no discretion over the balance of spending that is formally directed through it.[8] Indeed local government is so little valued that current local spending cumulatively will have fallen by over two-fifths between 2010 and 2018 – and capital spending by approaching 60 per cent.[9] Sir Albert Bore, chief executive of

Birmingham Council, says for example that by 2018 Birmingham will have cut an extraordinary 60 per cent of its controllable budget over eight years, so that many services usually provided by the council will simply have to cease. Job losses will climb to over 10,000 – the equivalent of two car plants the size of Longbridge being closed.[10] It was telling that Sir Merrick Cockell, Conservative chair of the Local Government Association (LGA), in June 2013 described the whole top-down approach of handing down such savage cuts from the centre with no consultation as 'feudal', warning that services will be stretched to breaking point.[11] The baleful consequences for our undernourished towns and cities are there for all to see: there are too few expressions of civic pride, little local individualism and scant support for local, intermediate economic and social institutions. Underfunded and overstretched town halls in large parts of the country preside over local economies whose private sector has been denuded to the extent that it provides little more than the foundations of life – utilities, retailing, petrol distribution; and is matched by a public sector that does the same in education, policing, health and welfare. This is the so-called 'foundation economy'.[12] The instruments that might allow local communities to energise their stagnant private sector are not allowed to exist; even Local Enterprise Partnerships have comically few resources. Karel Williams, author of the concept of the foundation economy, suggests that one means of reviving local energy and empowering local business would be to create a system of social licences for both foundational public and private activity, which could then be allocated to local business – but even that is impossible because local government is so powerless.

Local government is no longer even in control of the look and scale of its public spaces, let alone the overall neighbourhood. Without its own capacity to tax and borrow, its only tool is its powers over planning, attempting to strike bargains with private developers in return for planning consent that might achieve some public goals within a private project. Even here its room for manoeuvre is under assault, with a persistent reduction of its powers to challenge developers and, within planning law, to prioritise the use of land or space for public or social purpose.[13] European architects who work in both Britain and mainland Europe despair at our impoverished, weak municipal authorities.[14] Local authorities are unable to deliver buildings, parks and a wider urban ambience with a social and public ethos compared with those in Europe; the Swiss, hardly tribunes of the left, have a strong civic tradition and fabulously liveable cities. The robbing of the local of the capacity to shape its own destiny is a form of internal colonialism.

The need to empower our regions, towns and cities has been obvious for decades. The Layfield Report into local government in 1976 argued that Britain should either go the whole hog and make local government little more than the arm of central government, or properly empower local communities to spend, tax and borrow on their own account (within constraints) and shape their local area. It preferred the second option; its recommendations were buried. A generation later Sir Michael Lyons was asked the same question, and his 2007 report came up with the same answer: local authorities should be 'place-shapers'. He argued for more flexibility and autonomy over tax, in particular over council tax, and like Layfield suggested a local income tax. His report too was buried. The City Growth Commission, reporting in October 2014, made similar and no less imaginative proposals. Constitutional reformers, notably Charter 88 in their call for a comprehensive written constitution, have made local empowerment a key platform for reform. They too have been ignored. There has been the Local Government Association's consistent plea for a better deal, most recently expressed in its manifesto, *Rewiring Public Services*, published in July 2013. Again, it has been consistently ignored. New Labour did manage to establish devolution for Scotland and Wales, and set up the London mayor and London Assembly – but the amount of power transferred was minimal, with control over levels of spending, taxation and borrowing held tightly by the Treasury.

The Coalition government passed a localism bill which largely dodged the vital question of resources, trying to entrench the Conservative assumption that even in local government the principle should be a smaller public realm, fewer public goods and as little public initiative as possible. Even local powers to plan and shape a local area were further removed – an odd agenda for so-called localists. When in 2012, as observed earlier in the chapter, only two English cities voted for mayors in local referendums as provided for under the Act, a Conservative apologist could argue this was an endorsement of the party's endemic suspicion of government, local government included. But the success of the London mayor and events in Scotland are beginning to move even apathetic English opinion.

Scotland may have voted to say No to secession and decided to stay in the Union, but the strength of the Yes vote and the vigour of its campaign was a profound shock to centrist Westminster and Whitehall. The Scots had achieved what well-argued reports or the pleas of English local government over a generation for a better deal could not. It dramatised that the system was working so badly that the UK might break up. After all, the Scottish Nationalists' argument was that Scotland would never get the autonomy it needed within the framework of the current UK state or any modified variant. Genuine devolution from the 'Westminster' elite was impossible because the UK as a centralised polity could not offer the federalism of the US or

Germany, even if it were minded to do so. In any case England is so overwhelmingly large, with ten times the population of Scotland, that it would overwhelm any federal structure: and the solution of breaking it up into smaller self-governing regions to give more balance was impossible because there was no regional tradition on which to build. An artificial North-West or Midlands region is in any case not comparable to Scotland with its traditions of being a nation. Nor were the English going to embrace an English parliament; the House of Commons was their parliament, so there would always be junior parliaments in Scotland, Wales and Northern Ireland and the Big Brother sovereign parliament in Westminster – creating an asymmetry of power and legitimacy that makes a mockery of federalism. As for the idea that the House of Lords could democratically transmute into a senate to incorporate the federal constituents of the country along the lines of the US Senate or German Bundesrat – forget it! Only full Scottish independence, argued the SNP, would deliver the necessary capability to govern itself – painful though divorce would be.

This is a challenge that must now be met. By the standards of the rest of the UK, Scotland is a paragon of devolved government, in full control of half its spending, including that on health, education and policing, with the power to amend UK income tax and a wide range of legislative possibilities. But by the standards of an American state or German *Land* – or even of city government anywhere in the OECD – its powers are at the low end of the scale. All three mainstream British political parties offered yet more power over taxation and social security after the referendum in order to stem the SNP's advance. They were right – but to work, this must be part of a wider constitutional settlement. Britain's ancient unitary state, still monarchical not just in formal shape but in function, has to reform itself. There can be no more fudges to keep the

32-year-olds in the Treasury in control of the shape of the British economy and society. If Britain does not try to find its way to a more federal structure that works, expect the disintegration of the UK within the next twenty years. The SNP has been bested for the moment, but anybody who underestimates the force of its appeal should be disabused. There will be much mourning for the energy it unleashed – and envy from the rest of the UK about the even greater powers that Scotland will acquire.

There is a series of interlocking moves that should be made. First the Treasury should be disbanded into three essential parts.[15] The budgetary, economic forecasting and management functions need to be split out; English dimensions should be run by a new Prime Minister's department and where possible delegated to the new city regions, while all the functions relating to Scotland, Wales and Northern Ireland should be moved to create parallel first minister departments with complete discretion over all dimensions of domestic spending, borrowing and taxation. All aspects of English financial, regulatory and industrial policy functions would go to the Department of Business, Innovation and Skills to become a Growth Department, with analogous departments being created in Edinburgh, Cardiff and Belfast. Only international financial, global tax and debt management, co-ordination of the issues of bonds and debt by the varying arms of the federal state, and the setting of tax rates, transfers and spending envelopes, would be retained as the functions of what would now be a finance ministry. Scotland, Wales and Northern Ireland would now be in charge of health, education, housing, environment and policing with only the necessary functions of standard setting and oversight retained in London.

Cities and towns would be given the kinds of powers advocated by *Rewiring Public Services* and the City Growth

Commission.[16] Thus, as they recommend, local government should be able to budget over rolling three-year cycles for all the public activity in a locality in a single unified budget without being micro-managed by Whitehall. It should be given enhanced revenue-raising powers, allowing it to set local business and income taxes. It should be able to issue municipal bonds, and should be in charge of whatever should properly be devolved to it – from training to planning – as set out in Lord Heseltine's growth review. It should be the local champion of the consumer and citizen. A vibrant British economy and society, declare the core cities group, depends on a vibrant Manchester, Leeds, Birmingham, Sheffield, Bristol, Nottingham, Newcastle, Liverpool and Glasgow. All have the capacity to become smart cities capitalising on the new importance of intangibles and creating the frameworks that boost creativity and innovation; but that means they must have delegated power. They want to become the conduit for a major programme of national infrastructure and investment spending aimed at redressing the massive imbalance between London and the rest of the country, This, with their autonomy constitutionally entrenched as Scotland's is, would be the means to that end.

One last innovation would cement the federal settlement.[17] The House of Lords would be reconstituted as an elected senate with a balanced membership to reflect the new federal constitution. All the country's city regions would be represented, including Glasgow, Cardiff, Edinburgh and Belfast; English counties would send a couple of members each. It would be a proper second chamber, with full revising powers and a membership that reflected the character of the country rather than the accidents of birth and political patronage.[18] It would, as at present, have no power over budgetary questions, which would reside with the House of Commons and the various city and national assemblies.

The last matter is the so-called West Lothian question: what voting rights should Scottish, Welsh and Northern Irish MPs elected to the House of Commons have over domestic measures that will apply only to England? Conservatives will press for the House of Commons to transmute into a de facto English parliament, creating a second-class tier of Scottish, Welsh and Northern Irish MPs with no votes over English issues, which would become the preserve of English MPs, of whom Conservatives confidently expect they would represent a near-permanent majority. Although superficially fair, with Prime Minister David Cameron promising to address the issue of English votes for English laws, this would be a category error. First of all Britain's is the most prestigious and long-standing parliament in the world, and it cannot be taken away from Scotland, Wales and Northern Ireland and co-opted for narrow English concerns, in effect to sustain Conservative hegemony in England. In any case an enormous amount of legislation remains national. For example, almost the entire shopping list of reforms advocated in Chapters 5 and 6 of this book – from company, finance and innovation reform to the defence of public service broadcasting and the BBC – are national and remain undevolved. Even the proposed devolved spending, taxing and borrowing powers would be powers to deviate from nationally decided norms. To disenfranchise Scottish, Welsh and Northern Irish MPs and make them second class on a false prospectus is a recipe for breaking up the union. In any case the number of issues relating purely only to England in any parliamentary year are in a minority – generally restricted to some health, education and welfare issues but even then not all. mySociety finds that of 5000 votes in the House of Commons between 1997 and 2014 only 21 depended on the votes of Scottish MPs. The 2013 McKay Commission was set up precisely to examine the question.

Remarking that since 1919 there have only been two brief periods – 1964–6 and February to October 1974 – when a government has relied on the votes of Scottish MPs, the report firmly repudiated the creation of a balkanised parliament of MPs with different voting rights. But acknowledging the strong English sense of grievance as Scotland acquires more powers, it proposed developing the existing conventions of the House of Commons to address the question. Part of the Queen's Speech should be devoted to English-only issues, it recommended, which after agreement by a Grand Committee, the bill would be considered as it progressed through report stage, second and third readings only by English MPs. Full parliamentary assent, however, would require the vote of every MP from every part of the country.

The choice is stark. Either Britain lives with a compromise along these lines, while giving powers to English local government and its important cities that are analogous to those of the nations, so that in effect English democracy will be equal, and by accepting the few problematic areas sustains the union. Or Britain sets up an English assembly based outside London in, say, Manchester to match the Scottish and Welsh assemblies. This has its logic – but it would always be a cipher assembly sitting in the shadow of the House of Commons. The only course is to empower English local government, break up the Treasury, reshape the House of Lords and implement the McKay Commission and live with the necessary compromise given that England is ten times larger than Scotland but wants it to continue to be in the UK. This will not give the Tories the 'control' they want but it will keep Britain together. Messy perhaps, but then so is the British constitution.

Along with these structural changes, new technologies should be enlisted to put the creation of public value at the forefront of political debate. Chat rooms, online dialogue, and indicative polling should all be used in an effort to keep in constant touch with citizens' wishes. The new federal constitution should oblige all departments and public bodies to use public value as a metric to support budget setting and resource allocation. Publicness should be at the heart of public activity. In my review of public sector pay I proposed that leadership teams in the public sector put some of their pay at risk to be earned back around simple, easily understandable performance metrics – and that only when those were achieved should executives be eligible for a bonus.[19] The necessary pay metrics are obvious. Public officials throughout the federal UK should be rewarded for the public value they create – and penalised for the value they don't. There is no need to turn over our public assets to any old profit-maximising corporation, or contract out everything to the careless attentions of public service contractors. Rather we should affirm the imperative of public value generation as the animating value in our public and social intermediate institutions – and as the precondition for revitalising them. All that is required is belief, and the willingness to reform the state to deliver the results – not privatise it. Scotland will thus have triggered enormous change. Britain will have the institutions that will not only keep it together – but will ensure that together it prospers.

Crisis two – The end of the road for book-keeping as economic policy

The Chancellor's Autumn Statement of 2013 was a shocking event. It was not the plan to reach a balanced budget in 2018/19 that shocked. Rather it was that the entire burden was to be shouldered by cuts in public spending amounting to a cumulative £75 billion. Only 0.1 per cent of GDP is to be raised in taxation – and in any case this will mainly be achieved by small and hard-to-assess measures on tax avoidance and the taxation of non-residents which in any case are to be given away in compensating tax cuts. The impact will be devastating. On average, estimates the Office of Budget Responsibility (OBR), per capita spending on public services will have fallen 23 per cent between 2007/8 and 2018/19.[20] But because health is completely protected (as is overseas aid) and education and defence spending partially protected, the cuts elsewhere are close to incredible. Spending on the criminal justice system and local government will have fallen cumulatively by over 30 and 40 per cent respectively, as cited earlier in the book. Similar decreases are planned for environment, agriculture, tourism, culture and sport. From flood defences to class sizes, from the capabilities of our regulators to the effectiveness of our police, from assistance to the elderly to the quality of our performing arts – everything is under threat. Welfare spending is to be capped at just over £100 billion. In sum, as both the Institute for Fiscal Studies and the Office of Budget Responsibility confirm, spending on public services and administration as a proportion of GDP will be back at the levels of 1948[21] – indeed on some data back to 1938.[22]

The story is that this is all in support of 'hard-working' people, in order to freeze their tax burden, as the Treasury declares on its webpage – bizarrely reducing the central institution of the state to a mouthpiece of Tory Central Office. The assumption is that the public and social institutions built up over the last seventy years are unnecessary, and that they are held in the same contempt by 'hard-working' people as they are by a highly ideological Tory party. It is a bet that only politicians insulated from the reality across Britain could make.

What is happening is that, notwithstanding the many options, the Conservative leadership simply refuses to consider raising more taxation on property, business, inherited estates or the rich. For the same ideological reasons, there can be no increase in the income tax rate. Once tax revenues have been forecast, with no increase in tax rates, broadening of the base or wider reform, then – given the target of producing budget balance in 2018/19 – the level of public spending is computed as what is left: the residual, in the jargon.[23] With the ring-fencing of the NHS and the legal necessity to pay benefits, like pensions, that are earned as entitlements, along with some smaller protection for education and defence, what follows is as described earlier: the unprotected departments and the broader welfare budget are left to take whatever accounting adjustment follows.

There is no consideration of need, justice, equity, necessary infrastructure investment or any dimension of public value. This is just a form of book-keeping enforced by an institution dedicated to – and very effective at – financial control. Public spending – far from being out of control – has consistently come in under budget since the Coalition took office.[24] What has undershot is tax revenues – partly because the economy has proved weaker than expected, with wages growing less rapidly than prices, and partly because of the fixed idea that tax cuts fire up enterprise, stimulate more growth than public spending and are morally virtuous, giving back to people money that is already theirs.

Chancellor Osborne has thus taken every opportunity to cut corporation tax and the business rate rather than spend the equivalent on ensuring a reduction in carbon emissions, additional infrastructure or innovation. Although he has pronounced against tax avoidance, closing down some of the more arcane ruses and the secret use of Swiss bank accounts, he has been careful not to push his reforming zeal too far. Richard Brooks in *The Great Tax Robbery* has described how Britain does not tax the worldwide earnings of UK-based multinationals and, by continuing to indulge a network of tax havens despite calls for more transparency, is incapable of challenging the many technical schemes by which companies, especially foreign companies and individuals, pay little or no UK tax – and how the deal is sealed by persistently under-funding and under-resourcing HMRC's tax inspectors. The rich home-grown elite use the same ruses to write their own tax rules, preserving their ducal estates or protecting the income streams they gain from once public assets in overseas tax havens.

Ideology, blind faith and an overpowerful Ministry for Book-keeping – aka the Treasury – are governing Britain. It is not economics that dictates these choices. The IMF, after assessing the experience between 1980 and 2012 of 107 countries where growth has been constrained by banks reining back on lending after a financial crisis, finds that spending cuts are the least appropriate way to reduce the resulting budget deficit. Interest rate reductions and monetary policy are necessarily ineffective in promoting growth after a credit crunch: growth, after all, is the best context to cut public spending. After a credit crunch the private sector is reducing its own debts by deleveraging. As a result public spending cuts are particularly damaging. Instead they should be avoided as far as possible and a balance struck between tax increases and spending reductions to lower the deficit.[25] If British officials knew of this work, they did not allow it to impact on policy which has proceeded on the opposite and inane assumption. After all, public spending, particularly on infrastructure, has a doubly beneficial effect on growth: first, it creates additional demand which does not leak into imports as tax cuts do; and secondly the infrastructure itself enhances growth. More efficient transport, energy networks, roads, ports, bridges, dams, flood prevention, etc., help growth; it also affords the opportunity to incorporate energy efficiency and lower pollution – a step change in the struggle to contain climate change. Public borrowing at historically low interest rates to finance infrastructure spending when the economy is running below the capacity, as it is at present, is just very good economics: the IMF in its 2014 World Economic Outlook suggested that every dollar so invested increases output by three dollars so that in effect, taking the tax yield into account, infrastructure investment in times of weak growth essentially pays for itself. It is, as Professor Larry Summers has argued, a free lunch crucial in the wake of a credit crunch – a way for the government to strengthen its own finances and the economy alike.[26]

This has never washed with the book-keeper in chief: it was the Treasury that wanted the M25 to have only two lanes, and over the decades it has opposed the building of the M1 and Crossrail; it is now opposed to HS2. It has a deeply embedded anti-investment, anti-infrastructure culture – and is perfectly comfortable with putting targets for debt and deficits first and tax cuts second, with public spending to create public benefit, public goods and vital infrastructure being cast as the residual. Indeed Osborne's system of public accounting, disallowing the separation of investment projects to be funded by public borrowing, actively cements this self-harming approach to fiscal and economic policy. For example, infrastructure spending is to be financed off the public sector's balance sheet by pension funds and insurance companies that are not willing to do it at sufficient scale. Any ambition to lift research and development spending to the benchmark 3 per cent of GDP spent by the world's best, advocated in Chapter 5, can be abandoned. Britain is to stay in the lower division. These are deep-set institutional biases – not the result of economics.

The hysteria over the level of national debt compounds the irrationality. The national debt has been proportionally higher for most of the last three hundred years, with the low national debt in the three decades before the First World War and the three decades up to the financial crisis the exception rather than the rule.[27] Otherwise public debt levels have been higher. Moreover Britain is lucky in that its public debt is on average held in long-term bonds redeemable on average over fourteen years, and that a strikingly high proportion is held by British savings and investment institutions – which reduces the country's vulnerability to a sell-off from panicky international investors. With interest rates at a 300-year low, the country emphatically does not have a public debt crisis. It can comfortably service the stock of national debt and issue new debt at a pace it considers creates the proper trade-off between getting its budget deficit under control and sustaining economic growth. Nor is spending out of control. The entire discourse justifying the scale of public spending austerity is manufactured to serve the ideological end of shrinking the state.

The result is that Britain's public fabric and social settlement are being torn up at a rate that cannot be sustained. The speed and savagery with which public spending on crucial services like the criminal justice system, local government and the environment is being cut can and must be moderated. For the first time since the war an under-resourced British Army has suffered reverses, in both Iraq and Afghanistan: crude austerity is now weakening our security. Fiscal policy must be recast. Corporate welfare spending, totalling £85 billion, as cited earlier in Chapter 3, should take its proportional share of any cuts along with the proposed cuts in welfare spending on the disadvantaged. The demands of fairness, the need to reduce inequality and the imperative of boosting revenues means there must be an increase in tax revenues. I have already suggested that there should be a revaluation of British property, currently set at 1991 levels, to today's values. Alongside this there should be a radical reshaping of the council tax to make it more progressive, starting at higher values and continuing right up the property ladder with more bands. In addition there is no reason why foreigners should be excused property tax. Corporation tax is so low that foreign companies are taking over British companies artificially to move their headquarters here – a new gold rush and a needless transfer of the control of British corporate assets overseas. Financial services have been excluded from VAT; they should pay tax on the value they add. The VAT base should be broadened. Lord Nicholas Stern estimates that broadening the VAT base to include financial services, reforming council tax and introducing taxes on environmental pollution would together raise 2 per cent of GDP[28] – and that is before any additional extension and raising of, say, inheritance tax, capital gains tax, corporation and income tax rates.

For example, inheritance tax is not a death tax, as conservative apologists insist, deterring enterprise and initiative because the chief impulse of any entrepreneur is to pass his or her wealth on to their children. It is, as argued earlier, a 'we share in your good luck' tax, the fairest tax of all. The entrepreneur does not pay the tax; her children do, who have done nothing to deserve their inheritance except pop out of the right loins. If they want to exercise the product of their brute good luck in society, they should pay their proper dues – not even half of the legacy, but some useful fraction of it. Almost every society on earth has required such a due: only today's conservatives have had the brass neck to argue that wealth should be dynastic, with no obligation to the wider community in which the lucky inheritors spend it.

But, comes the counter-argument again, the top 1 per cent pay a third of all income tax and so deliver at least their fair share of taxation. They should not be 'penalised' any more. The proper retort is that it is right they should pay disproportionately more, because they are paid disproportionately more – and that focusing on income tax ignores the way the wider system is organised to allow them to protect their wealth. Income tax constitutes only 25 per cent of all tax revenue. The mass of the population pay VAT, excise duties and national insurance which contributes another 45 per cent. Taxes on property, companies, wealth, inheritance and capital gains have shrunk consistently. The burden of paying for public goods such as education, health and housing is increasingly shouldered by average taxpayers, who don't have the wherewithal to sustain them. There is thus a twofold undermining of the tax system: because the rich don't pay their share, the average pay disproportionately more than they should, so they add their voice to the calls for a smaller state and lower taxation. But we need public goods, public services and public investment. Taxation is the down payment for these goods and the civilisation that goes with them. Mass flourishing, great infrastructure and frontier innovation have to be paid for.

To remove some of the burden of lowering the structural deficit from spending cuts alone, and at the same time to find the wherewithal to fund the improvements advocated in this book – boosting R&D, increasing infrastructure spending, establishing flexi-security, investing properly in training and achieving the audacious goals proposed for innovation – would together cost some 3 per cent of GDP in increased tax revenues, built up gradually over the life of a parliament or longer depending on how the economy performs. These would come from higher taxes on wealth, business and property, from ending the UK's tax haven status, broadening the VAT base and taxing polluters. Revenue as a share of GDP would rise, but at below 40 per cent of GDP it would still be at the low end of the EU average – below that of the original six founder members and well below that of the Nordic countries. Conservative critics will complain that the aim is impossible and will damage Britain's 'tax competiveness'; but it is much more feasible, and fairer, than cumulatively cutting £75 billion from spending over four years. Britain should not be leading a race to the bottom, indulging in a competition to achieve ever-lower tax rates; but neither should tax rates be fixed at a point where they act as deterrents and potential disincentives.

At the same time fiscal policy should be reorganised. The aim should be to balance current public spending and public revenues over the economic cycle, but raising tax rates and revenue along with moderating spending cuts so that the burden of lowering the deficit is more fairly shared. Public goods, whether justice or infrastructure, matter; reducing the deficit cannot be so indiscriminate, given the affordability of Britain's national debt, that these become so cruelly neglected. Borrowing for capital investment should be allowed and boosted. This would represent a decisive shift in Britain's economic priorities and approach: but the attempt to return to business as niggardly, book-keeping usual after the profound shock of the financial crisis is a first-order strategic error. Britain can be re-energised. Don't do it and it's more of the same.

Crisis three – Conservatism hits the buffers

Over the centuries British conservatism has been more wrong than right. It is fine to promote self-betterment, to champion society's little platoons (as conservative philosopher Edmund Burke dubbed the subdivisions of society), to defend the primacy of family, to respect tradition, to accept hierarchy, to believe in punitive punishment and to distrust the state.[29] But these are prejudices rather than a coherent political philosophy. They do not begin to grapple with the role and importance of justice and equity in human affairs, the complexity of the inter-dependencies and reciprocal obligations that define society or the necessary and iterative relationship between public and private. In conservatism's canon public is simply bad and private – the domain of the little platoons and individual self-betterment – necessarily good. Through the appeasement of its prejudices conservatism can boast of a long and lengthening list of disasters, from the unthinking sale of five million council houses without building replacements to the condition of our prisons, from the near-breakdown of England's relationship with Scotland and Europe to the very real threat of imminent power blackouts as long-term investment for energy generation has been undermined by excessive reliance on market forces and the delusion that cheap gas is for ever. Common-sense establishment opinion may worry whether the economy was and is safe with the Labour party. Now common-sense mainstream establishment opinion wonders whether the state is safe in the hands of the Conservative party.

For most of the twentieth century the rise of socialism excused Conservatives from having to wrestle with the dilemmas that resulted from being the party that represented the least generous and most repressive human instincts, because socialism made far bigger and more dangerous errors. Toryism, which for most of the eighteenth and nineteenth centuries had been the party of the county and shire, suspicious of modernity in all its guises – resisting the widening of the franchise, opposed to free trade, doubtful about mass education, sceptical about the fruits of science and invention, hostile to the industrial revolution and the railway – was given the chance to reinvent itself with the rise of the Labour party at home and communism abroad, along with the accompanying collapse of the Liberal party.

Conservatism became the broad-church, non-socialist party,

combining the merits of practical common sense with owner-
ship of all the important signifiers that a Conservative was at
the pinnacle of society – accent, country houses, the events of
the English summer like Ascot or Wimbledon. Many former
Liberal MPs, like Winston Churchill, became Conservatives.
This fusion with the liberal tradition allowed the party to
become the one-nation party Disraeli had wanted it to be.
Harold Macmillan could champion the middle way; Michael
Heseltine fought his first parliamentary seat as a National
Liberal in alliance with the Tories. These broad-church Tories
embodied a non-socialist idea of Britain as the defender of
both enterprise and the country's core institutions before the
socialist challenge. They accepted the necessity for a
sufficiently activist state which discharged its obligations to
the less well-off in a Labour-designed social settlement, living
with the justice and equity it contained because that was the
price of social peace and winning elections.

But unlike German Christian Democrats or Eisenhower
Republicans, Britain's Tories were never the wholehearted
allies of industry, innovation and technology; nor were they
willing to subordinate the City and finance determinedly to
drive British companies forward. They saw no need to build
institutions that would support a more productive, innovative
capitalism. They were gentlemanly capitalists happy to live
on the bounty of two centuries of empire. They defined the
political and economic problem as the Labour party and trade
unions, rather than the City and the deep dysfunctions in the
way British companies were owned and their lack of investment and innovation.

Margaret Thatcher's genius was to use the language of the
then fashionable free market to combine Tory prejudices
into what seemed like a coherent philosophy and then use it
to slay traditional Tory enemies – unions and nationalised

industries – while boosting old allies in the City of London. She could use the prestige of her party as a party for all the nation instead to engage in a highly divisive and destructive economic and social programme. The intellectual tide, generated in right-wing think tanks in the US and aggressively proselytised by Britain's overwhelmingly right-wing press, was running in her direction. It seemed to have initial success, but – as detailed in these pages – we now know it to be another Conservative wrong turning, ranking with the biggest of them all. The simultaneous deregulation of the labour and financial markets, with no thought for equity, justice or the complexity of the relationships between society, work and business, was to be a major contributory cause of the financial crisis and all that followed from it. We now have a 30/30/40 society, a slow-growing economy, decreased social mobility and a country at odds with itself. The great cashing out – the selling of our utilities, our great companies, and swathes of property in our cities to foreigners – in the name of privatisation, wealth generation and being open for business has availed us little. The current Conservative strategy sustains the framework. The reduction of the deficit and debt is the growth policy – essentially shrinking the state even more aggressively than Lady Thatcher would have dared, while promoting surely the last of Britain's traditional credit and property booms. It has achieved neither sustainable growth nor the prospect of mass flourishing.

The disaffection of so many Scottish voters – and of English voters in English cities – has reduced the Conservative party to the party of the outer English suburb and shire. It was notable that despite David Cameron's attempt to modernise his party and give it a liberal conservative veneer – defending the NHS, promoting the Big Society, boosting the aid budget, being green, not talking endlessly about Europe – the Tories could only win 35 per cent of the vote in the 2010 general election. The press threw its collective weight behind him, as did the financial and business community; the Labour government was self-evidently exhausted and Prime Minister Brown widely disliked. Yet even in these circumstances the Tories could not win a parliamentary majority. The legacy of the Thatcher years remained toxic.

In reaction, the broad Conservative church is now suffering a schism. The libertarian wing wants to use its many sympathisers in the selection committees of what are in effect rotten boroughs to select eurosceptic libertarians, take over the party and use the machinery of the Tory hegemony – the inbuilt advantage of being funded by the offshore rich, the ruthless Toryism of the press and the remnants of its reputation as a common-sense national party – to drive home an ultra-Thatcherite agenda in common cause with UKIP. Britain will leave the EU, consolidate its position as a tax haven, shrink the state further and become a low-tax, free market paradise for the world's rich and multinationals. The dwindling group of modernisers, aware that the City and business see important advantages in EU membership, uneasy about the growth of inequality and doubtful that growth will happen so spontaneously, are more keenly aware that such a programme – even with the Conservatives' embedded advantages – is unlikely to command a majority. It is more likely to leave the Tories permanently marginalised, as their experience in Scotland – when the Prime Minister could not even campaign for the union – foretold. The party is increasingly incapable of cohering.

Here long-standing advantages are becoming liabilities. No reciprocal demands have ever been made of the hugely influential owners of Britain's press in a country that is blind to the significance of ownership; the owners of Britain's media are required neither to live in Britain, as they are in other countries, to adhere to a minimum framework of accountability nor to sustain minimal standards of professional journalistic reporting. Instead they can simply use their titles as ideological tools to promote their centre-right prejudices, consistently attacking any institution or policy that represents what they would describe as the liberal consensus. The failings of any public body, immigration, the EU, benefit fraud, unions, the BBC, 'political correctness', are relentlessly and disproportionately attacked with facts slanted, selected and omitted to suit the owners' prejudices.

The process reached its nadir with the Murdoch press empire effectively becoming a state within a state – in cahoots with the police, shamelessly flouting the law by undertaking the hacking of thousands of mobile phones, looking for concessions from ministers in return for favourable reporting.[30] The scale of hacking forced the closure of the *News of the World* and the imprisonment of its former editor Andy Coulson, who had gone on to be David Cameron's press secretary. The recommendations of Justice Leveson to establish an accountability framework, superintended by an Independent Press Standard Organisation (IPSO) under royal charter, to ensure fair reporting and make redress against outrages, has been fiercely resisted as an encroachment on press freedom.

The argument rages as to whether the royal charter represents state control of the press by the back door. Academic freedoms – but also responsibilities – are underwritten by the charters under which universities are incorporated. Journalistic freedoms – and accountability – could be similarly protected. Accusations that this ends centuries of press freedom hide an uglier truth. The owners of the British press do not want to be the providers of trusted information for citizens in the public square; rather, they want to be free to shape the square and the character of the information it supplies, with as little redress and accountability as possible. That's not press freedom; that is arbitrary press power.

Parliament has enacted Leveson but has not dared to insist that newspapers now follow its directions by enrolling in IPSO, which until it has members is only a shadow regulator. Instead, notwithstanding the law of the land, they are trying to create a system of de facto self-regulation that they hope will achieve Leveson's ends without a charter-backed IPSO. In effect the owners remain judge and jury of their own cases, albeit there is more power to fine and encourage whistleblowing than before.

Cameron's impotence before this insurrection is telling. The systemic biases of the Conservative press create the cultural backdrop that furthers the cause of his party's libertarian ultras and UKIP. Not one title will give the preoccupations of liberal conservatism a fair hearing – nor honestly set out the complexity of the challenges facing the country. Yet he is impelled by the press's very strength not to act as he should, fearing it might actively campaign for his deposition before the election. The Conservative party and its wider coalition becomes even more ungovernable.

The various Faustian bargains the Tories have made over the years are now crystallising with a vengeance. The resistance to voting reform and insistence on backing first-past-the-post voting means that the selection of MPs is firmly in the hands of activists in the constituency associations – who now increasingly believe that UKIP is the true Conservative party and nominate rabid eurosceptics as their candidates. Unreformed party funding means that there is little ballast from British-based mainstream funders who might insist that in return for donations, the party's policy positions stay sane. Instead the party's great fundraising dinners are populated with overseas billionaires, hedge-fund managers and supporters of the wilder fringes of American libertarianism.[31] One British ambassador told me of his embarrassment when a local billion-aire who had directed tens of thousands of pounds to the party through his wife (who had British residence) complained that he had not had sufficient access to the Prime Minister. These are not funders whose priorities include the interests of the British public.

Nor can the party honestly own up to the necessary realities that drive policy. There is an industrial policy, as described in Chapter 5 – but it cannot be acknowledged because that would be a retreat from the pure milk of Thatcherism. Ardent eurosceptic William Hague, as foreign secretary, in 2012 com-missioned a review of the balance of competences between the EU and the UK, identifying 32 areas of policy and legislation for examination, essentially aimed at backing the eurosceptic case with hard evidence. Embarrassingly, with 14 competences examined, the evidence is vastly in favour of Britain's continued membership, identifying problems only at the margins. But for the bulk of the now endemically euroscep-tic Conservative party, this is put down to Foreign Office bad faith rather than a possible representation of the truth. Climate change has to be challenged despite the evidence. The indis-criminate attack on lowering immigration rates has backfired because, self-defeatingly, universities have to cut back on the recruitment of overseas students and business cannot recruit overseas talent. There is allegedly no crisis in our prisons as suicides rise. The rise in demand for food banks is no evidence of weakness in the social security system. So it goes on.

The Conservative party has lost its head. Its right wing has become more of a messianic cult than the wing of a political party. As a result the party's relationship with its own base in business is fracturing. The Conservative establishment that supports it is at a loss. Magic circle law firms, big four account-ancy firms, major banks, leading British multinationals do not want to leave the EU. There is no strategy underpinning defence, to the private dismay of the chiefs of staff. The police, prison, probation and criminal justice systems are on the borders of disintegration. Ambassadors wonder what British interest they serve, teachers what future they are preparing their students for. Businesses withhold investment. The country reaches for no great goals. There is no sense of living in a society committed to justice and opportunity. Signs of social neglect and the entrenchment of privilege are all around us. Libertarian Thatcherism has not only proved an intellectual chimera and a false promise for economy and society. It has wrecked a once great political party.

The opportunity

Yet all this could be the moment for a national turn-round. None of the problems outlined in this book are inevitable and God-given. They are the results of wrong economic and political choices over many decades that in turn have their roots in following the prejudices of a now fracturing conservative establishment. There is no need for equity and justice to be so little reflected in public policy. There is no need for investment and innovation to be so low. There is no need for the flourishing of the mass of our people to be given so little focus and priority. We don't need to have the Treasury treating the provision of essential public goods as budgetary residuals once the more vital business of lowering public debt and deficits have been achieved. We don't need the sole yardstick of company success to be the share price – and every company in the land up for sale, with Conservative ministers ludicrously claiming that the steady one-sided cull of British-owned companies is a sign of success. The silting up of opportunity and decline of social mobility can be reversed. The fractures of the 30/30/40 society can be healed. We can manage immigration inflows and still remain open to the outside world. It is possible to husband the environment and reduce carbon emissions without sacrificing living standards. We can become the innovation hub of Europe. We can represent the good life, social obligations and social cohesion in our public and social choices. We can re-energise our democracy and transform our state into an instrument that creates public good.

For all the egregious mistakes made on its behalf, the country is not a wasteland. There are some outstanding successes on which to build and the failings and growing illegitimacy of the current regime create the opening. Young people are more entrepreneurial. There are clusters of new high-tech companies. Some of our great companies are trying to exhibit purposefulness in their business strategies, along with a commitment to innovation and high performance judged by criteria other than the immediate share price. There is a willingness to embrace the new: the possibilities of digitisation and the internet are more quickly seized in Britain than almost any other leading industrialised country. If we gave our people and businesses the tools, and institutions fit for purpose to support them, we would surprise ourselves at the results.

The good news is that there is no longer a unified elite standing four-square behind the Conservative party as it divides over Europe and temptation to be ever more anti state and libertarian. There is mounting concern about inequality, low productivity and indifferent economic growth – and a greater willingness to challenge the consensus of the last thirty years. The willingness of so many Scots to vote for independence has shocked the spectrum of political opinion. The Conservative hegemony, the single most important cause of Scottish disaffection, is under assault. It is harder to imagine that Treasury rule within unchanged state structures can continue for ever. There is a feasible programme of reform along the lines outlined in this book – a twenty-first-century Companies Act, reformed finance, modernised trade unions, a commitment to innovation, flexi-security, revitalised education, a commitment to a reinvented public sphere that creates public value, the creation of multiple intermediate institutions – that could command majority support and create the conditions for mass flourishing. They are interdependent, each proposal needing the introduction of the others to work best and all linked by the golden thread of representing justice and equity. It is enlightened stakeholder capitalism.

Not one single measure is blocked by Britain's membership of the European Union, cast as the author of our ills by the flailing political right in general and UKIP in particular. Indeed the opposite is the case. Access to a market as large as Europe's and to its governing councils is indispensable for our future prosperity. Whether a start-up with a new technology or an established company with established products, both need the prospect of scale production that the EU single market offers. The same is true of our financial services industry. Schadenfreude over the travails of the euro as an excuse for dissociating ourselves from demonic Europeans demonstrates amazing amnesia. Floating exchange rates are no panacea for a continent that wants and needs to come closer together in a single market; they hardly promote comity between nations and economic integration, coming from the same neoliberal economic stable that offered labour and financial market deregulation as unalloyed benefits. Floating exchange rates between the twenty-eight member states of the EU are a recipe for competitive devaluation, beggar-my-neighbour economic policies and the ceding of the determination of monetary policy to the pole country and its central bank – Germany and the

Bundesbank. The euro is certainly no bed of roses and has serious design faults that are only partially being addressed; but regression to the floating exchange rates advocated by the Tory right and UKIP are not the get-out-of-jail-free card they insist. The unmanaged gyrations of a floating pound have not offered sustained competitive advantage, as Britain's widening trade deficit is testimony: indeed the unpredictability and risk of extreme overvaluation is a deterrent to investment. The euro in some form will survive because a single currency is the indispensable adjunct of a single market and the hoped-for economic integration it brings; it is at the heart of the bargain between Germany and France, who wins a voice in the determination of European monetary policy through the European Central Bank it would not have if Europe returned to national floating exchange rates. Germany and enough of the euro's members will do all they can to ensure its continuance, despite the strains, and an European upswing will follow years of underperformance, because economies do have enormous natural resilience. The EU will once again start looking economically attractive.

The case for leaving the EU is no more economically rational than an economic policy consecrated to nothing else but debt reduction. It is simply an expression of an atavistic English nationalism (suspended when it comes to the USA) fuelled by dreams of creating a libertarian arcadia, to which the EU is cast as the enemy as well as being the home of dread foreigners who foster immigration. In reality the EU is the political structure through which we Europeans express our common interests, build our long-term prosperity and buttress our security. This is our bit of ground in our continent; we cannot escape the destiny of geography – nor should we want to. Building an open Europe that fosters the intermingling and creativity of its peoples is a great and noble project. Retreating to become an island fortress around policies designed to enrich hedge-fund managers and sustain the endless rule of eurosceptics actively hostile to building a great society is not an attractive option for the mass of our people – even though our press will seek to persuade them to abandon their best interests to serve the prejudices of its proprietors. I have witnessed many decent Conservatives despair at their party's insistence they cannot make common cause with their allies in other European countries to appease no more than unthinking prejudice.

Although there is enormous opportunity, simultaneously there is a sense of dark forces being unleashed. UKIP is no friend of justice and equity. It is not a movement founded on generosity, mutuality and liberality: its first instincts are an intolerant closure, protection against the menacing foreigner, and to punish and repress. Many of us are watching the best that Britain stands for – fairness, openness, tolerance, offering a helping hand – being assaulted by political vandals, first cousins to those parts of the financial and business elite that have plundered the country for its own gain. There is little doubt that if UKIP grows its many inconsistencies and contradictions will eventually overwhelm it, but until then it is pulling the centre of gravity of British politics more to the right than at any time for more than a century. It is more urgent than ever that the centre holds – and that Britain bests this insurgency to build an economic and social model that not only does much better, but inspires loyalty and affection from our own citizens and those in other countries who we want to influence through our soft power. Britain could and should become an exemplar of the good economy and society.

The open question is what political coalition will be built, by whom, to do what needs to be done. A less ideologically fixated party of the centre-right might be ready to embrace these recommendations, but with the Conservative party for the time being in thrall to broken ideas and chronically divided, the country must look to the Labour party, the Greens and the social liberals within the Liberal Democrats, custodians of the social liberalism that is so philosophically close to any Labour party programme that chose to implement the recommendations outlined here. With Liberal Democracy so severely compromised by the Coalition government and unlikely to be a force again in the near future, there is a new obligation on Labour to step up. It needs to become the one-nation, broad political church the Conservatives once were, welcoming the chance to become the proper heir to the British Enlightenment tradition and bind the great groupings of the country together to pursue the necessary renewal. The best in British business and finance, officialdom, unions, media and academia know that the old model is bust and Britain has to strike out anew. It is the great Enlightenment values – openness, daring to embrace the new, justice, equity, liberty – that should animate this coalition's ambition, rather than any hankering for economic and social transformation around traditional left-of-centre preoccupations.

The current national conversation is hardly conducive to the development of the ideas in this book. The political right, who could adopt much of it, is transfixed by delusions of a libertarian future in a country they say they are going to reclaim from Europe. That is both their diagnosis and their solution – which in the terms of the arguments presented here are beside the point. Labour? It is in transition. It knows the socialism it used to champion no longer functions: it knows neoliberalism does not work either. It experimented with Blairism, which for all its electoral success did not address the fundamental weaknesses in the British system. It knows it is a party for the mass of the British, with roots that must remain in the workplace and the day-to-day life of ordinary people. It is dedicated to their flourishing, and to the justice that must underpin it. The country at different times in its history has looked to its left and right traditions to do the correct thing. It now needs Labour to complete its transition, to pick up if not the programme in this book then something like it and implement the change that we need. How good we can be.

Notes

1 The State We Shouldn't Be In

1 For a closer definition of the idea of the ownerless corporation see Chapter 2, pp. 49–54 and 56

2 The High Pay Centre, 'How to Make Top Pay Fairer', July 2014, http://highpaycentre.org/pubs/reform-agenda-how-to-make-top-pay-fairer

3 Office of Budget of Responsibility, 'Economic and Fiscal Outlook', December 2013 1.1: 'Our forecast implies that the UK's budget deficit will have fallen by 11.1 per cent of GDP over the nine years from 2009–10 (around £180 billion in today's terms). Around 80 per cent of the reduction is accounted for by lower public spending. This will take government consumption of goods and services – a rough proxy for day-to-day spending on public services and administration – to its smallest share of national income at least since 1948, when comparable National Accounts data are first available.'

4 Report by the Quid consultancy for Barclays Bank, 2013

5 Ernst and Young, Inward Investment Monitor, 2010

6 According to the Startup Genome project, London has emerged as Europe's largest hub for technology start-ups, with more than 3000 fledgling tech groups. Quoted in the *Financial Times*, 19 August 2014

7 For example the Scale-up Review, an independent review for government by Sherry Coutu published in November 2014, urges a series of financial and educational measures to close the 'scale-up gap'.

8 Mark Carney, Governor of the Bank of England, Mansion House Speech, June 2014

9   This view was set out by Raghuran Rajan in *Fault Lines*, Princeton University Press, 2010, but it has been repeated by Adair Turner, Lawrence Summers, Joe Stiglitz and Andrew Haldane among many others

10 A. Hansen (1938), speech published as A. H. Hansen, 'Economic Progress and Declining Population Growth', *American Economic Review* 29 (1939): 1–15

11 Lawrence Summer, speech at the IMF Economic Forum, November 2013, and essay in Coen Teulings and Richard Baldwin (eds), *Secular Stagnation*, VoxEU.org eBook, 2014

12 For a good discussion of this, see Teulings and Baldwin (eds), *Secular Stagnation*

13 Adair Turner, 'Wealth, Debt, Inequality and Low Interest Rates', lecture to the Cass Business School, March 2014

14 Richard G. Lipsey, Kenneth L. Carlaw and Clifford T. Bekar, *Economic Transformations*, Oxford University Press, 2005, pp. 93–119, and also discussed in my own *Them and Us*, 2010, pp. 108–13. The idea of the GPT was developed in a series of papers by Timothy F. Bresnahan and Manuel Trajtenberg, culminating in Timothy F. Bresnahan and Manuel Trajtenberg, 'General Purpose Technologies: Engines of Growth?', *Journal of Econometrics* 65 (1995): 83–108

15 Chris Anderson, *Makers*, Random House, 2013

16 See the blog of Thomas Frey, senior futurologist at the DaVinci Institute, in the Futurist, 'Creating Cars that Talk to the Roads', September 2012

17 Carl Benedict Frey and Michael A. Osborne, *The Future of Employment: How Susceptible are Jobs to Computerisation?* The Oxford Martin School, University of Oxford, 2013

18 Moshe Vardi, 'Automation to Make Human Presence Obsolete in Future Workplaces', *Metro*, 15 May 2014; M. Goos and A. Manning, 'Lousy and Lovely Jobs: The Rising Polarization of Work in Britain', *The Review of Economics and Statistics*, vol. 89, no. 1, pp. 118–33, 2007

19 Cowen Tyler, *The Great Stagnation*, Dutton, 2012

20 Robert J. Gordon, 'The Turtle's Progress: Secular Stagnation Meets the Headwinds', in Teulings and Baldwin, *Secular Stagnation*

21 Thiel's venture capital firm, Founders Fund, uses the phrase as a subtitle to its 'What Happened to the Future?' manifesto

22 Eric Brynjolfsson and Andrew McAfee, *The Second Machine Age*, Norton, 2014, p. 81

23 Joel Mokyr, 'Secular Stagnation? Not in your life CEPR', in Teulings and Baldwin, *Secular Stagnation*

24 Birgitte Andersen, *Technological Change and The Evolution of Corporate Innovation: The Structure of Patenting 1890–1990*, Edward Elgar, 2001

25 *The Economist*'s special survey, 'Innovation in Industry', 20 February 1999

26 Birgitte Andersen, 'Shackling the Digital Economy Means Less for Everyone', www.dime-eu.org/node/872, 2010

27 John Maynard Keynes, 'Economic Possibilities for Our Grandchildren', first published in the *Nation and Athenaeum*, 1930, and later in *Essays in Persuasion*, Macmillan, 1933

28 Quoted in Peter Goodridge, Jonathan Haskel and Gavin Wallis, 'Estimating UK Investment in Intangible Assets and Intellectual Property Rights', an independent report for the Intellectual Property Office, 2014

29 Vernon W. Ruttan 'General Purpose Technology, Revolutionary Technology and Technological Maturity', draft paper, 2007

30 Mariana Mazzucato, *The Entrepreneurial State*, Anthem Press, 2013, pp. 94–112

31 Will Hutton and Philippe Schneider, 'The Failure of Market Failure', NESTA Provocation 8, 2008, p. 9

32 *The Economist*, 6 July 2013

33 Department of Business, Science, Engineering and Technology Statistics 2013, Table A 3.1

2 The Eclipse of Justice and the Diminution of Britain

1 See *Them and Us*, Abacus, 2010, pp. 49–63. I discuss reciprocity, desert, proportionality and the role of intentions as underpinning the concept of fairness. In particular I cite the lab experiments of Professor Marc Hausser at Harvard's Cognitive Evolution Lab, revealing universal human adherence to moral instincts, and other experiments devised by behavioural psychologists which show a predisposition to share and divide gains fairly rather than the winner taking all

2 Amartya Sen, *Development as Freedom*, Oxford University Press, 1999

3 Iain Duncan Smith wrote to the Trussell Trust in December 2013 in these terms: 'I understand that a feature of your business model must require you to continuously achieve publicity, but I'm concerned that you are now seeking to do this by making your political opposition to welfare reform overtly clear.' Justice Secretary Chris Grayling has equally been at loggerheads with the Howard League for Prison Reform, notably over limiting prisoners' rights to books and giving the organisation the access it needs for its work

4 *The Economist*, 'Rough Justice', 2 August 2014, p. 19

5 The Bureau of Investigative Journalism: http://www.thebureau investigates.com/2013/07/27/new-figures-reveal-the-cps-has-lost-more-than-20-of-its-legal-teams/

6 'Policing in Austerity', HMIC, July 2014

7 Winston Churchill, House of Commons Speech given as Home Secretary, 20 July 1910

8 Gary Craig, Aline Gaus, Mick Wilkinson, Klara Skrivankova and Aidan McQuade, *Modern Slavery in the United Kingdom*, Joseph Rowntree Foundation, 2007

9 The Office of National Statistics, quoted in the *Guardian*, 1 May 2014

10 According to Unison, 'official statistics now show that the number of claims received in October to December 2013 was 9801 – 79% fewer than in the same period of 2012, and down 75% on the period July to September 2013. Sex discrimination claims have dropped by 77% compared to the same period in 2012 and by 82% compared to the previous quarter. And there have been 83% fewer equal pay claims compared to the same period in 2012 – 85% less than the previous quarter.'

11 See American socio-economic commentator Richard Sennett's perceptive books *The Craftsman*, Allen Lane, 2008, and *The Corrosion of Character*, Norton, 1998

12 Alan Bogg and Tonia Novitz (eds), *Voices at Work: Continuity and Change in the Common Law World*, Oxford University Press, 2014

13 See Project 28-40, a survey of 25,000 people by Opportunity Now and PwC, 2014

14 Karen Hurrell, 'Race Disproportionality in Stops and Searches 2011–12', EHRC Briefing Paper 7, 2013

15 'Fraud and Error in the Benefit System: Preliminary 2012–13 Estimates', Department of Work and Pensions, May 2013

16 Tom Clark raises this point in *Hard Times*, written with Anthony Heath, Yale Books, 2014

17 Quoted in Clark, *Hard Times*, p. 232

3 The Vandals Within

1 The Kay Review of UK Equity Markets and Long-Term Decision Making, Department of Business, July 2012

2 Michael Hudson, *The Fear Index*, quoted in the *Daily Telegraph*, January 2012

3 'The Short Long', paper by Andrew Haldane and Richard Davies, presented at the 29th SUERF (Société Universitaire Européenne de Recherches Financières), May 2011

4 Andrew Haldane, Richard Davies, Metta Nielsen, Silvia Pezzini, 'Measuring the Costs of Short-Termism', Bank of England, 2 July 2013

5 *The Economist*, 6 July 2013

6 Kay Review, Table 1

7 Section 172 of the 2006 Companies Act states: Duty to promote the success of the company
(1) A director of a company must act in the way he considers, in good faith, would be most likely to promote the success of the company for the benefit of its members as a whole, and in doing so have regard (amongst other matters) to—
    (a) the likely consequences of any decision in the long term,
    (b) the interests of the company's employees,
    (c) the need to foster the company's business relationships with suppliers, customers and others,
    (d) the impact of the company's operations on the community and the environment,
    (e) the desirability of the company maintaining a reputation for high standards of business conduct, and
    (f) the need to act fairly as between members of the company

8 Kay Review, quoting ONS statistics

9 See Professor Colin Mayer's *Firm Commitment*, Oxford University Press, 2013

10 Reported in the *Guardian*, 2 December 2013

11 These stories are told in more depth in Chapter 6 of *The State We're In*

12 FRC Final Report of Disciplinary Hearing: MG Rover Group, Deloitte and Touche and Maghsoud Einollahi, September 2013

13 The Privatisation of Royal Mail, The National Audit Office, 1 April 2014

14 These are calculations by the infrastructure consultant T. Martin Blaiklock, made for the *Observer*, 10 November 2012

15 George Turner, *Money Down the Drain*, Centre:Forum, 2013

16 *The State We're In*, chapter 6, pp. 133–4

17 *The State We're In*, p. 160

18 PwC, 'PwC Valuation Index, Tracking the Market to Understand Value', 2011

19 See: http://www.uhy-uk.com/resources/news/uk-listed-companies-keep-shrinking-as-share-buy-backs-outweigh-capital-raising-by-two-to-one

20 *The State We're In*, p. 114

21 Bank of England calculations based on D. K. Shepard, *The Growth and Role of UK Financial Institutions, 1880–1962*, Methuen, 1971

22 I set out my account of the financial collapse in *Them and Us* and want to spare readers a repeat!

23 'Reinvention of UK Banking', KPMG, 2013

24 David Marquand, *Mammon's Kingdom*, Allen Lane, 2014, p. 137

25 George Osborne and Simon Walker speeches to the Institute of

Directors Annual Conference 2 October 2014, reported in the *FT* and *Guardian*, 3 October 2014

26 See http://www.oecd.org/corruption/ethics/integrityinpublicprocurement.htm

27 Kevin Farnsworth, *Social and Corporate Welfare*, Palgrave Macmillan, 2012, and calculations from his forthcoming report cited in the *Guardian*, 7 October 2014

28 Ibid.

29 Mara Faccio, 'Politically Connected Firms', *American Economic Review*, March 2006, pp. 369–86.

30 Marquand, *Mammon's Kingdom*, p. 172

31 This is the full quote: 'On the face of it, shareholder value is the dumbest idea in the world,' he said. 'Shareholder value is a result, not a strategy ... Your main constituencies are your employees, your customers and your products.' FT 'Future of Capitalism' series, 12 March 2009

32 'Businesses that Speak Out for EU Membership will be Punished, vows John Redwood', *Daily Telegraph*, 29 September 2014

33 See, for example, Owen Jones, *The Establishment*, Allen Lane, 2014

4 Inequality at a Tipping Point

1 Housing Strategy Statistical Appendix, Department for Communities and Local Government, 2014

2 Margaret Thatcher Lecture to the Centre for Policy Studies, 27 November 2013

3 Ronald Dworkin, *Sovereign Virtue: The Theory and Practice of Equality*, Harvard, 2000

4 See Robert Joyce and Luke Sibieta, 'Labour's Record on Poverty and Inequality', Institute for Fiscal Studies and Oxford Review of Economic Policy, June 2013

5 High Pay Commission Interim Report 2011, p. 24: 34.6 per cent of the top 0.1 per cent were company directors, 30.2 per cent worked in financial intermediation and 38.5 per cent in real estate, business services or related property jobs

6 The Top Income Data base, LSE, provided to the author by Brian Bell

7 Charles O'Reilly III and Brian Main, 'Economic and Psychological Perspectives on CEO Compensation: A Review and Synthesis', *Industrial and Corporate Change*, 19 (3): 675–712, 2010

8 Hutton Interim Report of Fair Pay Review, HM Treasury, December 2010, pp. 67, 68

9 *The State We're In*, p. 170

10   This argument is made forcibly by City economist Andrew Smithers in his book *The Road to Recovery*. Smithers argues that the disappointing record of business investment in both the US and the UK, together with the readiness to use surplus cash not for research and innovation but to buy shares back from shareholders (a phenomenon we saw with Centrica), is driven by the incentivisation of executive teams to be concerned only about immediate share-price performance. Economic health requires that executive pay should come back to earth

11   See Stuart Lansley and Howard Reed, 'How to Boost the Wage Share', Touchstone Blog, 2014

12   Paul Gregg, Stephen Machin and Marina Fernandez-Salgado, 'The Squeeze on Real Wages – and What it Might Take to End it', National Institute Economic Review Quarterly Bulletin, May 2014

13   Stephen Nickell and Jumana Saleheen, 'The Impact of Immigration on Occupational Wages', Spatial Economics Research Centre Discussion Paper 34, 2009

14   Alina Barnett, Sandra Batten, Adrian Chiu, Jeremy Franklin and Maria Sebastia-Barriel of the Bank's Monetary Analysis Directorate, 'The UK Productivity Puzzle', Bank of England Quarterly, Q2 2014

15   Tony Atkinson, 'Wealth and Inheritance in Britain from 1896 to the Present', CASE Working Paper 178, London School of Economics and Political Science, November 2013

16   Thomas Piketty, *Capital in the Twenty-First Century*, Belknap Harvard, 2014, p. 571

17   Ibid.

18   Savills Residential Property Focus, Q1 2014 (25-year Anniversary Edition)

19   John Hills et al., *Wealth in the UK*, Oxford University Press, 2014

20   Paragon Report on the Buy To Let Market, reported in the *Guardian*, 26 April 2014

21   Citizens Advice Bureau Advice Trends, Q3 2013/14

22   'Reshaping Workplace Pensions for Future Generations', Department for Work and Pensions, November 2013

23   Department of Business, Innovation and Skills, reported in the *Financial Times*, 28 May 2014

24   See Gregg et al., 'The Squeeze on Real Wages'

25   *The State We're In*, p. 197

26   Mark Carney, 'Inclusive Capitalism: Creating a Sense of the Systemic', at Conference on Inclusive Capitalism, 27 May 2014

27   OECD, cited in Andy Hull and Graeme Cook, 'Together at Home: A New Strategy for Housing', Institute for Public Policy Research, June 2012

28 Professor Danny Dorling in *All That is Solid*, Allen Lane, 2014
29 *The State We're In*, pp. 199, 203
30 The Social Mobility and Child Poverty Commission, State of the Nation Report 2013, Chapter 8
31 *The State We're In*, p. 215
32 *The Anatomy of Health Spending 2011/12: A Review of NHS Expenditure and Labour Productivity*, Nuffield Trust, March 2013
33 These statistics are drawn from Ruth Lupton, with John Hills, Kitty Stewart and Polly Vizard, 'Labour's Social Policy Record: Policy, Spending and Outcomes 1997–2010', London School of Economics and Political Science, 2013

5 What is to be Done?

1 Much of the thinking on ownership, finance and innovation in this chapter began with 'Ownership, Finance, Innovation 2.0', the joint presentation I made with Professors Colin Mayer and Birgitte Andersen, to selected politicians, advisers and officials, in March 2014
2 Office for National Statistics data from 1987 to Q3 2013
3 Jonathan Ford, 'A New Approach is Required for British Deal Making', *Financial Times*, 11 June 2014
4 *The State We're In*, p. 162
5 See Colin Mayer, *Firm Commitment*, Oxford University Press, 2013, pp. 240–1
6 Reported in *The Economist*, 1 June 2014
7 Chris Higson, 'Measuring the Public Interest in Foreign Acquisitions', private paper to the Department of Business, 2014
8 'Best Execution and Payment for Order Flow', Financial Conduct Authority Thematic Review TR 13/14), 2014
9 Paul Woolley, 'Why are Financial Markets so Inefficient and Exploitative – and a Suggested Remedy', in *The Future of Finance*, London School of Economics and Political Science, 2010
10 See Mayer, *Firm Commitment*
11 Ibid., p. 106
12 For more detail see the Ownership Commission Report published in March 2012 (chaired by the author) at *ownershipcomm.org/files/ownership_commission_2012*
13 The MacTaggart Lecture, Royal Television Society, August 2014
14 Jon Riley and Robert Chote, 'Crisis and Consolidation in the Public Finances', Office for Budget Responsibility, Working Paper 7, September 2014
15 Will Hutton, 'Good Housekeeping: How to Manage Credit and Debt', Institute for Public Policy Research, 1991

16 Oscar Jordá, Moritz Schularick and Alan M. Taylor, 'Betting the House', forthcoming

17 Adair Turner, *Too Important to be Left to Bankers*, Chapter 4, forthcoming

18 Ibid.

19 Anat Admati and Martin Hellwig, *The Bankers' New Clothes*, Chicago, 2013

20 Lancaster University's Ken Peasnell and I have already proposed such a scheme. See 'Credit Where it's Due: How to Revive Lending to British Small and Medium Sized Enterprises', The Work Foundation, 2011

21 For a fuller discussion of income-contingent loans see Robert Shiller's *The New Financial Order: Risk in the Twentieth Century*, Princeton Press, 2003

22 The case has been well made by Robert Skidelsky and Felix Martin, 'For a National Investment Bank', *The New York Review of Books*, 28 April 2011

23 Mazzucato, *The Entrepreneurial State*

24 See Birgitte Andersen, Muthu de Silva, Charles Levy, 'Collaborate to Innovate', Big Innovation Centre, www.biginnovationcentre.com, 2013

25 QS World University Rankings 2014: top 200

26 David Sainsbury, *Progressive Capitalism*, Biteback Publishing, 2013, p. 184

27 David Willetts, *Eight Great Technologies*, Policy Exchange, 2013

28 Office for National Statistics, UK Gross Domestic Spending on R&D, March 2014

29 See Richard Jones, 'The UK's Innovation Deficit and How to Repair it', Sheffield Political Economy Research Institute, paper 6, 2013

30 Ibid.

31 Aditya Chakraborty, 'How UK Wonder Substance Graphene Can't and Won't Benefit UK', *Guardian*, 3 December 2013

32 Mariana Mazzucato makes this point forcibly; see Mazzucato, *The Entrepreneurial State*, pp. 23–5 and 187–9

33 See Andersen et al., 'Collaborate to Innovate'

34 Tim Berners-Lee address to the IPExpo exhibition, reported in the *Guardian*, 8 October 2014

35 Hiba Sameen, 'Two Spheres that Don't Touch', www.biginnovationcentre.com, 2013

36 Quoted in *Financial Times*, 19 August 2014

37 Birgitte Andersen, 'Why Britain needs an Innovation Bank', *Guardian*, 4 May 2014

38 See Birgitte Andersen, 'Knowledge and Innovation in the Enlarging

European Union – UKNOW', published in *Intereconomics*, 45 (2010): 35–47 as an output from the EU Framework 6 programme

6 How Smart We Can Be

1 Edmund Phelps, *Mass Flourishing*, Princeton University Press, 2013, p. vi
2 Joel Mokyr, *The Enlightened Economy*, Penguin, 2011
3 Mrs Thatcher's interview in *Woman's Own*, 31 October 1987
4 For a good description of network effects, see Carl Schapiro and Hal R. Varian, *Information Rules: A Strategy for the Network Economy*, Harvard Business School Press, 1999
5 Christine Lagarde, 'Economic Inclusion and Financial Integrity', Inclusive Capitalism Conference, 27 May 2014
6 Rajan, *Fault Lines*
7 Michael Kumhof, Claire Lebarz, Romain Rancière, Alexander W. Richter and Nathaniel A. Throckmorton, 'Income Inequality and Current Account Imbalances', IMF Working Paper 12/08, January 2012
8 Office for Budget Responsibility, Economic and Fiscal Outlook, March 2014, p. 70 para 3.91
9 National Institute for Economic and Social Research, Quarterly Report no. 2, 29 August 2014
10 Reported in the *Guardian*, 13 May 2014
11 Office of National Statistics data reported in BBC News Online, 14 March 2014
12 Stephen Dunn's essay on the future of trade unions in honour of David Metcalf in June 2009 offers a useful discussion of the decline of free collective bargaining
13 A useful account of the Bullock debates is given in the Trade Union Forum, June 2010
14 See, for example, *Reconstruction after the Crisis: A Manifesto for Collective Bargaining*, Institute of Employment Rights, 2014
15 See Alan Bogg and Tonia Novitz (eds), *Voice at Work for Accounts of Good Faith Bargaining*, Oxford University Press, 2014
16 Vincent de Rivaz, 'Celebrating our New Social Covenant for Hinkley Point C', 21 July 2014
17 See the discussion in *Them and Us*, pp. 288–91. Betty Hart and Todd Risley show that by the age of three, middle-class children have cumulatively heard 30 million more words than children from lower socio-economic backgrounds
18 See Stephen Machin, 'Social Disadvantage and Educational Experiences', OECD 2006, Figure 1
19 See more at http://www.cypnow.co.uk/cyp/news/1145399/youth-

skills-commission-urges-employers-offer-apprenticeships#sthash
.F8RuZXy2.dpuf

20 Report from The Independent Commission on Fees, August 2014

21 A report by Dr Steven Jones, Manchester University, cited on the
Sutton Trust website

22 See *Them and Us*, note 52; Lans Bovenberg and Ton Wilthagen, *On
the Road to Flexicurity*, Tilburg University, 2008; and Ton Wilthagen
and Frank Tros 'The Concept of Flexicurity', *European Review of
Labour and Research* 10 (2), 2004

23 Quoted by Zoe Williams in the *Guardian*, 2 May 2010

24 Department of Communities and Local Government (DCLG),
Dwelling Stock estimates, Table 2, 27 February 2014

25 *Daily Mirror* investigation, 5 March 2013, using freedom of information requests with thirteen city councils

26 Karen Davis and others, 'Mirror, Mirror on the Wall', 2014 update:
'How the US Health Care System Compares Internationally',
Commonwealth Fund

27 King and Crewe, *The Blunders of Our Governments*, Oneworld Books,
p. 221

28 Independent Report on the London Underground PPP, Industrial
Society, 2000

29 See Mark Rowney and Will Straw, 'Greasing the Wheels: Getting
Our Bus and Rail Markets on the Move', Institute of Public Policy
Research, 2014

30 David Abraham, MacTaggart Lecture, 21 August 2014

31 *The State We're In*, p. 203

32 Ibid.

Three Crises and a Conclusion

1 Public value theory was launched by Mark H. Moore, *Creating Public
Value: Strategic Management in Government*, Harvard University Press,
1997. Essentially public officials need to do what the public value,
and set up processes that ensure it. This was followed up in the
Work Foundation, November (2006); L. Horner, R. Lekhi and R.
Blaug, 'Deliberative Democracy and the role of public managers';
and Professor John Benington and Mark H. Moore (eds), *Public
Value: Theory and Practice*, 2010

2 Richard Collins, 'Public Value and the BBC', a report prepared for
The Work Foundation's public value consortium, March 2007

3 The Work Foundation report, 'Public Value: The Next Steps in
Public Reform', set out how to create measurements of public value
in 2008

4 See both *Common Sense* and *The Rights of Man*
5 Sharon White's Treasury Review in 2012 highlights 'staff churn'. Staff turnover peaked at 38 per cent in 2008. The average age of staff elsewhere in the civil service is forty-five
6 See Richard Brooks, *The Great Tax Robbery*, Oneworld Books, 2013, p. 11
7 James Browne and Barra Roantree, 'A Survey of the UK Tax System', Institute for Fiscal Studies, October 2012
8 Lord Heseltine, *No Stone Unturned: In Pursuit of Growth*, 2012
9 Ibid.
10 *Guardian*, 14 September 2014
11 Sir Michael Cockell, quoted in Local Government Association response to spending cuts, 26 June 2013
12 This term was coined by Karel Williams at Manchester University's Centre for Research on Socio-Cultural Change; see in particular Karel Williams et al., 'Manifesto for the Foundational Economy', CRESC, 2013
13 See Anne Minton, *Ground Control*, Penguin, 2012
14 Ibid.
15 These propositions are made in Stian Westlake and Giles Wilkes, 'The End of the Treasury', NESTA September 2014, which has influenced my thinking
16 Local Government Association, 'Rewiring Public Services', 2013, and speech by Sir Michael Cockell, and City Growth Commission, RSA, October 2014
17 These proposals are informed by Dr Andrew Blick and Professor George Jones, 'A Federal Future for the UK: The Options', The Federal Trust, 2010
18 Gordon Brown similarly calls for the House of Lords to be reconstituted as a British senate in his strongly argued and passionate book, *My Scotland, Our Britain*, Simon and Schuster, 2014
19 Will Hutton, The Fair Pay Review, HM Treasury, 2011
20 Riley and Chote, 'Crisis and Consolidation in the Public Finance', para 1.19
21 The Office of Budget Responsibility, op. cit. Chapter 1
22 Riley and Chote, 'Crisis and Consolidation in the Public Finance'
23 Westlake and Wilkes, 'The End of the Treasury'
24 Ibid, Table 1, p. 15
25 Emanuele Baldacci, Sanjeev Gupta and Carlos Mulas-Granados, 'Debt Reduction, Fiscal Adjustment, and Growth in Credit-Constrained Economies', IMF working paper, November 2013
26 Larry Summers, 'Why Public Investment Really is a Free Lunch', *Financial Times*, 6 October 2014

27 Robert Nield, 'The National Debt in Perspective', Royal Economic Society Newsletter, January 2012

28 Nicholas Stern, 'Fairer Fixes for the Public Purse Lost in a Chancellor's Drawer', *Financial Times*, August 2014

29 Edmund Burke, *Reflections on the Revolution in France*, para 75 to 79, first published in 1790

30 See Nick Davies, *Hack Attack*, Chatto and Windus, 2014

31 See the Bureau for Investigative Journalism http://www.thebureauinvestigates.com/2014/10/12/doorstep-lender-and-property-moguls-amongst-guests-worth-22bn-at-tory-fundraiser/and http://www.thebureauinvestigates.com/2014/07/01/access-all-ministers-billionaires-and-lobbyists-at-lavish-party-with-david-cameron/

Bibliography

Essays, articles and papers

'The Anatomy of Health Spending 2011/12: A Review of NHS Expenditure and Labour Productivity', Nuffield Trust, March 2013

Birgitte Andersen, 'Knowledge and Innovation in the Enlarging European Union – UKNOW', Intereconomics, 45 (2010): 35–47

Birgitte Andersen, 'Shackling the Digital Economy Means Less for Everyone', www.dime-eu.org/node/872, 2010

Birgitte Andersen, Muthu de Silva, Charles Levy, 'Collaborate to Innovate', Big Innovation Centre, www.biginnovationcentre.com, 2013

Tony Atkinson, 'Wealth and Inheritance in Britain from 1896 to the Present', CASE Working Paper 178, London School of Economics and Political Science, November 2013

Emanuele Baldacci, Sanjeev Gupta, and Carlos Mulas-Granados. IMF Working paper

Dr Andrew Blick and Professor George Jones, 'A Federal Future for the UK: The Options', The Federal Trust, 2010

Timothy F. Bresnahan and Manuel Trajtenberg, 'General Purpose Technologies: Engines of Growth?', Journal of Econometrics 65 (1995): 83–108

Karen Davis et al., 'Mirror, Mirror on the Wall: How the US Health Care System Compares Internationally', Commonwealth Fund, 2014

Paul Gregg, Stephen Machin and Marina Fernandez-Salgado, 'The Squeeze on Real Wages – and What it Might Take to End it', National Institute Economic Review Quarterly Bulletin, May 2014

A. H. Hansen, 'Economic Progress and Declining Population Growth', American Economic Review, 29 (1939): 1–15

L. Horner, R. Lekhi and R. Blaug, 'Deliberative Democracy and the Role of Public Managers', The Work Foundation , 2006

Andy Hull and Graeme Cook, 'Together at Home: A New Strategy for Housing', Institute for Public Policy Research, June 2012

Will Hutton, 'Good Housekeeping: How to Manage Credit and Debt', Institute for Public Policy Research, 1991

Will Hutton, 'The Fair Pay Review', HM Treasury, 2011

Will Hutton and Ken Peasnell, 'Credit Where it's Due: How to Revive Lending to British Small and Medium Sized Enterprises', The Work Foundation, 2011

Richard Jones, 'The UK's Innovation Deficit and How to Repair it', Sheffield Political Economy Research Institute, paper 6, 2013

Oscar Jordá, Moritz Schularick and Alan M. Taylor, 'Betting the House', forthcoming

Robert Joyce and Luke Sibieta, 'Labour's Record on Poverty and Inequality', Institute for Fiscal Studies and Oxford Review of Economic Policy, June 2013

John Maynard Keynes, 'Economic Possibilities for Our Grandchildren' (1930), published in Essays in Persuasion, Macmillan, 1933

Michael Kumhof, Claire Lebarz, Romain Rancière, Alexander W. Richter and Nathaniel A. Throckmorton, 'Income Inequality and Current Account Imbalances', IMF working paper 12/08, January 2012

Local Government Association, 'Rewiring Public Services', 2013

Ruth Lupton, with John Hills, Kitty Stewart and Polly Vizard, 'Labour's Social Policy Record: Policy, Spending and Outcomes 1997–2010', London School of Economics and Political Science, 2013

Stephen Nickell and Jumana Saleheen, 'The Impact of Immigration on Occupational Wages', Spatial Economics Research Centre Discussion Paper 34, 2009

Robert Nield, 'The National Debt in Perspective', Royal Economic Society Newsletter, January 2012

Charles O'Reilly III and Brian Main, 'Economic and Psychological Perspectives on CEO Compensation: A Review and Synthesis', Industrial and Corporate Change, 19 (3): 675–712, 2010

Reconstruction after the Crisis: A Manifesto for Collective Bargaining, Institute of Employment Rights, 2014

Jon Riley and Robert Chote, 'Crisis and Consolidation in the Public Finances', Office for Budget Responsibility, Working Paper 7, September 2014

Hiba Sameen, 'Two Spheres that Don't Touch', www.biginnovation-centre.com, 2013

Stian Westlake and Giles Wilkes, 'The End of the Treasury', NESTA September 2014

Ton Wilthagen and Frank Tros, 'The Concept of Flexicurity', European Review of Labour and Research 10 (2), 2004

Paul Woolley, 'Why are Financial Markets so Inefficient and Exploitative – and a Suggested Remedy', in The Future of Finance, London School of Economics and Political Science, 2010

Books

Anat Admati and Martin Hellwig, *The Bankers' New Clothes*, Chicago, 2013

Birgitte Andersen, *Technological Change and The Evolution of Corporate Innovation: The Structure of Patenting 1890–1990*, Edward Elgar, 2001

Chris Anderson, *Makers*, Random House, 2013

Professor John Benington and Mark H. Moore (eds), Public Value: Theory and Practice, 2010; http://www.theworkfoundation.com/products/publications/azpublications/publicvaluefinalreport.aspx

Alan Bogg and Tonia Novitz (eds), *Voice at Work for Accounts of Good Faith Bargaining*, Oxford University Press, 2014

Alan Bogg and Tonia Novitz (eds), *Voices at Work: Continuity and Change in the Common Law World*, Oxford University Press, 2014

Lans Bovenberg and Ton Wilthagen, *On the Road to Flexicurity*, Tilburg University, 2008

Richard Brooks, *The Great Tax Robbery*, Oneworld Books, 2013

Gordon Brown, *My Scotland, Our Britain*, Simon and Schuster, 2014

Eric Brynjolfsson and Andrew McAfee, *The Second Machine Age*, Norton, 2014

Tom Clark and Anthony Heath, *Hard Times*, Yale Books, 2014

G. A. Cohen, *If You're an Egalitarian, How Come You Are So Rich?* Harvard University Press, 2000

Tyler Cowen, *The Great Stagnation*, Dutton, 2012

Gary Craig, Aline Gaus, Mick Wilkinson, Klara Skrivankova and Aidan McQuade, *Modern Slavery in the United Kingdom*, Joseph Rowntree Foundation, 2007

Nick Davies, *Hack Attack: How the Truth Caught Up with Rupert Murdoch*, Chatto and Windus, 2014

Danny Dorling, *All That Is Solid*, Allen Lane, 2014

Ronald Dworkin, *Sovereign Virtue: The Theory and Practice of Equality*, Harvard University Press, 2000

John Hills et al., *Wealth in the UK*, Oxford University Press, 2014

Will Hutton, *Them and Us*, Little, Brown, 2010

Will Hutton, *The State We're In*, Jonathan Cape, 1996

Owen Jones, *The Establishment and How They Got Away With It*, Allen Lane, 2014

Anthony King and Ivor Crewe, *The Blunders of Our Governments*, Oneworld Books, 2013

Richard G. Lipsey, Kenneth L. Carlaw and Clifford T. Bekar, *Economic Transformations*, Oxford University Press, 2005

David Marquand, *Mammon's Kingdom*, Allen Lane, 2014

Mariana Mazzucato, *The Entrepreneurial State*, Anthem Press, 2013

Colin Mayer, *Firm Commitment*, Oxford University Press, 2013

Anne Minton, *Ground Control*, Penguin, 2012

Joel Mokyr, *The Enlightened Economy*, Penguin, 2011

Mark H. Moore, *Creating Public Value: Strategic Management in Government*, Harvard University Press, 1997

Edmund Phelps, *Mass Flourishing*, Princeton University Press, 2013

Thomas Piketty, *Capital in the Twenty-First Century*, Belknap Harvard, 2014

Raghuram G. Rajan, *Fault Lines: How Hidden Fractures Still Threaten the World Economy*, Princeton University Press, 2011

David Sainsbury, *Progressive Capitalism*, Biteback Publishing, 2013

Michael Sandel, *Democracy's Discontent*, Harvard University Press, 1996

Carl Schapiro and Hal R. Varian, *Information Rules: A Strategy for the Network Economy*, Harvard Business School Press, 1999

Amartya Sen, *Development as Freedom*, Oxford University Press, 1999

Richard Sennett, *The Craftsman*, Penguin, 2009

Richard Sennett, *The Corrosion of Character*, Norton, 1999

D. K. Shepard, *The Growth and Role of UK Financial Institutions, 1880–1962*, Methuen, 1971

Andrew Smithers, *The Road to Recovery*, Wiley, 2013

Guy Standing, *The Precariat*, Bloomsbury, 2011

Coen Teulings and Richard Baldwin (eds), *Secular Stagnation: Facts, Causes, and Cures*, VoxEU.org eBook, 2014

Adair Turner, *Too Important to be Left to Bankers*, forthcoming

George Turner, *Money Down the Drain*, CentreForum, 2013

Thorstein Veblen, *The Theory of the Leisure Class*, OUP, new edition 2009

David Willetts, *Eight Great Technologies*, Policy Exchange, 2013

Martin Wolf, *The Shifts and the Shocks*, Allen Lane, 2014

Index

About the Author

Will Hutton is principal of Hertford College, Oxford, chair of the Big Innovation Centre and columnist for the *Observer*, where he was editor, then editor-in-chief for four years. He began his career in journalism as economics editor for BBC 2's *Newsnight* and then for the *Guardian*.